SED

A WARTIME MEMOIR

Rita la Fontaine de Clercq Zubli

To Guay. Enjoy the reading.

R de Clercq Zubli

12/26/2010

CANDLEWICK PRESS
CAMBRIDGE, MASSACHUSETTS

Text copyright © 2001, renewed 2007 by Rita la Fontaine de Clercq Zubli
Map illustration © 2007 by Steven Stankiewicz

Second edition 2007
Originally published in 2001 by Southfarm Press

Library of Congress Cataloging-in-Publication Data is available.

Library of Congress Catalog Card Number pending

ISBN 978-0-7636-3329-5

10 9 8 7 6 5 4 3 2 1

Printed in the United States of America

This book was typeset in Berkeley.

Candlewick Press
2067 Massachusetts Avenue
Cambridge, Massachusetts 02140

visit us at www.candlewick.com

In memory of my parents,

Paula and Vic,

my two younger brothers,

Ronald and René,

and my aunt, Tante Suus,

who are all so much part

of this book and my life

THAILAND

FRENCH
INDOCHINA

Straits of Malacca

*Gulf of
Thailand*

*South
China
Sea*

MALAYA

SARAW

*Indian
Ocean*

SINGAPORE

SUMATRA

Muntok

Djambi

BANGKA

Lubuklinggau

Palembang

Batavia
(Jakarta)

Java S

Sunda Strait

JAVA

Bandoeng

*DUTCH
EAST INDIES
(1942)*

RUSSIA

CHINA

JAPAN

Pacific Ocean

INDIA

VIETNAM

PHILIPPINES

CAMBODIA

MALAYSIA

Indian Ocean

SUMATRA

JAVA

AUSTRALIA

INDONESIA
(2007)

UNEI

DUTCH
BORNEO

CELEBES

oerabaja

Timor Sea

This book is a true account of the three and a half years of my life spent as a prisoner of war during World War II, after the Japanese invasion of Indonesia, then known as the Dutch East Indies. At the time my unique story began, I was twelve years old, living in Djambi, Sumatra, the western-most island of Indonesia and one of the largest islands in the world. It straddles the equator and stretches for 1,060 miles from the Andaman Sea in the north to Krakatoa and the western edge of Java in the south.

My family—which included my Dutch-Indonesian father, Victor; my mother, Paula; my mother's older sister, Suus; and my two younger brothers, Ronald and René— had moved to Djambi from the island of Java in April of 1941 as a result of my father's promotion to Regional Head of the *Post Telegraaf en Telefoondienst,* which was the postal service, including telegraph and telephone. I was the eldest child and only daughter.

About eight months later, in January 1942, the Japanese army invaded the Dutch East Indies. On February 17, 1942, they arrived in Djambi, and most of its Dutch and

Dutch-Indonesian residents became prisoners of war. For three and a half years—to the end of the war—I concealed my true identity from both my Japanese captors and my fellow prisoners. What no one could have foreseen—not my family and not I—were the tremendous and unusual responsibilities that would land on my young shoulders.

We now know that the Japanese conscripted "comfort women" from the local populations of the countries they conquered. Hundreds of thousands of young girls and women were forced into organized brothels, serving soldiers of Nippon as far north as Korea and China and as far south as Sumatra and Java. Dutch women were among those lured into sexual servitude.

I wrote my story, first and foremost, as a gesture of affection for my husband and my four children. I wanted to hand them a legacy. I wanted to tell them about my parents—their grandparents—and about my aunt, none of whom they have ever had the chance to meet. I wanted my children to know about personal sacrifice, especially about how my aunt, Tante Suus, sacrificed her own future to care for her sister's family—and, by doing so, became my hero.

Early in her marriage, my mother began to suffer from kidney and heart disease. Her health gradually deteriorated so much that she was unable to attend to the daily responsibilities of home and family. Thus, two years before I was born, her sister, Suus, came to live with my parents. The arrangement eased my mother's mind as she became increasingly infirm. Over the years, Tante Suus became her sister's personal caretaker, a trusted friend to my father, and a second mother to my brothers and me.

The Japanese people in this book are as the war made

them, and the same is true of the rest of us. A story of war is always a story of hate; it makes no difference with whom one fights.

May what I lived through give you the tools to strengthen your own resolve and to endure pain and hardship with courage. It's easy to give up; it's a challenge to persevere and to conquer.

PART I

DECEMBER 1941–FEBRUARY 1942

The nightmare really began on December 7, 1941, when the Japanese attacked the American naval base at Pearl Harbor, in Hawaii. Their goal was to destroy the American Pacific fleet to prevent it from interfering with Japanese expansion southward—through the Philippines and Malaya to the Dutch East Indies, the main prize. In 1941, the Indies produced 2.5 percent of the world's oil and tin, 40 percent of the world's rubber, and 93 percent of its quinine. All were valuable commodities. Quinine in particular was valuable, because it was used to treat malaria, a disease spread throughout the world by mosquitoes. Quinine was extracted from the bark of the cinchona tree, which grew abundantly in the East Indies.

In response to the attack on Pearl Harbor, the Dutch government in Batavia (now Jakarta), Java, declared war on the Japanese, even before the Americans did.

My father's office was connected to our house by a door in the dining room. He was not only the postmaster, but was in charge of all communications in Djambi, including telephone and telegraph. After Pearl Harbor, he received a cablegram from the main office in Batavia with instructions to be on permanent standby. He became deeply absorbed in his work. We saw him at mealtimes, and then only for as long as it took him to eat. He no longer pursued his favorite pastime, tennis, or his second love, billiards.

The Japanese Army's whereabouts was the main topic on the radio. The broadcasters gave continuous reports of the Japanese advance and impending war. Newspapers with lurid caricatures of Japanese invaders came into our home.

"What are you reading, dear?" my mother asked one day when she saw me sitting in the living room with a newspaper.

"I wasn't really reading, Mom. I was looking at this picture on the front page." It was a cartoon devil holding a scepter dripping with blood, stepping on people in his path and crushing them. Others were running away from him.

"Why is he doing that?" I asked. The picture frightened me.

My mother had a pained look on her face. "I don't know, darling," she mumbled.

A terrifying thought suddenly came to my mind. "Could this happen to us, Mom?"

"I certainly hope not!" she said.

I turned to the next page only to be confronted by another ugly scene in caricature. A Dutch government official was lowering a Dutch flag while a Japanese soldier looked on, proudly showing off his own country's flag— a white banner with a red ball in the center—which was obviously meant to replace the Dutch flag. The soldier was wearing a menacing grin and a pair of glasses too large for his face. He had large, protruding, crooked teeth.

I was too young to fully understand what was going on or what it all meant, but I got a clear sense that something was about to change our lives terribly and dramatically.

By the time my twelfth birthday came, on December 17, 1941, there seemed nobody left in Djambi to share it with. My birthday passed with a small, insignificant celebration and without my new friends, many of whom had fled the island with their families for safer regions. I, too, longed for safety. But where would we go if the whole world was at war?

Chapter 2

Daytime air-raid drills grew frequent and more frightening. Special radio bulletins repeatedly reminded us of curfew times and the locations of shelters. My father hung a map of Asia on the wall and marked the daily progress of enemy troops. He charted new information by moving colored pins across the map. None of us—only he—knew what the colored pins represented. Electrical blackouts were held in the evening as a precaution against air raids. Those nights were eerily quiet and unsettling. I was afraid to even stand near a window. I imagined that a big, ugly monster would jump out of the darkness and grab me.

Each night, Tante Suus told me and my brothers a bedtime story to distract us from the signs of war. The stories she told were rich with interesting characters and details. She told them again and again, and we loved each retelling. She had a gift for bringing animals and trees in the forest to life, making them talk, and making us believe that we were living every scene. Yes, Tante Suus was a remarkable storyteller. There was no other like her.

In this frightening, uncertain time, Tante Suus occupied herself with household duties. She did a lot of the cooking, assisted by our Indonesian *kokki*. The preparation of our meals required daily trips to the *pasar.* Because we had no refrigerator, vegetables, meat, or fish had to be purchased each day from markets where flies clung to and buzzed around the daily offerings. The cooking was done not on modern stoves, but on *anglos,* small charcoal-burning stoves.

My father established a set of rules for Ronald, René, and me. We were not to leave the house for anything except school, as long as it was still in session. In his stern voice, my father instructed one of our menservants, "Take the children to school and do not allow them to dally with friends along the way. Is that understood, Karto?"

"*Saja toean, ngerti!* Yes, sir, understood!"

My father turned to us and continued, "In case of an air raid, I want you to go to the post office's vault for shelter—IMMEDIATELY!"

Since Ronald, René, and I were restricted in our movements, we spent more time with our mother on days when she was well enough to enjoy us.

One morning at breakfast, with the ceiling fan slowly spinning above the table, the official radio station announced the closing of all schools. My father's instant reaction was to confine us to the yard. The urgency in his voice told me that conditions were growing worse.

Long, uneventful days followed. I had no playmates, but Ronald, nine, and René, five, had each other. Even though they had been born four years apart, they played well together. They played hour after hour with their toy cars. I was envious of their amazing ability to retreat into their own little world of innocence. I felt so alone!

My days were spent keeping an eye on them and making

certain they stayed near the house. I felt that it was my responsibility to keep them out of mischief and occupied, but the joy had gone out of my world. The laughter, the playfulness, the carefree moments of playing together, even the occasional fights among siblings, were absent. My only source of diversion in these sad circumstances was my accordion.

Four months earlier, I had discovered the instrument in its case on top of my clothespress. My father had bought the accordion when we were in Holland on furlough in 1936. He had taken private music lessons, which I enjoyed listening to. After the lesson, his teacher would play the songs the way they were intended to sound. Unfortunately, back at work as the postmaster, my father didn't have time to continue the lessons and the instrument was forgotten.

It was in a deplorable state when I found it. Mr. Meijer, a local craftsman, was approached for the job and he somehow managed to return a perfect-sounding accordion. I played it from that day on.

Miss Seau, our teacher and the conductor of the Saturday morning *zangles*, or singing hour, heard of my determination to play the accordion and suggested that I practice the songs we were rehearsing on my own. I took the challenge, but soon realized that it took much effort to progress, simply because I had never had music lessons and therefore never learned to read music. The only way I knew whether to move to a higher or lower note was to observe the position of the "little black balls" on the sheet. Unfortunately, when the war broke out and the schools were closed, I had to give up my Saturdays showing off as a musician.

Chapter 3

One day in January, the tense and uncertain atmosphere was shattered when our *kokki* returned from the market quite upset. She approached my aunt nervously and began whispering. I overheard her saying, "*Nja! Nja!* Many *tokos* are closed, and the Japanese store is not only abandoned, it is boarded up!"

"Shh! Shh!" Tante Suus reprimanded her, pulling the woman aside. "Please, not so loud. Calm down and tell me all about it." After the cook repeated her news, Tante Suus told her not to say a word to anyone else about what she had seen. She did not want to worry the rest of the family.

The town was disintegrating into chaos. Restless Indonesian natives rioted and looted throughout the area. Several local Dutch trading companies began demolishing their warehouses and everything in them to deter the looters and put them out of business. Still, stolen goods continued to find their way onto the profitable black market.

At home, even among the servants, the mood was depressing. Besides the *kokki*, we had a *baboe* who did the household cleaning and ironing, and a *djongos* who took care of the yard and bicycles, and waited on the table during meals. The fear of war was evident on their faces, though nobody dared speak about it. Days passed in silence and uncertainty.

In early February, 1942, from out of nowhere, came the rumble of airplanes. No sirens sounded to warn us. My brothers and I were outside playing, at first oblivious to what was happening. The planes flew so fast and so low that the ground beneath our feet shook. Instinctively, and now terrified, I grabbed the boys and ran for cover. We threw ourselves onto the ground, afraid of being blown up or shot. The house was only a few feet away but it seemed like miles. Then, with the planes still roaring over us, we ran to the house.

Safe inside our home, we blocked our ears and stood at the window watching the planes rip across the sky, shaking the house to its foundation. Then, finally, quiet returned and peace—however uneasy—was restored.

My father and Tante Suus concluded that the squadron of planes must have been on their way to Singapore, passing over Djambi, which had no airport. Were the planes Dutch, British, or American? Or did they belong to our enemy, the Japanese? My father was almost certain that they must be enemy planes.

"With only a short crossing by boat from Singapore to Djambi, if Singapore falls, the Japanese could march into town within a few days," I heard my father whisper to Tante Suus.

At that moment, I realized that my mother was not with us. I took René by the hand and walked toward her bedroom. Ronald followed. We found her sitting up, clutching the bed sheets, looking frail, frightened, and distraught. Her eyes reflected terror and unasked questions. We jumped into bed with her and, instantly, her mood lightened. She began to relax, and so did we. We felt safe being so close to her.

My father and Tante Suus remained on the lookout at the bedroom window awhile longer. Then they quietly announced, "Things seem to have returned to normal." If only those words had been true.

Later that day our *djongos* rushed into the dining room and, with a look of despair, handed my father one of the thousands of pamphlets that had been dropped from the planes and scattered around the town. The pamphlet was written in Japanese but included translations into Malay and English. The Dutch language was ignored. This left no doubt as to the nationality of the planes. The pamphlet was an introduction to our future rulers—the army of the Land of the Rising Sun. It announced their plans to arrive in town within a few days. This written proclamation also placed the entire Dutch community in Djambi under house arrest until further notice. It was exactly what my father had predicted.

Chapter 4

We had barely recovered from the plane incident when the latest radio news bulletin prepared us for a different kind of terror. Djambi, just a short hop from Singapore over the Straits of Malacca, was indeed the next target. This confirmed what my father had already surmised from the pamphlets.

Tension at the breakfast table reached an all-time high when my father, agitated by this latest bulletin, abruptly rushed into his office and shut the door. Silence engulfed us as we listened intently to the rest of the radio broadcast. The anxiety everyone felt was reflected in the faces of my aunt and mother. Frightening thoughts raced through my mind. What would happen to us if the Japanese army invaded our little town?

Suddenly, the office door swung open and my father reappeared. He took my mother aside and whispered something in her ear. Then, without even a glance at the rest of us, he quickly retreated into his office.

My mother seemed stunned by what my father had just told her. Tante Suus, concerned about her sister's health, immediately walked over to my mother and led her back to the table. She gently helped my mother onto a chair, then tenderly stroked her hair.

"Are you all right, Paula?" she asked softly, searching my mother's face for clues. "What did Vic tell you, dear? Please tell me," she begged.

My mother stared at her sister and then at the three of us, as if preparing to make a major announcement. Her eyes filled with tears, she cleared her throat, and then stoically whispered, "Vic just received orders from the main office to be on standby for final instructions." The *Post Telegraaf en Telefoondienst* was shutting down.

Under tremendous emotional stress, my mother began gasping for air and sobbing uncontrollably, crying out, "Suus, what do you think is going to happen to us? It is so terribly frightening."

"We are all frightened, dear," Tante Suus agreed, trying to console her. "At a time like this, we just have to be strong and pray to our Savior for protection." She stroked her sister's hair lovingly, trying to calm her. Seeing the two sisters under these difficult conditions made me understand for the first time the deep love between them.

"Was there anything else Vic told you that we should know about, Paula?" my aunt asked. My mother, still dazed, merely shook her head.

Later that day, as my brothers and I were playing in our front yard, we heard trucks rumbling in the distance. Fear overtook us as we remembered the low-flying planes; we held each other. A convoy of buses, trucks, and small vans approached. They were careening down the hill at high speed. The vehicles were packed with passengers, and

13

luggage was tied down and piled high on the roofs. People waved to us, but they were moving so fast we were unable to recognize anyone.

Suddenly, one of the last buses in the convoy pulled out of line and turned into our driveway. My brothers and I chased after it until it came to a stop at our front doorstep.

"They're coming to get us!" René said innocently.

"Hush, René, don't say things like that!" I snapped at him, not knowing how accurate his remark was. The commotion of the passing convoy and the approaching bus brought my parents and aunt to the front door just as the bus came to a stop.

When none of us made an attempt to board the bus, a woman the family knew as Stien exited and stepped briskly toward my parents. Her long strides, thin face, and stern expression showed displeasure. Disregarding good manners and ignoring everyone else, she addressed my mother, "Are you ready to go, Paula? We don't have too much time, you know."

"I know, Stien. Won't you please come in?" my mother responded nervously.

"No, thank you! I'd rather stand!" the surly woman snapped. "As I said, we don't have much time. Besides, this isn't a social call, you know! Are you coming with us or aren't you? That's all I am interested in hearing!"

"Not really," my mother responded reluctantly.

While the rest of us watched, uncomprehending, the now infuriated woman shouted, *"Not really?"* Rolling her eyes, she asked, "What do you mean? Are you or aren't you coming? Didn't the office of Mayor de Vries phone you about the evacuation?"

When she received no response, Stien became suspicious and more outraged. She looked my father straight in the eye. "Don't you know about the plans?" she screamed wildly. "Come on, people, will somebody say something sensible? We could have been . . . what am I saying? We should have been on our way by now!" With her hands on her broad hips, she paced in circles, trying to compose herself.

My mother, totally unnerved by the woman's outburst and almost in tears, stuttered, "I am very sorry, Stien, but I didn't expect to see you here so soon."

"Would it really have made a difference? Damn it!" she shouted, stamping her feet.

Before the woman had a chance to continue, my mother turned to Tante Suus and said, "Suus, I didn't know how to ask you this—"

"This is too much! That's all I need to hear!" the woman interrupted, once again raising her voice. "You haven't even told your sister about it?" She spoke slowly but harshly, accentuating every word. "My God, woman, what's the matter with you?"

My mother turned to her sister, ignoring the woman's ravings. "Suus," she cried, "you must take the children with you to safety. Vic and I have to stay here for the time being, but we'll join you as soon as we can."

Tante Suus, not knowing anything about the evacuation plan, was stunned and struggled to respond to her sister's pleas. I had not said a word up to that moment. I was convinced that the presence of this woman could destroy our family if we allowed it. I sprang into action. "I am not going anywhere, Mom," I cried. "I am going to stay right here with you and Poppie!"

The thought of being separated from my parents terrified me, and I was not about to allow it. Who would care for my sick mother if Tante Suus and I left? No! Definitely, no! The bus had to leave without us.

My brothers, who had been quietly watching, joined me. Ronald held on tightly to my father, and René clung to my mother's hand. They were bewildered and softly crying. The more my parents tried to talk us into going, the more we held on to them, tears blinding our eyes and choking our voices.

"Stien, I am terribly sorry for the inconvenience we've caused you," my father said, genuinely apologetic. "As you've seen and heard, we're going to stay together. I'm very sorry."

The outraged woman threw her hands up in disgust. Then, pointing a finger angrily at my father, she said, "If you knew your family was not going, why in hell haven't you let us know? We could have saved ourselves valuable time. Damn you!"

"But I really didn't know—" my father explained.

"Never mind!" the woman snapped, cutting him off. "I don't want to hear any more of your excuses." She turned and headed back for the bus, mumbling something about stupidity.

The bus backed out of the driveway and disappeared down the hill on its way to "safer regions." With relief, I sighed and hugged my mother. Our family was still intact, and that was all that mattered to me at the moment.

Once the bus was out of sight, my father put his arms around my mother and aunt and directed them to the dining room. My brothers and I followed. One of the servants was awaiting us with cool drinks and a snack.

My parents and aunt discussed what had just taken place. It was only then that my father divulged that he and my mother had received a call from the mayor, informing them of the evacuation to Padang, a city on the west coast of Sumatra. The plan was to reach the more isolated islands in the Indian Ocean from there and, if need be, to go as far as Australia. However, considering the strain of my mother's physical and emotional condition, my father had left the final decision to my her.

With everything that had transpired over the last few weeks, my mother had cried a lot and had difficulty coping. I knew that Tante Suus and my father were worried about her. They did all they could to keep her calm, although they themselves had a hard time remaining composed.

That evening my brothers and I gathered around our mother's bed as we did every night. She embraced us and held each of us longer and more tenderly than usual. Before we left the room, she took our hands and uttered something resembling a prayer. "Dear God," she said, "thank you for having blessed me with three beautiful and courageous children, without whose decision our family would have been torn apart. They were the ones who acted responsibly. They had the courage and strength to make the decision that I, as their mother, should have, but could not make. Bless them!"

At the time, I was not able to fully understand but could sense that the bus incident had been a critical moment in her life, one that had deeply touched her heart.

I believe that the prospect of losing her family was the very reason why my mother had never shared the news about the evacuation plan with my aunt. She was afraid to let us go, afraid that she might never see us again.

A few days later we heard rumors that some of the boats carrying evacuees had been bombed and sunk. If the Djambi group was caught in this attack, my aunt, brothers, and I might never have seen our parents again had we evacuated that fateful day.

It was poignantly ironic to consider that those who were seeking safety elsewhere might have died, while those who remained to face the uncertain future were spared and able to tell their stories. Yet circulating information alleged that some refugees did get away. On February 26, 1942, a Dutch river-steamer from Java, the *Rosenbaum*, received a call for help on its radio and picked up a hundred Dutch and British refugees at Padang. Though not designed or equipped to be a seagoing ship, she delivered her human cargo safely across the Indian Ocean, at Colombo, Ceylon, now known as Sri Lanka, on March 4, 1942.

Chapter 5

When my father received the long-expected cablegram from Batavia with the unpleasant order to incapacitate all radio and telegraphic equipment, he and his work crew began their final task of destroying everything in town associated with the postal service and with telephone and telegraph connections. Terrible, unsettling sounds of hammering and breaking glass were audible all around us. Elsewhere, another group of postal workers was burning all confidential correspondence and classified material. Three radio towers on the premises were destroyed. Heavy black smoke and a sickening odor filled the air.

Hours later, my father came home, depressed and exhausted. I had never seen him like that. He appeared to have aged.

"I'm glad that's over with," I heard him say to my mother and my aunt.

Our house overlooked the Djambi waterfront along the Batanghari River. All day long we heard explosions from the nearby warehouses and oil fields and periodically saw gaseous flames shooting skyward as the Dutch government continued to sabotage its own facilities in order to render them useless to the enemy. Fire seemed to engulf all of Djambi. A dense veil of smoke hung ominously over the harbor at dusk.

Throughout that night, I was unable to sleep, one thought prevalent in my young mind: the whole world is in flames. Perhaps this was to be the last day of our existence on earth. Perhaps we were doomed to be burned alive. I tried to shake those horrible thoughts from my mind, but they would not leave. *I, Rita la Fontaine, a twelve-year-old girl, am too young to die,* was my last thought before falling asleep.

On February 14, the Japanese landed on the island of Bangka, just off the east coast of Sumatra at the mouth of the Moesi River, intent on capturing and controlling the major oil refineries in Pladjoe and outside the city of Palembang before our own engineers had a chance to sabotage them and flee.

By chance, the Dutch Home Guard was out training that day near Palembang. They managed to almost completely wipe out the Japanese who were advancing up the Moesi River toward the refineries. This delayed the Japanese but didn't stop them.

Also on the night of February 14, an Allied fleet passed through the Sunda Strait heading northeast, intending to circle around Bangka and strike the Japanese invaders from the rear, thus impeding or preventing the invasion of Sumatra.

The Japanese, however, were fully aware of the threat. They organized continual high-level bombing attacks on the Allied ships throughout the following day and, as a result, the Allied fleet withdrew.

Singapore, across the Malacca and Berhala Straits from Sumatra, surrendered to the Japanese on February 15. It was also my aunt's birthday. By that time, provisions were very hard to come by. In her capacity as the family chef, Tante Suus, assisted by her Indonesian helper, managed to prepare a delicious dinner for her birthday, but none of the usual happy party noises surrounded the dinner table and there was very little conversation. It could well have been the last birthday celebration for a long time to come.

Shortly after breakfast the next morning, far too early for company to arrive, there was a surprise visit from our parish priest. Father Koevoets, a tall, lean man in his forties, graying at the temples, was a kind and well-respected clergyman in the community. He entered the dining room carrying a large bundle under his arm.

"Good morning, Father. What brings you here so early in the day?" My father welcomed the priest in a joking manner. It was not unusual for the priest to come to the house. What *was* unusual was the time of day that he appeared.

"Good morning, all. Good morning, children." Father Koevoets smiled at us as he always did, but I could sense unease in his manner.

"Good morning, Father," we called out in chorus.

The priest apologized for coming to the house uninvited and claimed that he was on a special mission. Before sitting down with us, he dropped the bundle at his feet, nonchalantly shoving it under the table. Tante Suus placed a cup of coffee in front of him.

21

"In answer to your question, Vic, I just wanted to make sure that you and the family were still in town."

My mother, who had joined us at the breakfast table that morning, explained, "Actually, Father, Rita and the boys made the decision for us. If it weren't for them, Vic and I would have been left behind, thinking of them right now, while they would be on their way to safety, wherever that might be. They made the choice to stay. I love them for it and I'll always be very grateful for their courage." Tears filled her eyes and her voice trembled as she spoke.

"I understand," Father Koevoets said solemnly. "That brings me to my second reason for being here this morning." Looking directly at my parents, he added, "Would you allow me to discuss a little matter in private after breakfast?"

I noticed that the priest's suggestion startled my parents and aunt. It brought a puzzled look to their faces. A little while later, the adults went into the living room.

Ronald and René went outdoors to play in the dirt with their toy cars and trucks, acting like the truck drivers they usually pretended to be. I joined them and took a book with me, but was unable to concentrate on what I was reading. Suddenly, Ronald was beside me. "Do you know why Father Koevoets is here?" he asked. I didn't, of course. Disappointed in my negative response, he went back to play.

Half an hour went by before Tante Suus appeared at the dining room entrance. All three of us stood up, expecting to join her. "No, dears, I just want Rita to come with me." The boys were disappointed, but they remained with one of the servants and I went with Tante Suus. With her arm around my shoulder, we walked through the hallway while she told me about a few things discussed at the meeting.

Upon seeing me, my mother stretched out her arms. "Come and sit down beside me, dear," she invited. "We have something to tell you, and we would like you to listen and try to understand what we're asking of you." She paused for a moment to compose herself.

I looked at her and the others but could not come close to guessing what they had been discussing and why it would involve me.

"You heard Father Koevoets say that he had several reasons to be here today, didn't you, dear?" she quizzed.

"Yes, Mom, I did!"

"Well, one of the reasons is you. Or rather, one of the reasons concerns you."

"Me? In what way, Mom?" I asked. What could they have been talking about that concerned me?

"Father Koevoets has a plan that will affect all of us, but you in particular. He has laid out his plan. Your father, Tante Suus, and I think the plan is solid and we have accepted it. We have agreed with him to carry it out."

I still had no idea what she was talking about, but I knew it had to be something quite serious. Swallowing a few times, my mother then asked me a very unusual question: "Dear, how would you like to spend some time as a boy?"

I couldn't believe that she would ask me that kind of question. I looked at my father and Tante Suus. I didn't know what to think.

"As a boy?" I repeated. "You mean like a real boy, with a boy's haircut, wearing boys' clothes and all that?"

"Yes! Yes! All of that!" my father interjected, sounding very excited, apparently relieved because he had not expected such an enthusiastic reaction from me. Everyone seemed genuinely pleased by my positive response. "How would you like that?" he then asked.

"To pretend to be a boy, you mean? I think I would like it. I always wanted to be one," I blurted out. I was simply ecstatic! I was being given the opportunity to see my wish fulfilled, so why not accept it? As I looked at the faces around me, I suddenly realized that this was not a game. This was serious! The expression on my face must have reflected my thoughts, because my father then attempted to explain the importance and necessity of the disguise. While he was explaining, I was thinking about my long hair. It hung to my waist. I couldn't bear the thought of having to lose it all, but if I were to change my identity, cutting my beautiful hair was inevitable.

My father interrupted my thoughts when I heard him say, "A boy will be treated differently than a girl. We have to make people believe that you are a boy and treat you accordingly. It is the only way we can think of to protect you."

"Protect me from what?" I asked. Nothing was making much sense. "Why? Why would people treat me differently if I were a boy?" I asked out loud. "Why?"

Father Koevoets recognized my hesitancy and confusion. "May I take over, Vic?" Attempting to emphasize the importance of the plan to me, he said, "Let me try to explain, so that you understand what your father was trying to tell you. You see, soldiers are mostly young men in the prime of their lives who are living and fighting a war in a foreign country. Unfortunately," he continued, "these young men often try to forget their loneliness by drinking and spending their time in the company of women."

In my very young mind, what he said about soldiers needing to have some fun when they could, especially in wartime, made sense. What I could not understand was what this had to do with me. Father Koevoets was talking about women, but I was only twelve years old. So where was the logic?

He heaved a deep sigh. "If only you weren't so innocent," he mumbled with sadness in his voice. Then he cleared his throat. "Women who seek the company of these soldiers come prepared with grown-up knowledge to protect themselves. A twelve-year-old girl is far too inexperienced and doesn't know enough about the rules to play these games safely. We want to protect you from soldiers who take advantage of innocent little girls like you. Do you understand what I am trying to tell you, Rita?"

Explaining to a twelve-year-old girl the intricacies of life without going into detail could not have been an easy task for Father Koevoets. He took a handkerchief out of one of the deep, bottomless pockets of his vestment and wiped his forehead and clammy hands with it.

As I understood it, a boy had nothing to fear from the soldiers, but for a girl, matters might be different and even threatening at that age. I knew next to nothing about what went on between men and women, and even less about the dangerous aspects of these interactions. I accepted whatever the adults had decided.

The priest took my chin between his index finger and thumb and turned my head so that I was looking directly at him. "Are you beginning to understand what I am trying to say? Do you know how important it is to let you become a boy for a while?" He spoke in a soothing tone of voice.

"To be honest, Father, I'm not sure."

Still somewhat hesitant about going through with the plan, I looked at my fragile mother. I knelt down beside her and asked, "Should I do it, Mom?"

She looked down at me and her eyes filled with tears. "It would mean the world to me, darling! It would mean the world to all of us!" She pulled me to her, hugged me tightly, and sobbed like I had never heard her cry before. It was a cry of relief, frustration, and agony, and I cried with her.

Father Koevoets directed me firmly but gently through the hall to the breezeway. The transformation was about to begin. Tante Suus followed closely behind carrying a large sheet, which she draped around my shoulders. She unbraided my hair and combed it out for ease of handling. I was not really thrilled about what was about to happen.

Father Koevoets was ready to proceed. His hands again disappeared into the deep pockets and he took out a brush, a comb, clippers, and scissors. "I am ready, Rita," he announced, holding up the comb and scissors. He tried to ease my discomfort with a smile. "How about you? Are you ready to look like a boy?"

I was about to lose something precious—my long, dark brown hair. But there was no turning back. I nodded. When nothing happened, I looked up, thinking he had not understood my answer. I mumbled, "Yes, I'm ready!"

Father Koevoets lifted my chin to force me to look him in the eye. "Would it help if I tell you that you are the bravest and most courageous twelve-year-old girl I have ever known?"

The lump in my throat prevented me from responding. I began crying quietly. Through my tears, I saw the first of my precious tresses fall to the floor.

During the entire process, Father Koevoets tried very hard to distract me. He told jokes and talked about the funny things he had experienced as a teacher in the Catholic-Chinese school system. Meanwhile, the falling strands around me could not escape my attention.

Finally, Father Koevoets triumphantly announced that he was through. "I hope you and your family approve of my talent as a barber!" He whipped the cloth from around my shoulders, brushed off the loose hair with the flair of a real barber, and turned me around to see the results of his handiwork.

I threw my arms around his waist and sobbed uncontrollably. I couldn't explain why I was crying, but the tears just kept coming.

"Now, now. Shhhh. What do we have here? Why are you crying? I've just created a handsome lad, and . . . lads don't cry. Just remember, Rita, this is not forever. You know that, don't you? Your hair will grow back, I promise you." He loosened my arms and handed me the handkerchief he had used before to wipe his clammy hands and forehead.

"I know that, Father," I said. "I'm sorry, I just couldn't help myself."

"That's all right, my child, just do what your parents want you to do, and I'm sure everything will work out." Then, rubbing his hands together—obviously proud of his creation—he suggested presenting me to the rest of the family. Standing behind me and placing his hand on my shoulders, he guided me into the dining room, where everyone was anxiously waiting. "Here she is, folks! Doesn't she look handsome?"

Nobody said a word. My parents and aunt hugged and kissed me. I knew I had their total approval. Neither Ronald nor René seemed to be affected. Ronald acted nonchalant, as if to say that it would be ridiculous to think that a simple haircut could change his sister into a brother. No! He was not impressed.

Meanwhile, Father Koevoets had moved to the dining room table, where earlier he had dropped a big bundle on the floor. He sat down, patiently waiting for the moment when he could unveil the complete transformation. "This is for you," he said, handing me the package, "to complete your new identity. There are four sets of boys' shirts, underwear, shorts, socks, and a pair of shoes. I hope I haven't forgotten anything and that everything fits, Rita. Why don't you try them on?"

Unable to say a word, I was overwhelmed by the thought that this priest, who hardly knew us, had come up with a plan to disguise me, to protect me from the enemy. It was a very generous and unselfish gesture.

"Thank you, Father. I will try them on right now."

I carried the bundle into my bedroom. Tante Suus followed. Putting on boys' clothes felt strange, and my sense of excitement increased with each garment I tried on. I couldn't wait to see what the next piece would do to enhance my new identity! In spite of my initial trauma, I found the change very appealing and the hairstyle quite suitable. I liked it.

As I looked at the image of the boy in the mirror, an odd sensation came over me, a kind of inner transformation. I knew that it would not take much effort for me to pretend to be a boy. I was confident and ready to meet the challenge. In fact, the charade might even be fun. As I twisted and turned before the full-length mirror, admiring myself, I realized Tante Suus was no less pleased with what she saw. Like two children with a surprise between them, we began to giggle!

"How do you like the change, Tante Suus?" I asked joyfully.

"I like it, darling. I like it very much," she responded with a twinkle in her eyes. "As a matter of fact, I love it! Nobody will know the difference. Come on, let's show the rest of the family." She started to pull me out of the room, but suddenly she stopped, nearly throwing me off balance.

"What's the matter, Tante?" I asked, surprised by her abrupt move.

"Nothing, dear. I just want to make sure that you're perfect." She fixed my hair and gave me a last going-over, then she took my hand and we walked dramatically to the end of the hall, preparing for a grand entrance. Unfortunately, our attempt was spoiled because Father Koevoets, who saw us coming, leaped out of his chair and assumed the role of an emcee. He announced, "Mr. and Mrs. la Fontaine, may I present to you my creation!" With a deep bow and an elegant swing of his arm, he pointed in our direction. "Don't you agree that I've performed the transformation of the year?"

My parents, delighted with what they saw and deeply

moved by what the priest had accomplished, thanked him repeatedly. My brothers looked me over with displeasure and simply returned to driving their toy trucks.

Later that evening, I reflected on what was to come, and my excitement returned. I was by now quite comfortable with my new identity. I was looking forward to my new life as a boy.

My parents, on the other hand, recognized the complexity of the situation. Although they agreed with the priest that this was the only way to assure my safety, they were also aware that the burden was on my shoulders. They had no choice but to have faith in my ability to carry the newly acquired responsibility. Their main concerns were my safety and well-being, which were now out of their hands. I, on the other hand, interpreted their agreement with the priest and his creation as a sign of their trust in me.

Now the question was how my two younger brothers would react. Would they understand the importance of keeping my identity a secret? After all, I was still their big sister, even though I was pretending to be their big brother. Ronald and René had not said much throughout the makeover, and nobody had paid much attention to them since it all began.

Wondering what they thought of the change, I walked over to them and jokingly held out my hand for a handshake. "Meet your new brother," I said cordially. Neither of them reacted. Could it be that they resented all the attention that had been bestowed on me? Surprised and somewhat disappointed to see them turning away, I asked, "Ronald, what do you think? Honestly, how do I look? Do you like the change?"

He looked at me disapprovingly and said, half-heartedly, "Why is it so important to make you a boy? I know you're not a boy; you're my sister."

"I know I'm your sister, Ronald," I responded, hurt by his attitude. "You understand why I must dress this way, don't you? But that's not what I'm asking you right now. I want to know what you think of the way I look."

He glanced at me again. "You look all right, but you're still a girl."

Those were his final words on the subject. I tried to hide the sting I felt at his lack of understanding and support. "You're just jealous, Ronald! But that's okay, you'll get over it. I'm doing what I have to do!" With that, I walked away.

My world, the world of a typical *Indisch Meisje,* a girl of mixed Dutch and Indonesian ancestry in the Indies, had unraveled.

The following day, February 16, 1942, I began what I perceived to be a challenging and adventurous life.

Chapter 6

When I awoke the next morning, I pulled aside the mosquito net that was draped around my bed and stuck my head out the window. A nauseating stench overwhelmed me. A layer of thick smoke was still lingering over the lower parts of town. I heard none of the usual city sounds of jingling bicycle bells or traffic. The clattering drumbeat of horses' hooves and the incessant chattering of vegetable and fruit vendors in their *sampans* on the river were all missing, too.

Only a few river merchants were crossing the waters with their wares, and that was unusual. The early morning hours were the busiest for them, and their boats, laden with things to sell, usually jammed the waterways. There was no doubt—the war was at our doorstep!

The atmosphere inside the house was subdued. It lacked the usual liveliness and spontaneous conversation. My mother and aunt were oddly quiet. The servants moved about in silence. Ronald and René played quietly in a corner of the living room. It seemed as if everyone was expecting something to happen.

What was everyone anticipating? To keep fear from overwhelming me, I had to keep my mind occupied. I considered playing my accordion, but that seemed out of place, given the circumstances. Unable to think of anything else, I decided to do it anyway and took refuge in my bedroom.

Seated on my bed in front of the full-length mirror, I strapped my accordion around my shoulders and rested it on my thighs. I was now able to see the mirror image of the broadside of the instrument and find the right chord settings. With my ear resting on the accordion, I pushed and pulled gently. The soft sounds I created allowed me to determine that the chords of both hands were synchronized. Totally involved in the music, I was, for a short time, in my own little world and completely oblivious to the grim reality around me.

The next day, February 17, we heard once again the roar of trucks. This time they carried Japanese soldiers instead of Dutch refugees. Jeeplike vehicles and sedans followed the convoy, which was headed in the direction of the military base on the other side of town. The Japanese had finally arrived to occupy Djambi!

Later that day, our *djongos* stormed into the dining room, forgetting his place as a servant as he cried out, "*Toean! Toean!* Every flagpole in town has a new white flag with a red ball in the center. They tore down the red, white, and blue Dutch flags!"

"Calm yourself, Karto! Relax!" my father insisted. "Tell us what you saw."

Karto, still highly emotional, told us about the Japanese

takeover. Some of the houses formerly occupied by Dutch families were now housing Japanese military personnel.

"As soon as an officer moves into a house, a flag is raised and a guard posted at the front door," he reported.

Suddenly, he realized that he had been disrespectful toward his master. His dark eyes closed, his head dropped, and he looked down. He fell to his knees and, with his hands folded on his chest, said, "Forgive me, *Toean*, for intruding."

"There is nothing to forgive, Karto," my father replied, gently pulling the man up.

"What will happen now?" Karto asked.

"We just have to wait and see," my father replied.

Two days after the military convoy invaded Djambi, we listened to the radio and heard a voice addressing the public in Japanese. The message was immediately followed by a translation into the Malay language. The Japanese army had officially captured and occupied Djambi! The Dutch were under house arrest. We were now prisoners of war.

The streets were suddenly bustling with cars and trucks carrying Japanese troops. They confiscated the cars the Dutch families had abandoned in their haste to leave. We felt alone. We hadn't seen any member of the Dutch community for days, nor had we any idea how many, if any, were still in Djambi.

Law and order returned to our city—Japanese law and order, that is. The rioting and looting of just a few days ago stopped. Through our servants we learned that there was no possibility of escape. All river exits and roads out of Djambi were guarded. A twenty-four-hour surveillance of the Dutch community and the riverfront was in effect.

Additional Japanese radio broadcasts provided information about current activities, the latest occupation developments, and the installation of a new town government. One particular announcement was directly addressed to the Dutch community.

"A special message for the Dutch citizens still in town! Remain calm, stay close to your homes, and be patient. The military authority will visit you soon with further instructions. Any attempt to escape by leaving town is punishable, and disobedience could be fatal!"

We had no idea how others in Djambi were reacting to this dire situation. Our only communication with the outside world was through our servants. Fear and anxiety were reflected in their faces. They had deep concern for us and for themselves.

On the fifth day of the Japanese occupation, February 21, 1942, a military vehicle with four *Kempetai* officials stopped in front of our house. At once, my father sent us all to a bedroom. "Stay out of sight and keep the children quiet, Suus," he ordered his sister-in-law. "Take care of them!"

We obeyed, but the bedroom door was slightly ajar and I peeked through the opening. Two of the four—one being an officer—entered through the front door. A third member stepped out of the jeep and headed toward the side of the house, where he had a clear view of the back entrance. The driver stood guard by his vehicle in front of the house.

The higher-ranking officer who had entered the house looked familiar to me but I was unable to place him at first. Suddenly, my mind cleared. He was the shopkeeper and owner of the Japanese store in town! Weeks before, he had boarded up his shop and mysteriously vanished. His was the shop that our cook had told my aunt about.

Strangely, there were no overt signs of recognition when the officer came face-to-face with my parents. He spoke perfect Dutch, the outward sign of a western education. No longer the humble and polite merchant trying to sell his wares, he was now our superior. We were his subjects.

"You, sir!" He addressed my father. "You must be the postmaster of this beautiful and peaceful little town?"

"Yes, sir, I am. My name is la Fontaine. How do you do, sir? May I introduce you to my wife?"

"How do you do, ma'am? Haven't I seen you in my store before?"

My mother admitted to having been there once, but said she could not remember having seen him.

Solving the mystery, he responded, "Oh, that is certainly possible. You see, I could observe my customers through a one-way mirror without their knowledge. That's why we have never met. Are there more members of your family?"

"Yes, sir," my mother answered, recovering from her embarrassment. "I have a sister living with us, and—"

"We have three sons," my father quickly interjected. Hearing him mention that he had three sons reminded me of my new identity and made me quiver.

"So, you have three sons!" I heard the officer say. "In my country you are considered a fortunate man. No! More appropriately, you are a blessed man. Do you realize that sons are a valuable asset to Japanese men?"

"Yes, sir, I do know that. Do you wish to meet the rest of my family?" my father asked, sounding a bit reluctant and uncertain.

"No! No! That is not necessary. I shall meet them later," the officer replied.

What he said next frightened me.

"Two of my men will come to the house in about an hour to escort you and your family to the police station. In the meantime, I want you all to pack a bag for a short stay away from home."

"A short stay?" my father repeated, not certain what the officer was implying. "For how long? What do you mean, sir?"

"A short stay of say . . . ten days. At the most, two weeks," the officer said nonchalantly. "At the police station you will register the entire family, after which you will all be taken to the school building across the street. There you'll stay and enjoy our free room and board until further notice. Do you have any questions, sir?"

My father gave no response.

"Don't take too much with you. Make sure, however, that you bring along all the necessary vital documents, such as passports, birth certificates, and the like," the officer added. With those words, the meeting ended. I saw him straighten his uniform and rearrange the sword at his hip. I quietly pushed the door closed.

The officer took it upon himself to make a tour of the house and began walking through the hallway, accompanied by my parents. After they passed our room, I opened the door slightly and peeked out again. The three were standing at the end of the hallway, peering into the dining room. The officer had noticed a portrait in the room. It was of a young woman. The long pause indicated that he was taking an appreciative look. He recognized the young woman in the photograph as my mother. "A beautiful portrait, madame!" he said. "You don't look a year older." My mother told me later that the officer had smiled seductively at her, totally ignoring my father.

After he and his entourage left, my father commented in a rather sarcastic tone, "What a flirt he is!" I didn't hear my mother's comment, if she made one, but I knew that she must have been made very uncomfortable by the officer's remark in the presence of my father.

While we were packing, I overheard my parents' conversation in their bedroom next to ours. "I have the dreadful feeling that we will not be allowed to return home," my father claimed. "I am almost certain that our stay will last longer than what they're telling us. The Japanese are using this opportunity as a pretext to gather and relocate all Dutch families to a central point. They will justify their actions by claiming to do it for the safety of the prisoners. Trust me! This is going to happen exactly as I see it!"

My father sounded so certain in his prediction that it frightened me. He also expressed worries about the confiscation and looting of our home and of other homes, if not by the natives then certainly by the military. "And another thing," he continued angrily. "Our personal belongings will be impounded as souvenirs, which these soldiers will take home. It makes me sick to my stomach to think that we cannot be here to fight them off or stop them." My father freely vented his outrage and bitterness. "Mark my words," he predicted. "All the things I have said are going to happen!" He must have been devastated to know that he and his countrymen were powerless against the new regime.

A short time later, two soldiers bearing rifles with bayonets arrived at our home. They walked up to my father, bowed, and addressed him in Japanese. Signaling with his hands and speaking in a potpourri of Dutch, English, and Malay, my father tried to let them know that we needed a few more minutes. One of the soldiers pointed to his watch and, using his fingers, indicated that he granted us fifteen more minutes.

While rushing through the house to finish our packing, we heard a truck pull into the driveway. Four soldiers jumped off the vehicle, reported to the guards, and entered our home. Totally disregarding our presence, they moved from one bedroom to the next, pulling all available mattresses and pillows from the beds. They carried them out to the truck and simply drove off.

Deeply disturbed by the incident and furious at the soldiers' ill-mannered behavior, my father shouted after them in any language he could think of. "What the hell is going on? Where are they taking the mattresses?" He yelled at the two soldiers who were guarding us. "Damn! You two are no help either," he fumed, unable to communicate in Japanese.

My mother jumped in and dragged my father away from them and back into the room, where I heard her begging him to calm down and finish his packing. To hear my father carrying on as he had, spitting out words that I had never heard him say before, left me stunned. Indeed, I had never known him to use such harsh words or to behave like that.

Minutes later, one of the two guards started to walk through the house, locking and sealing every door and window. The other approached my father and pointed at his watch to tell him that the time was up.

As we stood together outside waiting for the guards to complete closing up the house, the servants joined us for the last time. The sad circumstance caused these faithful servants to act beyond conventional custom, and quite unexpectedly, my brothers and I each received an embrace and a sort of kiss on the cheek. It wasn't really a kiss; it was more like a sniff or slight touching of our faces with theirs, according to their custom. My parents and aunt all offered rather emotional farewells because this loyal group of natives had been in my parents' employ for many years. They had traveled with us from Java to Sumatra eight months before when my father was transferred.

The guards interrupted our farewells and shouted orders to the servants, poking them with their bayonets to get them away from us. The servants did not resist and obediently moved aside. We waved our good-byes and were taken away. That was the last time we saw them.

I found out later, when I was much older, that it wasn't unusual in 1942 to be confronted by a Japanese officer who had lived and worked in your hometown for years in the East Indies before the war. They were spies, planted in communities across the Dutch East Indies by the Japanese military to learn about conditions throughout the islands in preparation for their invasion. In the late 1930s and early 1940s, Dutch harbor pilots had frequently been questioned by Japanese cargo ship officers who took notes and photographs of harbor installations across the archipelago. Some of them had better maps of the harbors than the Dutchmen assigned to guide their ships in and out.

On February 21, when we were herded to the Djambi police station and then the school building across the street, our fate was sealed. For how long, we didn't know. Java and the very southern and northern tips of Sumatra were still in Dutch hands. On February 15, the day Singapore surrendered, the day we celebrated Tante Suus's birthday, the British and Americans had dissolved their agreements with the Dutch to protect the Indies and pulled out of the area. The organized defense of the islands was completely in the hands of the Dutch.

Six days later, the Allied fleet engaged the Japanese fleet off the northern coast of Java, near Soerabaja. After three days, only four Allied ships out of fourteen had survived the battles that ensued. The Japanese invaded Java on March 1, and the Dutch surrendered the entire Indies at Bandoeng, Java, on March 9. A Dutch minesweeper managed to escape to Australia disguised as a tropical island.

The Japanese finally landed in northern Sumatra at the end of March to accept the surrender of the Dutch forces there. Resistance was mostly over. The Dutch East Indies, and my family, were cut off from the rest of the world for forty-one months. I was going to have to maintain my disguise as a boy for a long time.

PART II

FEBRUARY 1942–NOVEMBER 1942

The Japanese established headquarters all over town. Our home was no longer ours. It was theirs. The local school would become our home away from home, but before going there we had to register at the police station.

At the station we joined other Dutch companions in distress. My father looked around and expressed surprise at the number of former Dutch government officials who were in the same situation.

I quickly observed that our family was the only one with children. A few single men were in the group, along with some older couples and one single woman—my teacher, Miss Seau.

When my mother saw Miss Seau, she immediately walked up to her and pulled her aside in private conversation. Miss Seau knew that I was a girl! She was the one who encouraged me to play the accordion on Saturdays at singing class. She led the students in song while I accompanied them on my accordion.

Just as the two women began to speak in low tones, heads bowed, my father approached to inform my mother that he was being called in for the "registration." I watched the two women from a short distance away. An expression of surprise came over Miss Seau's face; then she walked away from my mother and in my direction.

"Hello, Miss Seau. Mom told you?"

She returned my greeting with a smile and a rather reserved, "Hello! You're looking good! The change is very becoming."

Something in the way she looked at me made me uneasy, so I asked her, "Is anything wrong?" She moved closer to me and whispered, "Your mother told me everything except . . ." She paused for a moment, looking around to assure privacy.

"Except what, Miss Seau?"

"Except . . . what do I call you, Rita? What is your new name?"

Her question caught me totally off guard. We had forgotten to give me a new name! Rita wouldn't do anymore. I needed a boy's name. In our excitement, none of us had thought of it!

"Shhh! Excuse me, Miss Seau!" I said in panic. "Please don't talk to anybody about me until I return." I fearfully looked around, afraid that someone might have overheard her call me by my real name.

When I whispered our oversight to my mother, she turned pale.

"Dear Lord, how could we have overlooked something so important?" She became frantic, realizing that my father was not there to discuss the matter. Tante Suus, noticing the commotion, came closer to see what was wrong. The two whispered and now it was my aunt's turn to be shocked.

At the same time, my father emerged from the office. When he approached them, Tante Suus sighed with relief and left my parents to talk.

From a distance, it was as if I was viewing a silent movie with the actors involved in a squabble. Then my father gently took my mother's arm and led her toward us. He seemed very much in control, relaxed, and confident, unlike my mother. As they reached us, my father said to me with a big grin on his face, "Hi, Rick!"

"Is that my new name, Pop?" I whispered.

"Yes! From now on your name is Richard. You may be called Rick." When I heard that, it was as if the little girl named Rita with beautiful long brown hair no longer existed. I felt that this new creation by the name of Rick, with the boy's haircut and dressed in boys' clothing, had completely taken over her life.

My father then gathered us around him for a talk. He told my brothers that they had to forget they had a sister. "You now have a brother, and his name is Rick." René, who was much too young to really understand what was going on, took it all in stride. Ronald, on the other hand, seemed annoyed.

"I was very lucky that the clerk did not do any cross-checking, especially on Rita's birth certificate," my father continued, addressing my mother and aunt. "I would not have known how to get out from under it if he had. It would have been disastrous, but . . . all is well. Thank goodness!"

I returned to Miss Seau to give her the news about my name. When I rejoined my family, Father Koevoets was there. He gave me two thumbs up and a wink as if to say, "Keep up the good work!"

Registration for all prisoners was completed that afternoon. We were ordered to gather up our belongings, line up, and march to the school across the street. Walking through the gate with the group reminded me of cattle being driven into a corral, just like in a western movie. On one side of the school yard, we rested on the grass in the cool shade of the trees. Japanese guards flanked the area, keeping a sharp eye on us.

Moments later, food was distributed. We had no idea where it came from or who had prepared it. During the meal, we tossed about many questions regarding our situation, but none of us knew the answers. One of the most crucial questions — "Will we stay together or be segregated?" — was left unanswered. Dread overcame us all.

I remembered what my father had said earlier, about how the enemy would have better control over its prisoners if they were all concentrated in one place. It was true, and it was happening now. There was no doubt in my mind that he had been right.

After lunch, the sharp sounds of slamming car doors cut through the already tense atmosphere. Voices at the front gate spoke what sounded like an order in Japanese, directed at us. Although none of us understood what was said, each of us instinctively jumped.

There he was again! The same officer, the shopkeeper, who had come to our home that morning. He carried his sword in one hand as he walked toward the podium set up for the occasion, which was no more than a pallet. His slow, careful march was a deliberate effort to impress us with his authority. He looked over the group and with a beckoning hand gesture invited everyone to come closer.

Before he had a chance to begin, voices in the crowd yelled out, "How long will we be here?" "Why are we here?" "What are you going to do with us?"

The officer held up a hand to restore order. He grinned, looked over the crowd, bowed deeply, and totally ignored the questions. "Did you enjoy your lunch?" he asked. Retorts flew from the audience. "You call that lunch! It was fine, but not enough! When is the next mealtime?"

"Yes! When is our next meal? We are all quite hungry!" other voices echoed.

"Answer our questions, damn it!"

Once again, he ignored the remarks, and standing erect and confident, he began his speech. First he introduced himself. "I am Captain Matoba. Many among you know me as the storekeeper in town. Some of you have been in my store. Because of that and my ability to speak your language fluently, my superiors appointed me to this post. As long as you do what is expected of you, we won't have any problems getting along with each other."

A deathly hush fell. Except for the sound of someone sobbing behind me, there was total, eerie silence. I moved closer to my father and placed my hand in his. Staring straight ahead and seemingly unemotional, he, in return, squeezed my hand tenderly.

Captain Matoba was officially the commandant of the Djambi prisoner-of-war camp. He instructed us in the procedures of bowing to our superiors and the importance of showing respect to all military personnel. He demonstrated a proper bow and instructed us to participate in the practice. "I expect all of you to respect and obey all orders," he shouted.

"How long are you going to keep us here?" demanded a man in the group.

"Please do not interrupt!" the captain fired back. "You will have an opportunity to ask questions after I have said what I came to say. Thank you!"

Silence returned. He spoke of the camp's rules and its guard roster. He described all the important buildings surrounding the school, such as the military and police headquarters. "I am telling you this so you won't try anything stupid to get yourself in trouble or attempt to escape." General groans of disapproval went up from the crowd, but no one spoke words of discontent. Matoba had gotten across his message of intimidation.

After a short pause, he invited the women to gather in front of the school. Worried looks passed between the men and women. The dismantling of family—the critical structure of our lives—was about to take place.

With one hand on his sword, the captain strode from the school playground. The women followed. In front of the building, he turned around and faced them for the first time in his capacity as commandant of this camp.

At this point, Mrs. de Vries, the mayor's wife and the oldest female, was instructed to divide the women into three groups, assign them to the three available classrooms, and elect room captains. They were then allowed to enter their assigned rooms and told, "Pick a spot, deposit your luggage, then join the men outside."

The room where my mother, aunt, brothers, and I would stay had mattresses lined up against the walls and piles of pillows nearby, all of which had been confiscated from our homes earlier that day. My brothers and I were the only children in the whole group of about fifty.

Meanwhile, outside, the men awaiting their families' return were in a state of despair. The captain, in conference with his staff a few steps away, returned to the podium. Without further delay, he announced, "You may not want to hear this, but the men will be going to the jailhouse."

The women wept uncontrollably, grabbing their husbands for comfort. One woman fainted.

Suddenly, above all the weeping, the grief-stricken voice of a woman wailed, "Why didn't you tell us up front that you planned to take our husbands away from us? Why couldn't you have been honest with us? We don't deserve this kind of treatment!" She spoke with such passion, such heartbreak, that all began to weep anew.

Another woman responded, crying, while she slowly walked up to the podium: "Because they are bloody cowards. They came to our homes to make sure that we would all show, so that they can lock us up and do whatever they please with us, including separate us from our husbands. From the very beginning they knew what they were going to do with us." She stopped and faced the captain, lunged at him, and whacked him with the sack that held her belongings. "Oh, you contemptible louse!" she screamed at the top of her lungs.

Two guards ran to Captain Matoba's rescue and pulled the woman away. Fighting them, she shouted all kinds of obscenities and clawed at the empty air. A man, probably her husband, jumped out of the crowd to go to her aid. Pointed bayonets stopped him.

Taking full advantage of his official role, Captain Matoba addressed the woman harshly. "You leave me no choice but to place you in isolation at the police station if you don't stop your outrageous and childish outbursts." His words made the prisoners even angrier.

A slender woman with long blond hair stepped out of the crowd. Without a word, she walked straight to the captain, stopped directly in front of him, and spat in his face. The captain reacted instantly. He slapped her across the face several times. She did not fight back.

Following that, a woman with birdlike features began to shriek. She burst out of the crowd, shook her fists, and ran up to the pallet. The guards stood fast and stopped her. All the while, her husband pleaded, "Please, Sjaan, for God's sake, don't do this! We are facing enough trouble as it is. Please?"

Captain Matoba stepped down from the platform, walked over to the woman, and slapped her soundly in the face. We gasped at the loud crack of his hand against her skin. "This, woman, is for not listening to your husband, who told you to be quiet!" he hissed. "You should have listened to him!"

From a distance her husband cried out, "She never could keep her mouth shut!" Tears ran down his cheeks.

Captain Matoba returned to the platform and said, "Are there more protesters among you? Please come forward and get all this hostility out of your system. Now!" He spoke calmly and with the complacency of authority.

Two military trucks arrived at the front gate. The male prisoners were instructed to get ready to board and to say their good-byes. Last-minute instructions about medications, rest, delicate backs, and other concerns were the caring words they heard from their wives.

In the final moments with my father, not much was said, but expressions of love were plentiful. My mother was the last to cling to him before he jumped onto the truck. We all waved until the two vehicles carrying our men were totally out of sight.

I missed my father immediately. I felt cheated out of a happiness I needed and deserved. Joy was now out of my reach.

After the men left, the women began readying their allotted cubicles for the night. Lacking tools of any kind, they found large rocks along the edge of the yard and used them as hammers to drive nails into the wall to hook up the *klamboes*. In the tropical climate, mosquito nets were a necessity. Mosquitoes spread horrible diseases.

Tired and unable to blot out the realization that we were now prisoners of war guarded by Japanese soldiers, I thought of the only thing of importance to me—my father.

I imagined him sitting on a dirty, filthy bed in a jail cell. How could he cope without my mother and Tante Suus doting on him? How humiliating for him to live under the same roof as common criminals! Obeying someone else's rules would not be easy for him, either. The more I thought of his predicament, the more it saddened me. I covered my head with my pillow to hide my tears. I did my best to remove images of that small figure sitting on a bench in a damp prison cell all by himself, except for the *kakkerlakken* and *koetoe boesoek,* the cockroaches and bedbugs that ran rampant in such places.

I was thinking so intently about my father that I imagined I heard his voice. His encouraging words told me, "Be brave and strong! I count on your strength and courage to stand by your mother, aunt, and brothers while I'm gone!"

This telepathic communication somehow gave me a boost and the confidence that all would turn out well. The belief that my father had spoken to me through the darkness of the night allowed me to fall asleep peacefully.

Our plight was simply unimaginable. Just a few weeks before, we were living a life of total comfort. Now we were restricted to a life of total confinement. It was hard to have my father taken from me. How difficult it must have been for my mother and the other women to have their husbands taken away. The mean Japanese had done this to us.

Not everyone shared the same thoughts about the Japanese, though. While some felt disdain, others showed outright hatred. There was yet another group who looked at the war philosophically. They considered the presence of the Japanese simply an inevitable episode of the war. According to that group, the war, not the Japanese, was to blame for all our misery. The Christians, who lived by the Bible, preached about loving the enemy. So there it was! Nobody was to blame for anything, yet there was suffering and unhappiness all around us, in fact, all around the world.

The previous months had taught me that life was a precious gift and that it could be taken away in an instant. Life should be cherished, not destroyed. Would compassion and understanding be better instruments for peace?

I was only a young child, but it worried me to see adults fight and go to war to get what they wanted. To involve the whole world was even more unbelievable.

Chapter 8

The next morning at six o'clock we were awakened by the pounding of a boot against the door and a loud shout in the Indonesian language. Like waking up from a bad dream, I had to remember where I was and how I came to be lying on a mattress on the floor of my former classroom. Then in a rush it all came back.

An hour later, the captain arrived, casually dressed this time. With a hand signal, he invited the women to follow him. When we were all gathered around, he asked in a friendly manner, "Ladies, have you forgotten to do what I taught you yesterday?"

Nobody had remembered to bow. Embarrassed, but realizing what he meant, we bowed the way he had taught us, and he returned the greeting. He then demonstrated how we should greet him in Japanese. "*Ohayo gozaimasu, Matoba-san.* Good morning, Mr. Matoba. *Ogenki desu ka?* How are you?" He taught us two other greetings, one for the afternoon, "*Konnichi wa,*" and another for the evening, "*Komban wa.*" After this short lesson in Japanese etiquette, he asked the women how they liked their new home.

"What home are you talking about, sir? The one where we have to sleep on the floor?" asked one, pointing at her classroom.

"And get up aching all over?" added another.

"And we have not even mentioned how drafty the rooms are," yet another blurted. "You call this home?" Her snarling remarks resounded throughout the school yard.

Captain Matoba said little during the women's outburst, but stared at them with piercing eyes. That look quickly reminded them of the events of the previous day. The protesting women stiffened and were suddenly quiet. Seemingly unaffected by the incident, he continued in an upbeat manner. "I am sorry to hear that you find your accommodations not satisfying, ladies. I've tried to find you bunk beds or cots. Obviously, I was unsuccessful. I sincerely hope that you will accept the current conditions and try to have better nights. It will not last long."

A voice came from behind. "Better nights? Without our husbands?"

"As I said before, it won't be for long!" His voice became harsh.

"Why is it that I don't believe you?" the woman snapped back.

Captain Matoba looked her straight in the eye and said sternly, "Let me assure you that life will be easier if you make an effort to adjust yourself to these present circumstances instead of showing all this hostility. It won't get you anywhere—or haven't you learned anything from what happened yesterday?" He gave the woman a frown of disapproval.

He handed Mrs. de Vries two sheets of paper. One

57

contained the names and personal information of the prisoners. He wanted her to verify their accuracy. The second sheet contained a row of Roman numerals and their equivalents written in Japanese. She was to teach the women to pronounce these numbers during *tenko,* roll call, which was done every morning.

At the end of the visit, he appointed Mrs. de Vries camp manager and charged her publicly with the responsibility of the prisoners' welfare. He also suggested that she select a committee to assist her in her daily duties.

Soon after the captain left, two natives entered the grounds under guard. They carried two small, open steel containers on a large stick that rested on their shoulders. This was breakfast!

The food had been prepared at the jail and carried on foot in this manner for more than two miles. The uncovered containers exposed the contents to the hot sun, filthy dust, and a myriad of insects that inhabited the island. We were prisoners, but we expected to be treated humanely. Knowing that our next meal would arrive in the same manner, some of the women wrote a note of grievance to Captain Matoba.

Immediately after that, Mrs. de Vries called her first meeting. The agenda consisted of the official confirmation of the elected room captains and the business of establishing several work projects and assigning work crews. Volunteers stepped forward and were appointed to a variety of tasks. Since my mother had fulfilled the role of food distributor on the previous day, she remained in that capacity.

The verified list of names and our attached note of grievance, describing the unacceptable arrangement of meal transportation, were sent to the commandant. To everyone's surprise, an improvement in the way our food was delivered was clearly noticeable the very next day. Lids were on the containers.

The following morning, standing in line for the required *tenko,* we were taught to count in Japanese. It took some time to do it correctly, but we finally succeeded. The officer of the guard was pleased.

Several days passed without the captain visiting us. When he finally did, he had this to say: "The officer of the guard informed me that the counting at roll call in Japanese was satisfactory." He smiled, and added, "He also suggested that a little more practice could do no harm in perfecting the performance. I am sure that you'll be working on it." Everyone laughed!

That was the first visit in which he was accompanied by the official camp management team, Mrs. de Vries and her assistants. He commended the women for their domesticity, knowing that they were used to a leisurely and pampered lifestyle. "For women who have been spoiled with the luxury and convenience of having servants, you are doing a tremendous job in maintaining your living quarters." He smiled approvingly.

"Thank you, sir. Realistically, what choice do we have?" Mrs. de Vries responded with a grin.

"That's right, Mrs. de Vries. You have no choice, and that's why I am glad that you have the common sense to not let yourselves go." He then mentioned a special project he wanted to discuss and see implemented. "It is a project that will keep some, if not all, of you ladies occupied for the duration. It will certainly benefit everyone in the end."

As it turned out, the special project was to start a vegetable garden. "There is plenty of land behind the school and it's free for the taking. So, why don't we take advantage of it?" Cheerfully determined to win them over to his plan, he continued, "I want to give you something to do to keep you from becoming bored. Let's get down to business, shall we? Who is the captain of the garden detail?"

From the back of the crowd, my aunt, a shy, five-foot-tall woman, walked toward him. There was a look of surprise on his face. Recovering from whatever it was that surprised him, he asked her several technical questions. He wanted detailed information regarding ground preparation, fertilization, and ultimately, planting. "The land has never been farmed," he added.

A gardener most of her life, Tante Suus responded with confidence. She informed him that she would need several months to do what needed to be done.

"Several months?"

"Yes, sir, certainly, considering that my crew has never held a hoe or even worked in a garden. More importantly, working in an open field, the women will be exposed to the hot, scorching sun. To work under these conditions, they will need special protection."

"Yes, you are right!" he agreed.

"And with regard to the time," my aunt continued, "I have to warn you that there will be a period of slow progress in the beginning. After all, these women have to perform the work of a plow. They have to break up the soil and cut furrows in preparation for sowing. Until the team gets over these first hurdles, things might not begin to happen. It can be done, and it will be done, but adequate time is absolutely necessary."

I had never known Tante Suus to be such a talker. Suddenly, she became a teacher and leader in agricultural matters. I was never so impressed.

Tante Suus was a woman of skill. Her hobby was experimenting with pollinating dahlias, roses, and other flowers. She had created several award-winning species. Beyond working with flowers, she always grew a small vegetable garden. In short, she had a green thumb in addition to all her other talents, including being our *keuken prinses* (family cook), our *dame van de huishouding* (housekeeper), our *gouvernante* (nanny), and my mother's nurse and caretaker.

The commandant praised Tante Suus for her knowledge and self-confidence. "I can see that the project and its workers are in very good hands." Then he spoke to the group. "This little woman has the spirit we all need. So, it's settled!" From that day on, he referred to Tante Suus as "the little woman."

Just as the situation seemed to be resolved, one of the women ridiculed my aunt's optimistic plan. "Suus," she shouted indignantly, "what are you saying? We won't be here that long."

The captain interjected angrily. "That may be so, ma'am, but that should not be a problem. And it should certainly not be *your* problem. The work can still be done, even if it is just to keep you all occupied and give you"— he turned to face the woman—"something to do other than be hostile."

The woman challenged him. "What is the point of starting something, knowing that it cannot be finished?"

Toying with her, the captain answered, "The point is, my good woman, as I mentioned before, it'll keep you from boredom!" He turned to Tante Suus and snapped, "You have the tools and the people and you know what to do! Start tomorrow! Make it happen!" He left abruptly.

Mrs. de Vries took the woman aside and reprimanded her for her conduct. Then ground-breaking procedures were discussed and scheduled to begin the next day. Just as Tante Suus had predicted, the first day did not go without difficulty. The main obstacles were lack of experience and the unrelenting heat.

Captain Matoba didn't show up for several days. When he did, he apologized to my aunt for his rude behavior at the last meeting, then announced, "I've come expecting a full progress report from you."

Tante Suus gave him a list of her needs. The first item on the list was straw hats. The women needed them desperately. Hearing about the project gave him great satisfaction.

When she was done talking, the commandant said, "Would you please be kind enough to gather your girls at the usual meeting place. I have an announcement to make! Thank you!"

Tante Suus was rather puzzled by his request and kept the uneasy feeling to herself. She gathered the women together, who now stood waiting for him to speak. They tried to read his face to determine what topic he would unfold this time, although some of them had already made up their minds as to what the message would be.

"Ladies, due to unrest among the natives in the state,

my government thinks it best to keep you in custody for as long as necessary. We do not know how much longer, but until we have resolved the problem on the outside, you'll be safe and protected right here."

I heard someone mumble softly behind me, "I knew it! I knew that would come sooner or later."

Although the news was upsetting, it was really not a surprise, and the women, by now familiar with the consequences of reacting, kept quiet.

After receiving this sad news, the women gathered together and discussed the situation. They found one way to cope with grievances, vent their anger, and fight fear and anxiety: to talk about these things with one another. They could voice their opinions and agree or disagree among themselves.

The days that followed were fairly routine. The women carried out their daily duties, and my brothers and I played games together or helped out where needed. With the latest news about our extended stay, another of my father's predictions came to pass.

Chapter 9

A week later, without advance warning, a truck stopped at the camp's front gate. Two teenagers, a boy and a girl, jumped out, followed by several women. All were wrapped in blankets and looked numb.

The officer who escorted them was unable to give Mrs. de Vries any information. "I am sorry, but I can't tell you what to do with these people," he said. "My only instructions were to bring them here. I assume they are to remain in this camp. I would suggest you take over. Do what you think is right, ma'am."

Mrs. de Vries and her entourage met with the group and took them in without any hesitation. The newcomers spoke English and told us that they were survivors from a ship that had attempted to sail from Kuala Lumpur, Malaysia, to safer regions.

The ship captain's wife, Mrs. Schook, a Dutch woman, and her blind, eighty-year-old mother, were among the survivors. Their ship had joined others in the open sea when a squadron of Japanese planes suddenly appeared and opened fire. Their boat sank, taking Captain Schook down with it.

The planes we had seen flying low over our house just a few days before came to mind. Had those planes bombed the ships? It was an eerie thought.

All of the people, including the old woman, had been in the water for forty-five hours. The group was eventually picked up by a Japanese patrol boat and transported to the mainland. Our camp was the closest to the scene of the attack.

Some survivors had no recollection at all of what had happened. Others were able to provide vivid accounts of every dreadful moment. They had seen ships burning and wreckage and debris floating in the water. They had heard desperate cries for help all around them but were unable to respond. While floating helplessly, they saw many of the passengers drown or die from injuries sustained during the bombardment. A few gave religious testimony, praising God for their miraculous escape from the deep, dark, threatening ocean.

We learned that a medical team was in the group: two physicians, one German, the other a Scot; and four nurses, two Scots and two English-Eurasians. The two teenagers, Norma and Peter, and their English-Eurasian mother were in the group, too.

Mrs. de Vries, as camp manager, assumed that this group was to stay with us and so arranged accommodations. Captain Matoba arrived shortly thereafter and was pleased that Mrs. de Vries had welcomed the newcomers. With his hands clasped behind his back, he followed her and her staff as they led him on a tour, showing him the accommodations she had organized.

"My compliments on your hospitality, your efficiency,

and your kindness toward the new arrivals, Mrs. de Vries! I am sure that you'll advise them of all camp rules and regulations."

Although my brothers and I were unable to communicate with Norma and Peter in English, we got along just fine in play. Peter taught us a song, "She'll Be Coming 'Round the Mountain." We had a lot of fun.

A few days later in the school yard, an unfortunate accident occurred. Being a real tomboy, I climbed a barbed-wire fence, lost my balance, and caught my left foot on a rusty barb. Trying to regain my balance, I grabbed a wire but slipped, causing the barb to penetrate my skin even deeper. Ronald ran for help. When my mother appeared at the scene, she tried to free my foot, but caused me to suffer in the process. I screamed all the while. My foot was bleeding profusely and I was in excruciating pain.

Finally freed, I was carried to our quarters. The Scottish physician, Dr. MacDowell, stopped the bleeding, then cleaned, dressed, and bandaged the wound. Having lost her medical bag during the bombardment, she was not able to do more. Within minutes my foot swelled and I began to run a fever.

Mrs. de Vries requested that Captain Matoba come right away with medical assistance. He arrived accompanied by a Japanese military doctor who immediately opened his black bag and prepared an injection for me.

After the doctor administered the shot, he handed my mother some medication. With the captain as his interpreter, he explained its application to her. During this entire time, Captain Matoba acknowledged no recognition of my mother.

After the Japanese physician's departure, Mrs. de Vries, Dr. MacDowell, and the captain engaged in a conversation. I heard Mrs. de Vries inform the captain that there was a medical team among the newcomers. He hinted that they might be scheduled to work in the local hospital.

He turned toward me, ready to leave, and became aware of my mother's presence. He smiled. "Mrs. la Fontaine, how good to see you. Forgive me for not realizing to whom I was talking just now. I am so sorry; my mind was with the accident and the welfare of the boy. How are you?"

My mother bowed politely. "Fine, thank you, sir."

"So, this must be your son. One of the three you and your husband have—am I correct in my recall?"

"You remember well, sir," she replied a bit uncomfortably. "Rick is our oldest. He is twelve."

The conversation was cut short because Mrs. de Vries needed to speak to the commandant.

"I am sorry, Mrs. la Fontaine," he said. "It seems as if someone needs my attention. It was very nice seeing you again, ma'am. Make sure that your son takes his medicine. I'll talk to you again soon." He bowed and left to join Mrs. de Vries and her staff.

A few days later, promptly at seven-thirty a.m., a guard arrived to take the medical team on their two-mile-long walk to work at the hospital. We watched them march away.

One of the women said with envy, "Limited as their freedom might be, it is better than having to stay in this guarded compound."

My injury allowed me to get to know one of the Scottish nurses. Her name was Helen MacKenzie. She was kind, gentle, soft-hearted, and very tall. She took it upon herself to nurse my foot every evening after her day's work at the hospital. I felt comfortable in her care.

Although I did not speak English and she did not speak Dutch, it was somehow possible for us to piece together what we were saying. We had help from a Dutch-English dictionary I found in the school's small library. I consulted the book many times to assist us in our conversations, and the bond between us turned into a special friendship.

On one of her days off, Helen and I settled in the shade of a small grove of teakwood trees. While she mended a garment, I told her that I could help her with her sewing if the repairs were not too difficult.

She looked at me oddly. "Help with sewing? Sewing is no job for a boy!" she said.

Her remark stunned me for a moment. I had forgotten about my disguise! To the world, I looked like a boy, but inside, I was still a girl. This woman didn't know I was a girl. I debated whether I could trust her enough to tell her my secret.

For some time, not many words were exchanged between us. From the corner of my eye, I could see Helen throw glances in my direction as if she were trying to read my mind. It took a while, but then with concern in her voice she asked, "Rick, are you all right? You seem to be preoccupied all of a sudden. Is something wrong? Did I say something to upset you?" Her hands rested in her lap as she waited for an answer.

"Well, would you be surprised if I told you that Tante Suus taught me how to sew?" It was true; she had taught me how to sew.

"Well, that's good to know. I'll keep that in mind," she

responded, rather amused. She seemed to know there was more on my mind. "Is there anything else you want to tell me?" she asked.

"What makes you think there is more to tell?" I countered. Had my face revealed my anxiety?

"Come on! Out with it! Tell me!" she teased. "It is written all over your face. Well?"

She looked at me with such kindness that I felt obliged to speak up. I told her my secret. After I had said the words, she looked me over as inconspicuously as she could, swallowed hard, and said in disbelief, "Really? I can't even tell that you are not a boy. This is unbelievable! It can't be true!" Suddenly, she laughed long and heartily. "Are you serious?" she asked, still laughing.

"Of course I'm serious. Would I tell you a lie?" I asked, confused by her reaction.

"I am so sorry," she apologized. "I was not laughing at you. I laughed out of amazement. To think that I have been caring for an injured boy, who now tells me that he is a she! I never expected anything like this. I am so, so sorry. It just tickled my funny bone."

She hugged me and we laughed together. I felt tremendously unburdened now that I had revealed my secret to her and shared her laughter. Recovering from the revelation, she turned and said, more soberly, "Your family must love you very much to agree to such a plan. I'm proud of you for making it work."

"It really is no effort. I enjoy playing a boy," I admitted.

I explained how the disguise had come about. She listened quietly, her pale blue eyes looking into mine. She assured me that my secret would be safe with her.

"You fooled even me, a nurse, you brave little rascal," she said, mussing my hair. "Keep up the good work, Rick!"

Following our confidential chat, I spent some months sewing her a dress by hand. Considering her height, over six feet, sewing sixteen strips of the skirt was quite an accomplishment. It was a joy to do that for her in return for the care she had provided me.

Three months before we were detained, my period had started, but two months into confinement, I suddenly realized that it had ceased. I was concerned but not alarmed. Who needs to cope with that female inconvenience? I could do without it, especially now that I was pretending to be a boy. I decided to wait and see before mentioning it to my mother or Tante Suus. But four months went by and it still had not returned. I assumed that my body was in shock from being interned, or concluded it had made a mistake and that I was too young to be bothered with the monthly happening. Whatever the case, I was glad to be rid of it. Lucky me!

Peter and Norma—older than us—and Ronald, René, and I became good friends during the months of living together as prisoners. We were especially fond of Peter because he taught us card and marble games. He was also very good at keeping us interested in doing things. He was instrumental in helping break the monotony of daily life in a prisoner-of-war camp.

Chapter 10

Although the hospital team had permission to accept edible gifts from grateful patients, the coffee and tea they received could not be shared with the rest of us because there were no cooking facilities. The discovery of an unused brick stove in an abandoned shed in the backyard promised a welcome change in our lives. Mrs. de Vries was informed about the find and she asked the commandant if we could use the stove. The request was granted and it wasn't long before a large bag of charcoal was delivered.

The captain came for his weekly visit a few days later. He inquired about the cooking. There was nothing to tell other than that the women were grateful and delighted to experience some familiar domestic chores in their daily routine.

"Is there anything else I can do to please you ladies?" he asked. The captain was in a jovial mood.

"Such as . . . ?" Mrs. de Vries queried, curious as to what he meant.

"Such as?" he repeated after her. "Isn't it customary for European women to have cookies at teatime?"

Mrs. de Vries looked around for support to answer the question. "Yes, we do, Matoba-san. A cookie or two at teatime would certainly be appreciated," she responded teasingly, still not sure where the conversation was heading.

The captain had a boyish glimmer in his eye. "Would you like it if I'd suggest that one of you be designated as the cookie lady, say, to make your wish come true once or twice a week?" he asked. His playfulness indicated to the women that he was in a good mood and really meant what he suggested. They surely wanted to take advantage of this moment of generosity.

"Do you need to ask?" the women exclaimed, looking at one another in great anticipation. "We would love it!"

Captain Matoba promised to deliver everything needed to start the bakery as soon as he could arrange it. "That's settled, then!" he concluded.

Some women were apprehensive about the whole thing. "This is not an empty promise, is it, Matoba-san?" one of the women gingerly asked.

"Certainly not! It is a genuine promise, you'll see."

A few days later, he was as good as his word. A small supply of flour, sugar, cooking oil, and other ingredients was delivered. The women were overwhelmed and ecstatic at the prospect of this new privilege. From the start of our internment, Captain Matoba's willingness to grant some of our wishes made several women accept and appreciate him more as a provider than as a cruel adversary. To show their gratitude, they baked cookies and made him an honorary guest at a tea one afternoon. He was visibly touched.

Days in the camp became routine. The women resigned themselves to a temporary life without their spouses. They kept themselves occupied with camp duties and chores for most of the day. Evenings were filled with friendly gatherings, talking, singing, and card playing, especially bridge.

I found textbooks on a variety of subjects in the classroom cupboards and discovered that I enjoyed reading. My favorite pastimes now were solving math problems, reading about different cultures, and studying geography. I sometimes played school with Ronald and René, but they were not always interested. Ronald's most common complaints were, "You're too bossy and too strict," or "Why do you always have to be the teacher?"

Then one day something happened to cause a break in the monotony of a day at camp. My mother, the food distributor, was scooping out the vegetable soup to fill the small dinner bowls when she noticed something floating on the surface in one of the containers. Not thinking that it might be anything but a vegetable stalk, she kept on distributing the soup equally among the bowls. An occasional attempt to scoop up the stalk failed. It was as if something heavy kept it down. By now she was quite suspicious.

"Attention, ladies! I do not want to alarm you, but please leave your soup bowls on the table for now, until I have solved a mystery in the soup."

"What is it, Paula?"

"I don't know yet," she said, trying to scoop up whatever it was. "I am experiencing something strange here and as long as I don't know what I'm dealing with, your bowls must stay right where they are."

"What do you see? Can you tell what it is?"

"No, but I'm expecting the worst."

"For heaven's sake, what is it?" a woman yelled.

"I believe it's a rat's tail!" Mommie was joking at the time, not realizing how close she was to the truth.

"No, it can't be! Could it?"

The women grimaced at the thought of a rodent bobbing around in their soup.

"Say it's not true, Paula."

"It might very well be," my mother responded, still trying to scoop up the object. "One moment . . . and I will be able to present the culprit to you."

In the meantime, the women had all moved closer to observe the unveiling of the mystery. My mom scooped up the foreign object. It was indeed a boiled rat, and a big one at that. When it came into full view, the women scattered in all directions, horrified. We did without soup that day. The women requested permission to prepare their own meals in the future, but the request was denied.

Several days passed without anything happening that was nearly as exciting as the rat soup. But something pleasant occurred that brought a happy moment into my mother's life. One of the carriers who delivered our meals from the prison secretly handed her a small piece of paper which she very quickly slid into her apron pocket. After distributing the food to the women and children, she slipped into the bathroom and read the brief message. It was from my father.

Tante Suus had seen the clandestine delivery of the note and was waiting for my mother to tell her about it. She suspected this would not stop at just one note and worried about the consequences. Thus, when my mother showed her the note, there was instant reaction.

"Paula, I'm happy and pleased that you have received word from Vic. Really I am, but can the carrier be trusted not to mention it to anyone? How did he know to whom to give the note? What would happen if the man were caught?" My aunt kept firing questions.

"I don't know the answers, but so what?" my mother fired back, upset with the interference and big-sister act. "I'm going to return a note to Vic along the same route. Vic is entitled to an answer!"

"I knew you'd do that." Tears of frustration glistened in Tante Suus's eyes. Her younger sister once again had the upper hand. Because of my mother's delicate health condition, she almost always got her way. Sometimes she acted like a spoiled child. I had seen it happen many times before but never as clearly as that time.

"Nothing much happens in this place. We may as well live dangerously," my mother stubbornly declared.

I knew she was overreacting and how that kind of attitude affected Tante Suus every time. The two were totally different in character. My mother was the happy-go-lucky sister, the one with the devil-may-care attitude. Tante Suus, the smaller of the two, was the serious, protective older sister.

At the end of the confrontation, realizing that she had again lost to her more daring sister, Tante Suus begged, "Paula, please be careful! Think of your children. I don't even want to think of the consequences if something goes wrong."

"Nothing ventured, nothing gained, dear sister," was my mother's response. "Nothing is going to go wrong. Be positive!" My self-assured mother walked up to her sister.

"Oh come on, Suus, don't worry. You know how I like to live dangerously."

After uttering those words, she realized that being flippant wasn't helping the situation. "I was just kidding, Suus! Of course I'll be careful, but you have to let me do this, OK? I wish you wouldn't be so heavy-hearted." Her tone had become more compassionate. Looking into each other's eyes, they ended the argument with a hug and a kiss, and the reassurance of each other's love.

One day the presence of a pet monkey at the *Kempetai* office next door came to my attention. I had seen the soldiers outside a few times earlier, playing with the bouncy, excitable young animal. Somehow, the monkey had escaped, and the entire staff came out of the building to recapture it. Leaping farther away and out of their reach, the young animal was simply having the time of its life. Eventually, it made its way into our camp.

We tried to help capture the monkey, but each time we tried to lure it, it went the opposite way. In fact, the monkey was much better at teasing us than we were at catching it. The chase, a welcome distraction from our everyday life, went on for a while. It was a lot of fun until the monkey found its way to the two outdoor lavatories. Miss Beck had just entered one lavatory with two pails full of water to take her bath. Miss Beck was a rather hairy, old-fashioned, plain-looking woman in her early thirties.

We saw the monkey climb up and land on the center beam of the two side-by-side lavatories. From a distance we were able to watch the monkey's every move. It looked down at the bather, showing its teeth in a wide, friendly smile. It shook its head, screamed loudly, and jumped up and down on the ledge. We all laughed, but it must have been terrifying to Miss Beck.

The monkey made all kinds of comical, chattering noises. It clapped its hands and swung its long arms excitedly, jumping up and down again and again on the narrow beam. It was like watching a funny movie. Suddenly, the monkey reached down with its long hairy arm and grabbed the towel. Then it grabbed the woman's clothes and threw them on the ground outside the lavatory.

Miss Beck began to scream for help. "Will somebody please get this beast away from me? Please? Oh, please?" she begged. "I can't stand it any longer."

The guard and a couple of *Kempetai* men debated the best way to catch the scoundrel. Meanwhile, the animal became wilder and screeched louder. There was no way for the woman to get herself out of the situation—without a towel or clothes and with people standing outside.

It took some fancy maneuvering, but the monkey was finally captured and Miss Beck got her clothes back. When she walked out of the lavatory, she was as white as a sheet and shaking like a leaf. She was a good sport, however. Eventually, she laughed about it.

The commandant kept a close eye on the progress of the garden project and showed up more and more frequently. After two months of hard work under the hot tropical sun, Tante Suus and her girls proudly announced that they were ready for the next step, the fertilizing process.

The fertilizer the commandant promised was in the backyard. The girls were standing only a few feet away from it. "What better fertilizer than what is right here on the premises?" Captain Matoba noted, pointing in the direction of the septic tank. "It won't cost anything, there are no delivery fees, and . . . you have to agree that it's the very best fertilizer there is—human waste!"

The idea disgusted Tante Suus. She felt terrible for her girls, but she had learned not to argue with her superiors. She only hoped that her team understood when she stated, "If that is what you want us to use, sir, then that is what we'll use."

Her complicity pleased the captain. "Good! Good! I am glad you see it my way, little woman." He liked Tante Suus's humble attitude. He reached one hand into his pocket and pulled out several face protectors and rubber gloves. "As you see, I come prepared! I don't want anything to go wrong!"

He urged my aunt to be strict about the rules and regulations concerning this particular assignment. "I do not want to hear about any mishaps as a result of negligence." They walked up to the septic tank. Captain Matoba introduced an essential accessory to do the job: buckets. The different sizes signified different functions, which he explained to my aunt.

The procedure was to scoop out the fecal matter with the small buckets and deposit it into larger ones. Two women would carry the buckets to the field on a long stick and then empty the oozy, sloppy, stenchful stuff into trenches alongside the plants. Workers were assigned jobs long-term, but Tante Suus and the captain decided to alternate the fertilizer duty to be fair.

Immediately after the captain departed, a meeting was called to explain the fertilization plan. The women didn't like it but they went along with it, as they, too, had learned to cooperate for the sake of the group.

When the captain returned two days later, he was overwhelmed by the noxious odor. He covered his nose with a handkerchief and asked Tante Suus, "Any problems with the fertilizing?"

"Two women fainted the first day, but they have recovered and are back at work." She also mentioned that two additional volunteers, despite the unpleasant working conditions, had signed up for permanent garden duties. He was quite pleased to hear it and happy because everything was going well.

He then asked Tante Suus which vegetables she would grow. She mentioned a few greens, and within days the seeds and seedlings arrived. A personal note from the captain accompanied the packages, saying that he admired my aunt and her courageous and devoted team for their hard work. He wished them well in their endeavor and added that he was looking forward to their first crop.

He visited the garden religiously, frequently asking Tante Suus and her workers to show him their hands. He praised the women who had the most calluses.

Unable to go anywhere, we found most days in the prison camp to be boring and dull. The only thing I had to look forward to was Helen's daily visit. Faithfully, every evening after work, she dressed the wound on my foot. She told me it would take a while to heal due to undernour-ishment.

After frequent consultations with Dr. MacDowell, Helen recommended a certain treatment involving touch-ups around the edges of the wound with a pencil-like applicator releasing an ointment. It was a simple enough procedure, but one that created more pain than relief. For-tunately, I had to undergo it just once a week.

One evening during such a treatment, we heard a commotion coming from the lavatories. Women who were nearby and heard the screams ran to the rescue. They found one of the young English-Eurasian nurses uncon-scious on the path. When the woman came to, she said that somebody had tried to rape her. When she had resisted and screamed for help, he covered her mouth and dragged her off to a dark area.

"I must have lost consciousness," she sobbed, "because I don't remember what happened after that." She was unable to tell what the man looked like because he had grabbed her from behind when she came out of the lava-tory. She concluded, however, that her assailant must have been a large, strong person, "because he picked me up as if I was the size of a child!" She had fought him off. Her struggle to free herself had prevented the rape. She cried hysterically.

Shortly after the incident, a plain, soft-spoken woman named Stella told Mrs. de Vries that she had seen a big man running toward the guardhouse at the time of the attack.

"Toward the guardhouse?" Mrs. de Vries was shocked and pulled Stella aside for privacy. In a whisper, she grilled the woman: "Are you sure of what you saw, Stella? You realize that you are accusing a guard of a crime. Is that what you are saying?"

"Yes. I saw the silhouette of a rather large person running toward the guardhouse as if he were in a hurry to get there," she vowed. "I didn't think much of it until I heard the nurse mention the size of her attacker."

Both Mrs. de Vries and Stella said in unison, "Ohrita!" From their vantage point they were able to confirm that Ohrita, one of the *heiho*s, was indeed on duty. *Heiho*s were Indonesian natives trained by the Japanese to be guards. The two women decided to go to the guardhouse to report the attack on the young nurse. They agreed beforehand that Mrs. de Vries would do all the talking. She gave her statement to the Officer of the Guard, never mentioning that Stella could point the finger at Ohrita.

On the way back to the classroom, Mrs. de Vries explained why. "This way, Stella, Ohrita will think that he is in the clear and that there was no witness to the crime. But we know better, don't we?"

The woman nodded.

"More importantly, you'll be safe until we have a talk with Captain Matoba tomorrow morning."

The next morning, the two met with Captain Matoba. He was infuriated. After a talk with Stella, he checked on the nurse to make sure she was all right. He promised that he would take care of the matter.

After roll call two days later, Mrs. de Vries, Stella, and a guard walked across the street to the police station. Captain Matoba was waiting. The testimony Stella gave them must have been instrumental in their decision to remove the brute. He was never seen in our camp again.

Several days later, my brothers and I were playing cards with Peter in the cool of a shady banyan tree. A commotion, followed by a loud, blood-curdling scream echoing from across the road caught our attention. We looked up and saw two military personnel dragging a struggling man out of the building into the backyard. The man was blindfolded. They stopped at an old swing set and two more military men joined them. The prisoner put up a mean fight and kept on screaming. His screams gave us goose bumps. The four soldiers stuffed a gag into the prisoner's mouth and tied him spread-eagle to the swing set.

A high-ranking officer appeared and addressed the prisoner. He then turned around and walked back about twenty feet to where a squad of six riflemen stood. A command sounded, then another. Shots rang out and the man's body turned limp. We froze, unable to move, like statues transfixed on pedestals. We had actually witnessed an execution.

At the sound of the shots, my mother and the rest of the women strained to see what was happening. We told them what we had seen and stood with them as the soldiers and the officer left the grounds. They left the body hanging there, for all to see.

My mother ordered us to play on the other side of the building until the body was removed. It remained there through the night. A guard told us why: "Public viewing of the corpse serves as a reminder that the Japanese are in command."

That incident had a tremendous impact on me and made me wonder if the same fate awaited us somewhere along the way. Perhaps that inhumane and cruel act and the caricatures in the newspaper subconsciously instilled in me the strength, vigilance, and ingenuity to stay alive.

In the meantime, our stay in the camp, which was to be no more than ten days, had stretched into nine months. I could not help but think back to the day I heard my father make the prediction. Now that prediction had come true.

Chapter 11

"Would any of you ladies be interested in joining a party across the street?"

"That's the commandant's home, isn't it?" one of the women asked.

"Indeed it is!" the officer responded. "The commandant has sent me over to invite you ladies to join him and his guests."

Sarcasm filled the air. "A party? What do you know? We are in time of war and there is yet room for parties?"

Ignoring the cynical remarks, the officer repeated the invitation, "Can't you hear the singing? The party is well under way. So please, would anyone be interested?"

To everyone's amazement, several women accepted the invitation without hesitation. They dashed inside to dress in their best attire. I heard them giggle, as if they were adolescents getting ready for their first date. I could not understand why these women—some of them married—would agree to go to this party!

Was this a right thing to do? If that were the case, why wouldn't my mother go? She had always liked parties and she loved to dance. What about the husbands of these women? I was quite sure that they were not treated to anything special like this. No, it could not be right!

Minutes later, the women reappeared. They must have searched into the depths of their suitcases for cosmetics. With powder-patted faces, rouge on their cheeks, and accentuated lips, they looked like dressed-up dolls. The officer complimented them and they walked away with him, swinging their hips.

I was never one for girlie stuff—playing with dolls, makeup, wearing jewelry, and the like. So, seeing these grown-up women pose the way they did was quite embarrassing and, frankly, it made me nauseous. My mother, noticing the disapproving look on my face, put her arm around me and suggested I get ready for bed.

In my prayer, I asked God to look after my father. I asked Him to forgive the women who went to the party. "Please, Lord, don't be mad at them," I prayed, "and thank you for my loving family. Amen."

Unable to fall asleep while thinking about the women who had left for the party, I heard the same officer return and ask for someone by the name of la Fontaine. My mother responded to his call.

"The commandant would like to see the member of your family whose name is engraved on the accordion we have in our possession, ma'am," he said politely.

"That will be difficult, sir," my mother replied. "I can't produce my husband. He's in the jailhouse. He's the one who plays the instrument." She knew all the while that it was I whom they sought, but she could not think of a way out.

The officer, puzzled by my mother's hesitation, said, "No! No! You don't understand. One of the women at the party mentioned that your eldest son used to conduct the music hour in the school on Saturdays. Isn't that true?"

"Yes, that is true," my mother admitted.

"Captain Matoba requests the presence of that person, your son, to entertain his guests."

The thought of being reunited with my accordion excited me.

My mother, upset to hear that the captain was behind the request, tried very hard to dissuade him by saying I was asleep, but the officer gently insisted that she wake me up.

"You can't be serious, sir. My son is only twelve years old. You could not possibly expect him to entertain adults. He is too young."

"I am just following orders, ma'am. Would you let your son come if I promise to be personally responsible for him?"

"Can I count on you, sir?" my mother asked, looking the young officer straight in the eyes.

"Yes, you can count on me, ma'am!"

Realizing that she had no choice, she came to wake me and found me already sitting up under the mosquito tent.

"I heard. The commandant wants me to come and play the accordion!" The thrill of the moment made me insensitive to my mother's feelings.

Hurriedly, she combed my hair and straightened my shirt. "Be sure not to take any alcoholic drinks, dear, and watch yourself," she whispered. "You understand?" She held me at arm's length and scrutinized me. She leaned forward, hugged and kissed me, and whispered, "Be careful, darling—you are going to be in unfamiliar territory. God be with you, sweetheart!"

Tante Suus, having stayed in the background during all this, embraced me and wished me well on my way out. She, too, was worried.

The young officer bowed to my mother. "I'll take full responsibility for Rick, ma'am. Please do not worry."

I heard the lump in my mother's throat as she said, "I appreciate your offer, sir. Thank you!"

As the officer and I walked away, I noticed disapproving looks on the women's faces.

During the walk to the commandant's house, I forgot all about prison camps, mattresses on the floor, rats in the soup, Djambi on fire, and even Mr. Meijer, who had repaired my accordion. The officer tried to engage me in casual conversation, but all I could think of was getting to my instrument!

Before we entered the dining room, I had to take off my shoes as everyone else had before me. This, I learned, was a traditional Japanese custom.

To reach the host, I had to pass by the Japanese guests and the women prisoners. They were all seated on the floor on individual pillows in front of several long, low tables. The women were already settled in and at ease with the Japanese guests.

Welcomed with a loud cheer, I made a grand entrance. "What has taken you so long, Rick la Fontaine?" shouted the commandant from the far end of the table. He pronounced the name in the typical Japanese way. He motioned for me to come to him. The accordion was on the table and I had no doubt that it was mine. My father's engraved name tag confirmed it.

"I knew you were the musician," Captain Matoba said in an intoxicated slur. "Now that you're here, I expect you to produce merry tunes for my guests. Play something!"

Pulling my arms through the straps, I felt as if I were embracing an old friend. I touched the keys lightly and familiar sounds came out, making me feel complete and relaxed. Until that very moment, I hadn't realized how much I had missed the happy tunes my accordion and I could produce.

I knew no Japanese songs and told the captain so. He merely looked at me and slurred, "It doesn't matter! Just play anything, as long as you fill the room with happy sounds and bring this party to life."

He had put me on the spot and I wasn't sure what to do. Everybody was watching. My body shook, my hands were clammy, and my fingers were uncooperative. By this time, the guests were impatient and calling for music. I started to push in some keys, but my mind drew a total blank. I couldn't think of a song!

Noticing how I struggled to find a start, Captain Matoba tried to put me at ease. "Take your time, Rick!" he said. Then, asking for the attention of his guests, he added, "Friends, give the boy an opportunity to compose himself. He'll come around when he's ready."

What a relief! Now I had time to acclimate myself to the situation. The party had to settle for the Dutch songs I had learned for the music hour at school, and I had to play them from memory. It was the first time I realized I could play by ear. My effort paid off. Loud applause and requests for more followed each tune.

At one point, the guests took over by singing Japanese songs, so I hummed along and tried to find the right settings on the keyboard and basic chords. I became totally involved in the challenge of producing a version of a Japanese tune entirely on my own. While fiddling with the instrument, I saw, from the corner of my eye, one of the guests lean over and whisper to the captain while keeping his eyes fixed on me. I had noticed him watching me earlier, and it made me nervous.

Suddenly, he was beside me, addressing me in Japanese. Captain Matoba interpreted for me. The man was fascinated that I played the accordion without having sheet music in front of me, so I told him that I played by ear. My statement made him decide to teach me a few songs by humming them, giving me a chance to come up with my own rendition.

Obviously enjoying the party and having had a little bit too much to drink, the man raised his glass to offer a toast to his "new friend, a talented, young, and handsome Dutch boy!" He was even more impressed when Captain Matoba told him that I was only twelve years old and had never had a music lesson in my life. I bowed politely and smiled. The guests began singing new Japanese songs, and I memorized a few of them.

As the evening wore on, the inebriated officers and their lady guests became more and more physical, exchanging kisses and other forms of affection. I was embarrassed. I didn't know what to do or where to look. I played with my accordion, trying to avoid the scene. Suddenly I was startled by a heavy hand on my arm. It was the captain! He was quite drunk. "I have something to show you," he slurred, "but I need a strong arm to get to it."

I welcomed his suggestion to leave the room for a while. He had had much more to drink than I had anticipated. With his eyes closed, he placed a finger over his lips in a hush gesture, held on tightly to my arm, and directed me to an adjacent room that resembled a study. At the doorway, he let go of my arm. Stumbling into the room, he attempted to make a gracious bow to honor the woman in the picture on the wall. The move made him dizzy, and he held his head with both hands. I helped him to a chair. With a thick tongue, he asked, "Do you recognize the woman in the picture, Rick?"

"It's my mother."

He confessed to having admired the portrait since he saw it at our home a few months earlier. "I decided that before your home was officially sealed off, I would make arrangements to have the portrait taken to my quarters." He also told me about the accordion. It had been on the floor in one of the bedrooms. To him it looked as if the owner had only just taken it off his shoulders and put it down. Knowing he would find the musician, the captain took the instrument home.

Just then, the commandant's caretaker came into the study looking for his boss to take him to his sleeping quarters. I went back to the party to put away my accordion. What I saw was totally unexpected. Two young geishas, Japanese women trained to entertain men, were in the middle of a performance. One of the dancers was dressed in a silk water-blue kimono with swirling ivory lines to mimic the current in a stream. Glistening silver trout tumbled in the current, and the surface of the water was ringed with gold wherever the soft green leaves of a tree touched it. The *obi,* a broad sash worn especially with a Japanese kimono, also woven of pure silk, was embroidered in pale greens and yellows.

Her face was painted a kind of rich white, like the wall of a cloud when lit by the sun. Her hair, fashioned into lobes, gleamed as darkly as lacquer and was decorated with ornaments carved out of amber and with a bar from which tiny silver strips dangled, shimmering as she moved.

The other dancer had on a yellow kimono with willowy branches bearing lovely green and orange leaves. It was made of silk gauze as delicate as a spider's web. The *obi* had a lovely gauze texture too, but was heavier-looking in russet and brown with gold threads woven throughout.

They both wore light straw slippers and moved across the improvised stage with elegance and grace. Their tiny steps made it look as if they were gliding. What impressed me most were their amazingly unusual hairdos. For an instant I remembered the loss of my own beautiful, long hair.

Except for a few guests who were asleep, the room was practically empty. I detected a faint smell of vomit, although there were no telltale signs. Since there was no trace of the women prisoners, I assumed they had returned to camp. I was too tired and too sleepy to lose myself in conjectures about them. My escort finally showed up to take me back across the street. When he informed me that the women would be home later, the significance of what he said didn't even register.

My mother and Tante Suus were waiting up for me. Both sighed with relief when I entered the room. While I prepared for bed, they asked about the party and how it felt to play my accordion again. I told them as much as I wanted them to know about the evening. I knew deep down that there were more questions they wanted to ask me but didn't.

For days I wandered around with questions whirling in my head, contemplating whether I should tell my mother about the party. I was a very confused twelve-year-old. I didn't know what to do, although I knew that eventually I would need to talk about it to make peace with myself. Telling my mother or aunt about what I had seen was simply unthinkable; it was too embarrassing. How would they react? Would they believe me? It was a terrible dilemma and I needed guidance.

The women's behavior at the party had baffled me. I was unable to shake it; the thought stuck with me and kept me awake. I lost my appetite and withdrew from being with people. Again and again the same questions surfaced: How could these women, separated from their husbands, inter-act with other men in such an intimate manner? Weren't they ashamed? Had they lost their dignity? How could they show affection and allow these men to fondle them in the presence of others? In *my* presence! The more I thought about it, the more depressed, confused, and angry I became. Frustration at not being able to find a reasonable answer to all these questions moved me to tears. I felt completely lost.

In the meantime, Tante Suus and my mother realized that they had never talked to me about growing up, sex, and other aspects of life. They both felt they had let me down. It certainly would have disturbed them even more had they known what I had witnessed.

I decided at first that the less said about the situation, the better, but I was wrong. When my mother probed me for details about the party, I used such adjectives as *good, fine,* and *much fun,* but she realized that I was holding something back. Despite her decision to leave me alone for a while, she worried.

Eventually she decided to talk with me again. We were on the playground. She began the conversation by casually mentioning the happy times we had as a family. Smoothly and tactfully bringing up times of laughter and fun we both remembered, she set me at ease. Gradually, we reached the main topic: the party. I told her about the geishas, their beautiful kimonos, and about my discovery of playing a tune by ear. She was not surprised. Then she wanted to know more about the party.

I told her about the officer who was amazed to see me play the instrument without reading music and how the same man taught me several Japanese songs. I told her about my efforts to accompany the singing guests. "It was great to play my accordion again," I said. "It was like getting together again with a friend I hadn't seen in a long time. Can you understand that, Mommie?"

My mother was happy to see me opening up, but at the same time she felt there was more, and of course she was right. Then she began to question me about the women. I was uncomfortable talking about them, and I responded rather rudely.

Sensing my inner struggle, she said that keeping it all

to myself would only confuse me more. "If you don't tell me anything, or ask me any questions, I can't help you," she said in despair.

Questions kept coming up in my mind. Is drinking and being affectionate with strangers all right for adults? Were those women acting so freely because their husbands were not with them? What about all the kissing and fondling in view of everyone? Was that all right? I suddenly burst into tears, tears of frustration because it was so hard to tell her about the women.

My mother held me tight and whispered encouraging words, suggesting I let all my emotions out. And I did. I told her everything about the women and how I felt when it happened. Though she didn't say a word while I poured my heart out, tears rolled freely down her cheeks, making it difficult for me to continue. Each time I stopped, she encouraged me to go on. "Don't hold anything back, dear."

I could tell that what I related made my mother unhappy, but I was glad to be relieved of the burdens I had been carrying around.

"You poor darling," she said when I was done. "Your aunt and I should have told you about such things long before now. But we never dreamed that you would be exposed to them at this young age."

I tried to console her. "It's nobody's fault, Mom. Don't feel bad. It couldn't have been helped." We embraced and held each other for a while. I had such love for my mother at that moment. Then she added, "After what you saw at the party, you must have a better understanding about what Father Koevoets wanted to protect you from."

After the talk, the confession, and the cry, I felt good

and wonderfully lightened. I was free of a burden that had been pulling me down. "Do not condemn the women who attended the party," she insisted. "It's no one's business to judge anyone else's behavior. We all have the right to choose our own way of life. Your responsibility is to concentrate on your own destiny, and try to live your life the best way you can. I don't ever want you to forget that!"

My mother and I felt especially close that day. We spent most of the day together, talking about everything.

When I told her about her portrait hanging in the commandant's study, she was surprised and embarrassed at the same time.

"I wonder what your father would say if he knew about it," she said with a mischievous twinkle in her eye.

Chapter 12

Sounds of the Dutch national anthem, *"Het Wilhelmus,"* broke the peaceful hours of the night and woke me up. I thought I was dreaming, but then I noticed that Tante Suus and Mommie were awake as well. The voice was that of Mrs. Arends, a middle-aged Dutch socialite whose behavior had been erratic since the beginning of imprisonment.

"Why," I asked, "is she singing so loudly? What's wrong with her? Why is she singing *'Het Wilhelmus'*?"

"I don't really know, dear, but it is obvious that the woman has problems adjusting to a life in confinement. Poor Dina."

From the commotion in the next room, it was clear that Mrs. Arends was out of control, flailing and kicking every time someone tried to calm her. The pain in her voice made us all feel her anguish. Her cries came from deep within. Was she crying out for help?

I blocked my ears, buried my face in my pillow, and started to cry, too. My mother rubbed my back without saying a word, lost in her own thoughts. It was soothing and comforting, but no less sad.

The appearance of the commandant brought a pause in the commotion. Mrs. de Vries told him that Mrs. Arends had been acting strangely during the last weeks, and that Dr. MacDowell had been treating her with success until now. Everyone agreed that the woman needed hospitalization for treatment before she seriously hurt herself or others. Several people had to hold Mrs. Arends so Dr. MacDowell could administer a tranquilizer. The ambulance arrived and moments later she and the patient left for the hospital.

The next day the medical team reported that Mrs. Arends was resting comfortably and isolated from other patients. The windows of her room were barred and a special guard was posted at her door at all times. Subsequent reports indicated that her condition was gradually worsening and her appetite was waning dangerously. The violent attacks became more frequent. Days later, sad news reached us. Mrs. Arends had climbed onto a chair, lost her balance, and hit her head against the side of the steel bed. The fall had been fatal.

Dina Arends was our first camp casualty. Everyone was distraught and yet felt that it was a blessing. She might have suffered more in the long run.

My second performance as an entertainer took place some months later in a downtown Djambi restaurant. Before the war, the eatery was popular and well known to businessmen. Luncheons, dinners, banquets, meetings, and other special occasions were held there.

The commandant invited me to the party in the presence of my mother and, again, she had no choice but to let me go. It was the second time she faced such a dilemma.

That afternoon, my mother and I had another talk about life and the women's attitude in particular. She was still rather apprehensive about letting me go. On the other hand, she felt confident that, after our talk after the first party, I now had a better understanding about grown-ups and would be able to handle an unwelcome situation.

That evening, a car carrying the captain and one of his lieutenants stopped at the front gate to pick me up. Arriving at the restaurant, I followed the officers. I entered the lobby with uneasy anticipation and then noticed a group of splashy women. They were heavily made-up and unattractive. They were dressed in distasteful, multicolored, out-of-style clothes, but they seemed to be the main attraction for the men.

I had seen women of this type before in downtown Djambi. I knew they were called "ladies of pleasure," but I didn't know what those words implied. Assuming that they could not possibly be part of our party, their presence did not particularly bother me.

Entering the large party room, I noticed alongside the walls several private booths with curtains. Most of them seemed to be occupied, and sounds of giggling were occasionally heard from behind the curtains. A long table in the middle of the room immediately drew my attention. Seated around it were many of the guests I had met at the first party. Recognizing one another, we bowed politely. Several women from the camp were also there.

I sat next to my accordion while drinks and appetizers were served. The commandant asked me to start the background music. Softly, I played the few Japanese songs I had memorized. I even dared to present my own improvisation.

Generally, I felt good about my role as an entertainer and was happy to oblige.

The man who had taught me a few songs came over and welcomed me with a bow and what I assumed were kind words. I still did not understand his Japanese but graciously accepted his kindness. I was happy to see him. He stayed by my side. He had a sparkle in his eyes and a glimmer of recognition when I opened my repertoire with a song he had taught me. Obviously pleased, he listened critically, corrected whenever it was necessary, and applauded enthusiastically after the first performance. He was a proud teacher whose pupil had just made an important contribution.

I was invited to join the host when the main course was served. The women were beginning to enjoy their night out and started acting the same way they had acted at the first party.

Remembering the talk with my mother, I did my utmost to focus on my food and to look away from the distractions, the booths, but it was not easy. People kept popping in and out of the booths and there were giggles. What was going on behind those curtains?

I could not see a difference in the behavior of the hired ladies of pleasure and the women prisoners. That disturbed me. They all seemed to be there for the same reason: to entertain the military in any way they could.

Was this what life was about? Was I too opinionated about the women's behavior? Was I judging them too harshly? Did I, a child, have a right to even have an opinion about the situation? My mind, refusing to quit, went even further. I started to wonder about the language. How did they communicate? Did one know what the other said or needed? These were questions I could not possibly ask my mother. Despite our talk, I remained confused. The longer I thought of the rights and wrongs, the more frustrated I became.

I was glad when the meal was over. I went back to playing music and concentrated on my songs. I loved performing because it made me forget where I was. Music always had the magical ability to take me into my own little fantasy world. The guests were generous with their compliments. They applauded loudly. I, in return, made a point of playing each Japanese song a bit louder.

After a while, I started to feel the weight of the accordion pressing heavily on my thighs and decided to take a break. However, looking around, I was reminded of my current environment. I chose not to stop playing but instead adjusted the instrument to ease the discomfort.

The hour was late and the guests and their lady companions were now showing the results of the extensive intake of liquor. Everyone, including the commandant, was having a good time, absorbed in their personal pleasures. A sudden urge to slip away overcame me, but I suppressed the thought and returned to playing the accordion. My heart was not in it any longer, and the discomfort in my thighs was worsening by the minute. I became anxious and extremely uncomfortable. Frustration and confusion were gnawing at me. I felt totally alone, neglected, and lost. I didn't want to be there. I wanted to be in bed with Mommie and Tante Suus, in the safety of the guarded, protected prison camp.

I have no memory of leaving the restaurant. The next thing I remember is stepping briskly along a deserted but familiar street toward camp. I was in a daze. I had walked those streets many times before, but never under such conditions, and never in the dark by myself.

There was a slight, refreshing breeze, unlike the smoky party room in the restaurant. It felt good to be outside breathing fresh air, walking with the wind blowing in my face and playing with my hair. At that particular moment I felt free, until I realized where I was and what I was doing. In spite of it all, I had no fear, but I was certainly aware of the consequences if somebody were to find me walking the streets unguarded. I tried to think of how I had been able to leave the restaurant without anybody stopping me.

In a state of denial at that point, preparing myself for what was to come, I heard the sound of a fast approaching vehicle behind me. From the shouting and yelling, I could only assume that it was the *Kempetai*. I kept walking, although I felt like running for my life. Since I was the only pedestrian on the road, it wasn't hard to figure out they were after me. I could hear shouting in Japanese and Indonesian. "There he is! There he is! Hurry! Grab him!" I assumed that someone at the restaurant had discovered my absence and reported it.

I stopped on the side of the road, waiting for the vehicle to come alongside. I stepped in voluntarily and we took off. Probably stunned at how easy it was to get me into the car, nobody asked me any questions or even talked to me during the short ride to the camp. I jumped out before the vehicle came to a final stop, ran through the gate toward our classroom, and totally ignored the quizzical looks and remarks of the women, who were enjoying their usual cool night-gathering.

I headed straight for our place, buried my face in the pillow, and cried my heart out. I cried until I could hardly breathe, tasting my own salty tears. I was afraid, confused, angry, and utterly frustrated. I felt guilty for running away and was prepared to be punished for what I did. The thought of facing the commandant for what I had done was giving me more reason to be anxious. It was a frightening prospect!

Tante Suus and my mother were by my side. Neither said a word. My mother lifted me up and took me in her arms, cuddling me, soothing me, rocking me back and forth. We both sobbed. Tante Suus joined in the embrace. I felt safe again.

I tried to explain what had happened because I didn't want them to worry too much or make them think the worst. My mother was satisfied and visibly relieved when I told her that nothing physical had happened to me. She held me tight and shed even more tears.

I overheard her say to my aunt, "Suus, believe me, this is going to be the last time I will allow her to go to another party! I don't care if the emperor of Japan invites her, I will not let her go!" She sounded quite adamant.

I cried myself to sleep that night. At daybreak, the sound of a noisy vehicle awakened me. From the giggling and chattering, I gathered that the women were returning after their evening of fun. Unfortunately, two of the women roomed with us. They did not look as attractive as they had the night before. Their clothes were wrinkled; their hairdos were flat; they looked terrible. Unpleasant odors of liquor and cigarette smoke permeated the room.

Captain Matoba showed up later that morning and asked to see me. My mother joined us and we walked to the playground for privacy, under the curious eyes of the others.

"Mrs. la Fontaine, it's nice to see you again. I wish that the circumstance could be different, but so be it. I assume that the two little guys you left standing there are Rick's brothers?"

"Yes, sir, they are," my mother responded.

"I haven't met them before, have I? No, I haven't!" he concluded, answering his own question. "Will they be okay there?"

"Yes, sir. I've told them to wait for me. Thank you for your concern."

"You have a beautiful family," he complimented.

"Thank you, sir," my mother answered curtly.

The captain turned to me. "Well, young man. Tell me. What happened last night? What made you decide to go for a walk?" He smiled and placed his arm around my shoulder. "Was the party that boring?"

"Not at all, sir," I defended myself. "I enjoyed playing my accordion and the food was good. But I wish I had not been there," I blurted.

There was no hint of anger in the commandant's voice when he encouraged me to tell him what had happened. I was afraid that my emotions might get the better of me, but with my mother present, I felt strong and spoke up.

"What made you decide to leave the restaurant? You just wanted to take a walk?" the captain asked jokingly.

I started clumsily and stuttered a bit. "Well . . . I . . . I was surprised to see the hired women. They wore too much makeup," I admitted, emphasizing my observation. "Then there were the booths. I heard giggling and other sounds behind the curtains." I turned around to look at my mother. She had tears in her eyes, but they did not stop me from continuing my account.

I looked down at my feet. "What embarrassed me the most, though, was the women from our camp . . . acting like the others. You know?" I had to stop and swallow. My mother squeezed my shoulder, sympathizing. I didn't dare look up at the captain. I continued.

"I guess I left without knowing it. I found myself on the road in the middle of town. I wanted to be with my family, where I would be safe."

What I told the captain was news to my mother. I hadn't had the chance to tell her about it. Captain Matoba listened attentively. I knew he believed my story.

"I apologize for leaving the restaurant without telling anyone, and probably causing a disturbance. It was not my intention to do that. I am sorry. I shouldn't have done that."

To my surprise, he complimented me for being such a level-headed young man. He then spoke of the soldiers and how, with a drink or two and female companionship, they allowed themselves to unwind, relax, and forget their loneliness for a while. "You can believe me," he confided, "when I tell you that I know what it is to feel lonely."

He paced in front of us, then added, "Keep in mind that whatever those women did is their business."

"That's what Mommie told me," I confirmed.

"I am sure your mommie knows what I'm talking about. I understand your confusion and anger over what you have seen at the parties, but that, my boy, is part of life. Your parents must have taught you to concentrate on all the right things and to be a good judge of people." He smiled and continued his lecture.

"Some things that happened are in conflict with what your parents have taught you. My advice is to take all these happenings to heart and consider them lessons of life. You are in the advantageous stage of your young life where experiences like these will only strengthen your judgment of right and wrong in relation to human action and character. All of this will be beneficial as you grow to manhood." He continued, urging me to be a good student in whatever else life had to offer and to always pay attention to what my parents taught me.

Addressing my mother, he made a promise. "Mrs. la Fontaine, you have a good, well-mannered, sensitive son. I solemnly promise you that Rick will not be invited to any future parties as long as I am the commandant of this camp. I will miss his music, and my guests will miss him as much. I am certain of that."

Suddenly remembering the accident I had a couple of months before, he asked, "By the way, how is your foot? You don't seem to be limping anymore. Has the wound healed?"

I told him that the wound had not healed, but that my foot felt fine. I could walk on it without too much discomfort. He was happy to hear that.

He turned to my mother and again apologized for what

had happened. Then he asked my mother, "Would you and your children oblige me by joining me for dinner tonight?"

"Dinner, sir?"

"In my quarters across the street." He gestured in the direction of the house. "The guard will walk you and the children over at seven o'clock. Is that agreeable?"

My mother accepted his invitation graciously. Before leaving, the captain joked that he needed to see the "little woman" in the garden about the vegetables for that night's dinner.

My mother knew that he was not aware of the fact that his protégé was her sister. At that particular moment, she just could not resist bringing it to his attention. When she told him, he stopped in his tracks, looked my mother straight in the eye, and with a smile said, "*The little woman* is your sister?" accentuating every word.

"Yes, sir, she is. We are opposites in many ways," my mother admitted, after she had noticed the look on his face, as if he were mentally comparing the two sisters.

"So you are," he said agreeably. "Bring her along, too! She deserves a good meal for all the hard work."

After the captain left, the women swarmed around my mother and pressed her for news of what had taken place. Limiting her comments to only telling them about the dinner invitation, she left them guessing.

That evening, Captain Matoba himself met us at the front door. Dressed in a beautiful silk kimono and wearing straw slippers, he was certainly handsome. He welcomed us most graciously and requested that we put on the slippers he provided for us. We left our footwear at the front door. He then addressed my mother and requested her to follow him into his study. We followed.

"Rick must have told you about the portrait." I heard him say.

"Yes, sir, indeed," she replied. "I had intended to thank you for saving it, but was too embarrassed to speak of it before now."

Captain Matoba smiled. "How do you like seeing yourself on the wall in my study?" he asked, flirtatiously smiling at her and pointing at the photograph.

My mother's face turned scarlet and she was unable to find the right words to respond. Finally she said, "I'm happy that it gives you pleasure to look at it, sir." She paused. "My husband had the portrait made before our marriage in 1922. It has hung in every dining room we have had. It always faced him from where he sat at the dinner table."

"Very romantic," Captain Matoba admitted, and started to walk toward the dining room.

As I remembered from the first party, the guests sat on the floor, cross-legged on individual pillows in front of low tables. When I played the accordion, I was spared from joining them on the floor. This time, however, I had no excuse and was forced to experience how it felt to sit in that position for a long time.

Appetizers were already arranged on the table. Tea was poured into small Japanese cups. Toasts were made and, while we snacked on the appetizers, a variety of dishes arrived and filled the room with the delicious aroma of

Japanese cuisine. This time, I had the opportunity to really enjoy the party and taste the food.

Our host was a charming man who had the ability to make us feel at ease. I believe that the combination of a Japanese host, a conversation in Dutch, my family's native tongue, and the Japanese cuisine helped create the cordial and relaxed atmosphere.

My mother and aunt experienced a moment of embarrassment after dinner, when both had difficulty in rising from their unusual sitting position. It took them a while before their numb legs were restored to normal. We all laughed about their attempts to help along the blood flow by shaking and massaging their legs.

Captain Matoba took us on a tour of his quarters and showed us a photograph of his family in Japan. He had a wife and three teenagers, two sons and a daughter. To remember this special occasion, he gave my mom and aunt each a genuine Japanese fan.

With this last gesture, the unforgettable evening ended. At the front door, he offered me his hand, which struck me as a very non-Japanese custom. "From man to man, Rick!" he said. We shook hands, and I felt proud, honored, and respected. Then he took a step back and bowed in the Japanese way, bidding us all a good night. We did the same. We then returned to the prison camp, escorted by a guard.

The women anxiously awaited our return to hear how our dinner date went and what we had for supper. My mother, who had expected this kind of medialike frenzy for information, waved her hand, letting them know that she had no desire to talk about the matter.

"It was a delightfully pleasant, cordial, and enjoyable evening. The food was excellent and the captain is, as you all know, a gentleman," was all she said.

The curiosity of the women was understandable, but to my mother their interest was merely prying and . . . rather annoying.

Chapter 13

A scream from a field worker caught everyone's attention. The woman screamed nonstop, jumping up and down, swaying her arms wildly and pointing to something in the distance that we couldn't see. We all ran to a spot at the edge of the field to get a better look. What we saw was amazing: On the other side of the field were men carrying spades, hoes, and other garden tools. Guards walking alongside them led us to believe they were prisoners: our men. Some of the women called out their husbands' names in hopes of hearing a familiar voice in return. The men waved back.

"Who do you think they are, Mom? Do you think Poppie is with them?" I asked.

Her only response was, "I don't know, dear. I only hope that the Japanese are not working them too hard."

Even though we waved to them and they waved back, we couldn't tell if they were our men. The distance was too great to hear anything or to recognize anyone. The women, however, were absolutely convinced that the men they were waving at were their husbands.

The group passed by again that same afternoon and on subsequent days. In anticipation, the women would gather at a spot in the field where they could best observe the parade. Mrs. de Vries suggested keeping the calling and screaming to a minimum. The women complied reluctantly and acted as discreetly as possible.

I, too, pretended to be waving at my father, but I knew those men might be just a work detail of real prisoners, not prisoners of war. Whoever they were, I had no illusion that one of the men was my father. I was satisfied with the thought that I was waving at him, simply to enjoy the thrill of the moment.

The parade came to an abrupt and unexpected end one day. The men just didn't show up anymore. Our entire camp seemed to be in mourning after that. At the same time, this episode had strengthened our hope and given us the courage to face the future. The seemingly insignificant incident gave us the much-needed encouragement to persevere and to carry on.

After nine months in captivity, everyone seemed to have accepted imprisonment as a way of life. Most days were pleasant, fruitful, and agreeable, while some were less so. Captain Matoba visited at least once a week to pick up his personal crop of vegetables. He kept a keen eye on the growing plants and enjoyed spending time with the garden crew. He joked with them, answered their questions, and was always willing to please them in any way to make their lives and work more tolerable.

This close acquaintance made the women grow fonder of him and he, in return, gradually gave more of himself by showing a gentler and more compassionate side. He was their friend, a sensitive person who possessed a deep and genuine understanding of the circumstances and situation they found themselves in.

Early one morning, he came through the gate in his usual manner, his hands clasped behind his back, stopping here and there for a chat. On this particular day, however, the expression on his face showed something different— unhappiness. To no one's surprise, he called for an important meeting.

After an initial greeting, he cleared his throat and spoke to the crowd. "Today is a sad day for me, personally," he started. "I am afraid it will be for some of you as well. However, for yet a few others, today might well be an exceptionally happy one."

There were sounds of restlessness. None of us had any idea what he was talking about or where all this was leading. "I came to tell you that I have just received my transfer papers, which means I am going to have to leave my post as your commandant."

Several of the women cried out emotionally, interrupting his speech. After order had been restored, he continued. "I do not know when or where I will be stationed. But, ultimately, I will have to leave you." His voice quivered. "Some of you will be glad to see me go. That is all right," he added. "To those, I sincerely apologize for not having been able to win your trust and friendship."

He stopped and looked around as if he were trying to find a group of women or a face to whom he could address the depth of his feelings.

"To the ones with whom I have been closely associated during the past months, I want to extend my genuine thanks for cooperating with me under sometimes difficult situations. Thank you for your friendship. I am going to miss you all. You can be sure of that!"

After a deep breath, he looked up. Raising his arms to prevent the women from asking painful questions, which he knew they would do, he continued. With sadness still showing on his face, he tried to sound a bit happier for the next announcement.

"I have other news, good news for a handful among you." He paused. "Some of you will have the good fortune to return to family life and to enjoy freedom on the outside."

A sense of surprise and wonder came over all of us because we had no idea how to react to this unbelievable news. It caused an emotional stir and raised many immediate questions.

"Ladies! Ladies! Please! As I said, only a few among you will be fortunate enough to enjoy the happiness of a reunion. Let me read off the names."

As the ultimate surprise, our family's name was on the list. My mother, aunt, and I looked at one another in total amazement. We were not certain what it meant and were thus unable to fully grasp the reality of it.

The commandant continued. "To the families in question, I want to add that starting tomorrow your husbands will be coming down to join you. The idea is that the two of you will be allowed to leave camp to do house-hunting in town. That's all I'll say for now. Tomorrow morning I'll provide further instructions.

"To those staying behind, again, I'm terribly sorry that the privilege of caring for you has been taken away from me. I also feel badly that you must say good-bye to people who have become your friends. I wish you all the very best. Thank you."

His piercing eyes took in the expressions on our faces, as though he wanted to etch a final picture in his mind. Several of the eyes fixed on him had become teary. He left behind a group of women with heavy, unhappy hearts, women who had to go through yet another separation and adapt to new leadership.

We never found out what brought about this transaction. It was curious that only Dutch-Indonesian families were considered for the release, with one exception—Mrs. Schook and her blind eighty-year-old mother. They were Dutch. The age of the older woman must have been the reason for including them.

I felt fortunate for the news bestowed on our family but was rather saddened by the prospect that we had to leave the others behind. We had been through so much together. Somehow, through it all, everyone—including the commandant—felt obligated and had actually managed to work in harmony for the sake of peaceful coexistence at the prison camp.

The next morning after roll call, the captain of the guard told the soon-to-be-released women to get ready. A small truck carrying the men arrived. Poppie was on the truck. I waved at him but didn't dare to call out. My mother and Mmes. Rijken and van Zanten, who would be our new neighbors, waited nervously.

Captain Matoba had the men follow him into camp. My father looked well but was skinnier. Seeing their wives just a few steps away, the husbands, including Poppie, could not resist and rushed over to reunite with them.

The captain had not anticipated the spontaneous move, but did nothing to stop them. He asked the couples to follow him to the playground, away from the rest of the crowd. Tante Suus, Ronald, René, and I sat ourselves down on the grass within hearing distance.

"Well, here we are," I heard the commandant say. "There are a few things that you need to know before you face the world out there. It is a bit different than what you are used to." He stopped and looked around. "You may go in any direction you wish to find the house of your choosing."

"Excuse me, sir," Mr. van Zanten interjected. "Does that mean we cannot return to our own homes?"

"That is correct," the captain confirmed, tactfully avoiding further elaboration on the subject.

"You may take as long as you need to find your new home. One day, two days, or even a week. However, at the end of each day that you are out there, I want you to be at the drop-off point by exactly six o'clock and not one minute later!" He looked the group over and continued, "At the end of the day, I want the women to leave a note with the guard informing me about their progress in finding a home. In case another day is needed, the same truck will be back the next morning with your husbands so that you can continue looking. If you have found a house, an inspection for approval will be arranged. Is all this understood?"

Each one of the group received a name tag made of cloth representing the Japanese flag. The name was written in two writing styles: Japanese characters and English lettering in black india ink.

"One last thing. A friendly warning: disobedience

115

may have serious consequences. So, stick to the rules! Good luck!"

"Thank you, sir," they responded in unison.

The group was dismissed, and my brothers and I stood up. When the captain saw how anxious we were to meet our father, he winked and said, "Oh, Mr. la Fontaine! Please say hello to your anxiously awaiting little people. Go ahead!"

Poppie ran toward us. He hugged my brothers, me, and then my aunt. There was so much passion in his embrace that it made me tear up. "Love you all!" he whispered. "It'll not take long. We'll be together again soon. Be good! I love you!"

Facing the commandant, he then said, "Thank you, sir. Thank you for allowing me to embrace my family." He had tears in his eyes.

Seeing my father, touching him, feeling his embrace, and kissing him felt good. However, to hear that we could not move back into our home was very disappointing and occupied my thoughts all day. What choice of house would my parents have? The only houses I could think of were primitive, crudely built cabins in less desirable locations in town or in the woods. Most were not even outfitted with any conveniences, such as electricity and running water.

Another concern was that we would have to live among the natives, which was not only a painful thought for my parents; it would be socially degrading as well. Having to live a life at the same level as our servants with no other option was humiliating, to say the least!

When my mother came home that evening, she was very tired. She told us that she and my father had located a small house in the woods at the outskirts of town.

"It isn't much," she warned us. "We will not have fancy stuff or servants as we are used to. There is running water but no electricity. I don't care about all that. What's important is that it'll be a place where we'll be together as a family again!"

She was trying to prepare us for a simple, primitive lifestyle, one with which we were unfamiliar. She also wanted us to realize how important it was to be together no matter what the circumstances or conditions.

"Together, we can make the smallest shack our paradise and create our own happiness." This statement indicated to me how important this reunion was to her.

The next day was almost a carbon copy of the one before. My parents saw two other houses, enabling them to compare locations and conditions. Finally, on the afternoon of the third day, my mother returned with the news that it was definite. They would take the first house they had viewed.

Again, she reminded us that it would not be a life of luxury. She was unconsciously teaching us children to adjust and accept a different lifestyle, a lifestyle that was totally foreign to us.

The next day, Poppie came to our camp again. He and my mother were escorted across the street to Captain Matoba's office for the final approval or rejection of their choice of house. Mommie returned to camp a couple of hours later, alone, and declared that the captain approved of the house, meaning we could leave camp the next day. She was jubilant.

My brothers and I danced around, announcing the news. Most of the women were happy for us. Some were genuinely worried about life outside the camp, a life without protection, and yet others were envious.

That evening, I said a special good-bye to my nurse friend Helen MacKenzie, who urged me to come to the hospital on a regular basis for medical care for my foot.

While we waited for my father to arrive the next morning, we said good-bye to Peter and Norma. They were sad to see us go. Peter suggested we think of him when we sang the songs or played the games he had taught us. The truck finally arrived. Captain Matoba was already at the meeting site to be present at the joyous moment. We quickly loaded our belongings and were ready to go when Captain Matoba turned to my father and said, "You certainly have a son to be proud of, Mr. la Fontaine." He smiled at me and mussed my hair. "I'm going to miss this young man," he said, placing his hand on my shoulder.

My father thanked him, apparently flattered, although he had no idea what the man was referring to or talking about. At that point, my mother hadn't had the opportunity to tell him anything about our experiences in the previous months.

"You'll need this to tide you over until you have found yourself a job," he said, handing my father some money. "Remember, you are responsible for your family from now on!"

My father was very appreciative. "Thank you, sir. Thank you for everything."

At the end we all bowed to one another and waved as we left to meet the challenges of the second phase of our World War II days.

PART III

NOVEMBER 1942–NOVEMBER 1943

Our new home was not much of a house; it was a shanty. *Is this it?* I thought in disappointment. What a place! We were moving to the *kampong* (a native village) in the woods. It suddenly became clear why my mother found it necessary to prepare us for this moment.

Behind the house, near the woodlands, were remnants of what was once a vegetable garden, now choked with weeds. Scattered sticks, once supporting tomato and cucumber plants, littered the ground.

When I entered the house, I immediately realized how very different this life would be from what it had been before the war. We were now facing the primitive lifestyle of our servants, a lifestyle that was very intimidating, especially to my parents. But if they felt humiliated, there was no evidence of it. They seemed to take it in stride for the sake of family togetherness.

The interior of our little shack was unfinished and consisted of an assortment of overlapping planks that formed the walls. The unevenness in the construction resulted in cracks through which the wind blew. There were no ceilings.

The roof, clearly visible and supported by heavy beams, was made of dry straw and palm leaves. The floors, wherever there was covering through the house, were pieces of wood placed side-by-side on bare ground. Walking on them was wobbly, to say the least.

We had two small bedrooms and a sitting room. Each was about twelve feet square and had a window. A door in the sitting room led to a large back room divided into two sections. The section to the right was an open area without a roof. That was the laundry and bathing facility. I was intrigued by something in the bathing area: a large, water-filled drum. It stood on a wooden platform. I started to wonder how I was supposed to take a bath in privacy. There were numerous chinks between the planks of the walls, some large enough for a person on the outside to peek in and watch someone take a bath. It was of no consequence for my brothers, of course. They were still too young and innocent to let something like that bother them. For me, however, it was a bit more complicated, especially disguised as a boy.

An enclosed toilet was in the far corner. The section on the left was completely taken up by an oversized multi-purpose bench. It served as our dining table and my father's workbench. Against the back wall was a rickety wooden counter crudely constructed of scrap boards. We cooked on two *anglo*s.

At mealtime, we three children sat cross-legged on the bench while our parents and aunt took their places on wooden stools alongside. Poppie used a small part of the bench as a place where he would clean the glass chimneys of the kerosene lamps and fill their small reservoirs. He followed the procedure without fail every day. Those lamps were our sole source of light.

Poppie became an expert in repairing our footwear as well. Someone suggested that he soak cut-up pieces of raw rubber and set them overnight in a container filled with gasoline. The process produced a welcome and useful commodity: glue. The new invention saved us money on footwear for the entire family.

Tante Suus provided me with an answer to my bathing fears. She found a *sarong* for me to cover my body with while I bathed. "Wrap yourself in the *sarong* like this," she said, demonstrating how to do it. "Hold it up with one hand and use your other hand to scoop water out of the drum with a *gajoeng* and pour it over you. To soap yourself, you may want to use both hands, which is a bit trickier. In that case, clench the *sarong* between your teeth, like so." We practiced the tricky technique.

I executed every step as she had modeled. It didn't take me long to find out how difficult it was to keep the *sarong* up as a cover. I felt like a juggler and it took some getting used to, but I managed.

On our first day in the *kampong,* a pick-up truck arrived. The son of an Indonesian acquaintance of my father had heard about our release. The young man arrived ahead of his parents to deliver household goods, furniture, and other necessities.

"I brought you a few things," Joesoef explained after introducing himself and shaking everyone's hand. "Nothing is new, you understand, but everything is usable and in reasonably good shape."

Joesoef's generosity touched us. We hadn't expected

anyone to know about our release, let alone welcome us in such a manner. He carried in the furniture, pots, pans, plates, glasses, some silverware, kitchen utensils, and more. He helped us find a place for everything.

"My parents will be coming over later with food," he said, "to celebrate your freedom and the beginning of a new life. We regret that the celebration will be under primitive conditions, which you are not accustomed to."

"We're grateful to be reunited as a family," my father responded. Looking around the house, he added, "We will work hard and make this shack our home."

My mother corrected, "No, it will be our paradise and haven. You can be sure of that!"

That afternoon, Tante Suus, Ronald, René, and I went on a scouting tour outside the house and walked to the edge of the woods. A nature lover, our aunt was in her element and promised to go into the woods the next day to see what she could teach us about edible greens. She said she hoped to start a vegetable garden to replace the one she had sadly left at the prison camp. The boys and I promised to help.

Before we went back into the house, we noticed a small flock of curious native children gathered on the path in front of the house. Dirty faces, stringy, greasy, unwashed hair, and ragged clothing set them apart from any other children we had ever seen. A few among them were even stark naked, a common occurrence in many out-of-the-way villages.

As they stared at us, we stared back at them. We didn't know whether to play with them, talk to them, or ignore them. As I started to approach with the intention of introducing my brothers and myself, a loud, authoritative voice called out. I could not quite make out what was said, but the children quickly scampered away. It was as if the caller had been watching us and thought I wanted to harm the children. Seconds later, silly little noises came from the window of a house across the path. The house, built on stilts, stood about fifteen feet off the ground. A further attempt to make friends with the children and pursue the mystery of the voice was interrupted by the arrival of Joesoef's parents.

The couple had brought enough food to feed an entire community, so we invited our friends and neighbors, the Rijkens and the van Zantens, to join us in our reunification celebration. Our first meal outside the camp was an extremely special and memorable event. The rice looked whiter and seemed to have more flavor. The meat dishes were tastier and just as we remembered them. It was a feast with good food, refreshing drinks, desserts, and friends. Before going to bed that evening, my family held hands and thanked God for our good fortune to be a family again. It was simply unbelievable.

The following morning, my brothers and I explored the area around the house. We played hide-and-go-seek while my parents and aunt were busy getting settled indoors. Later that afternoon, Tante Suus took us into the woods. Together, we examined various species of greens, ferns, and mushrooms to determine their edibility. During our first lesson—and she was serious about it—she pointed out the difference between the edible and poisonous varieties and taught us to recognize the greens that were safe to pick and eat. Under her supervision, we harvested enough vegetables to last us a day or two.

Our first family dinner was quite different from the prewar

dinners I remembered. The eight months of separation and camp life had taught us invaluable lessons. Among them was the ability to communicate with one another. The dinner table was now the place to share thoughts. We could speak freely with no fear of being punished. That positive awareness brought the family closer together and, surprisingly, the change happened quite naturally. It gave me a sincere feeling of family that I had never experienced before.

Ronald, René, and I were assigned chores in and around the house. Work became part of the daily routine of our new life. It taught us responsibility, and working so closely together gave us quality time as siblings. Family life was much more meaningful this time around.

Whenever my brothers and I were outside exploring, playing, or doing our chores, we knew we were being watched, although there was no sign of our little native friends. We discovered that they were secretly spying on us from their lofty post fifteen feet in the air. We heard giggles but saw nobody. On rare occasions we glimpsed the top of a head or little dark eyes peeking down at us over the windowsill. Why did they keep their distance? Was it because of who we were, how we looked, or was there another reason? We never found out.

Eyes of a different kind were upon us as well, those of the Japanese authorities. We were, after all, still prisoners of war. Two days after we moved in, an officer and two soldiers drove up. We were busy cleaning up the yard. The officer stepped out and bowed, as did we in return. He handed my father five name tags and instructed in English, "Make sure all members of your family wear these name tags every time they leave the house. If not, they might end up at the police station!"

The officer asked my father if he had found a job yet. My father had not and told the officer that he had been too busy with the house.

"Don't wait too long," the officer reprimanded. Then noticing me, he asked, "How old is the boy?"

"Almost thirteen, sir."

"Then he must work, too. He is old enough to help support the family!"

"What can you suggest for him, sir?" my father asked politely, though immediately overtaken by nervousness and fear, considering what Joesoef's father had told him about the hiring of young boys to work in Japanese households. Undesirable activities such as physical and sexual abuse, the use of drugs, drinking, and smoking had been reported. Being confronted with the possibility that his own child— his only daughter, in disguise—could be employed as a house boy, my father became determined to do anything in his power to prevent that from happening. "If it is necessary for my son to work," he said to the officer, "I want you to know that he has spent many hours assisting me in a variety of office duties during the time I was postmaster."

My father struggled to impress upon the officer what kind of work he wanted me to do. "Rick is good at what I ask him to do, and he is very conscientious. He has the potential to develop into a first-rate worker if given the opportunity." My father rambled on. "I would appreciate it if you could find him a job at an office. I am sure he will prove himself to be a great asset to his employer."

"The best thing for me to do is contact Captain Matoba and pass the information on to him. He might have a suggestion."

The officer's response had a great impact on my father. It was as if a heavy burden was lifted from his shoulders. The tension of the last few minutes had been so intense that he had a difficult time staying composed, and after the officer left, he broke down in tears.

That afternoon, Poppie took me aside and told me about the fate of young boys hired as house boys in Japanese households. Only then did I understand why he tried so hard to see to it that I got employment elsewhere. My father also admitted that involving Captain Matoba was a welcome sound to his ears. Knowing about the friendship between the commandant and me, he was almost certain of a favorable outcome.

The following day he went out to look for a job and was hired on the spot as a clerk at a rubber export company. A few days after that, the English-speaking officer stopped by with good news about a job for me, but I wasn't home. He left a note with the necessary information and, in exchange, my mother told him about my father's new job. It greatly pleased him.

The officer's note said that I was to report to the Department of Finance in the government building at eight the next day and to ask for Mr. Soepradono. I jumped up and down with joy and relief; then I suddenly sobered up and became quite nervous. I was not yet thirteen years old and I had a job! It seemed incredible that I was not in school, concentrating on homework, studying for a test, or working on a science project. Instead, I was happily looking forward to being a clerk and getting paid for it as well. It was unbelievable! My reaction both surprised and saddened me. I had always loved school. What was happening to that love? Would it ever come back?

I began to think about what was to come next. I couldn't imagine myself working in an office. What kind of work would I be doing? What did I have to offer an employer? I had no typing skills, or any other clerical skills for that matter. Oh, I had occasionally spent pleasant hours with my father in his quiet office on weekends and joined him during school vacations, when he would let me. He even allowed me to use his private Royal typewriter occasionally. It had been fun pretending to be a typist, but all that fiddling on the machine had definitely not made me competent.

The first thing my father heard when he came home was the news about my job. Naturally, he was very pleased. "See, what did I tell you, Paula?" he bragged. "Captain Matoba came through for us. No, let me correct that; he did it out of courtesy for Rita and you."

Both my parents were happy that I was going to work in an office where I'd be safe. Poppie congratulated and hugged me and pointed out that this was a special opportunity to prove myself. Then he kidded, "Just remember who your teacher was and who taught you everything you know." He laughed heartily.

My father was acquainted with Mr. Soepradono, a customs officer who had an office at the harbor. Not so very long ago, he had been instrumental in releasing our furniture when it arrived by boat from Java.

Chapter 15

A gray-haired Indonesian gentleman sat behind a desk opposite two Japanese officers seated behind their own desks. I bowed politely when I entered the room, as I was taught in camp. Not one of them reacted to my presence, so I thought I had entered the wrong door.

"I'm sorry. I must be in the wrong office," I apologized in Indonesian.

"Who are you looking for?" the older man asked.

I told him my purpose for being there and introduced myself. He said in Dutch, "You're in the right place. I am Mr. Soepradono," and invited me to sit down.

Recognizing my last name, la Fontaine, he asked if I was related to the former postmaster. I explained that I was, and that my father had asked me to give his regards. Mr. Soepradono asked me to return the salutation and was happy that my father had found employment.

"Mr. Tanaka from the *Kempetai* came by and asked me about a job fit for a teenage boy. Could you be the one he was referring to?"

"Quite possibly, sir," I responded.

"Well, I'm glad he had the good sense to send us such a young and eager person. As you can see, we need some young blood in here!" With a comical expression he made a quick sweep of the room, emphasizing the considerable ages of the three of them.

While in conference with Mr. Soepradono (whom I thought of from then on as Mr. S.), I observed the curious looks on the faces of the two Japanese gentlemen on the opposite side of the room. They were probably wondering who I was and what I was doing there.

Before approaching his two Japanese bosses to introduce me, Mr. S. opened what seemed to be a pocket dictionary, the kind one consults on travels in foreign countries. Skimming through it, he placed his fingers between certain pages as markers.

"This is my *boekoe pienter,* my book of smarts, without which I would be lost. I'm preparing to introduce you in Japanese," he said, beckoning me to follow him. "Promise you won't laugh when I stutter and stumble over words I can't pronounce correctly."

I promised, but I couldn't help smiling.

We stood in front of the desks and bowed deeply. The two Japanese men returned the greeting. Mr. Ito was the younger of the two. Mr. Sato, balding and starting to gray around the temples, was rather plump. Both wore eyeglasses.

Mr. S. addressed the two men in Japanese. If he stuttered, I would not have known. They talked for a while longer, leading me to assume that it went well. I had no idea what details, if any, Mr. S. knew about my background, but I assumed he gave the men an adequate introductory profile because neither man asked me any questions. Nods of approval were the only telltale signs that I was accepted.

Back at his desk, I asked Mr. S., "How do you communicate with them?"

"With a lot of difficulty," he confessed. Even with the help of his book of smarts, he admitted, the situation sometimes became frustrating. In view of the existing problems with the language, he suggested I start a dictionary of words or sentences of my own.

He pointed to a smaller desk next to his with a typewriter on it. "That's yours! How does it look?"

I smiled when I saw the typewriter and told him about my early playful attempts to type on my father's Royal. "It has not made me a typist, though," I joked.

"You'll have plenty of time to practice and work your way up to becoming one," he teased.

Mr. S. invited me to walk with him to the back room, where he introduced me to the rest of the staff, a group of six Indonesian men. They addressed me in Dutch, making me feel very comfortable. Right away they began to tease me about my age, being the youngest in the group and having to put up with three old men in the front office. One of them asked, "Do you realize you're going to spend your days in the least lively part of this department?" Mr. S., apparently used to this kind of kidding, just smiled.

I fired back, enjoying the repartee: "If I get bored in the front office, I know where to find all of you for some action, right?" They loved it. Though I was the youngest among them, their offer of friendship made me feel good, and I realized they respected me for who I was.

The last employee I met was Mr. Tamboenan, the

cashier-bookkeeper. An older, no-nonsense man, Mr. Tamboenan's heavy dark-framed glasses gave him a stern look, but he was a gentle giant. I was assigned to assist him with his heavy workload. He told me straightaway to conduct my duties responsibly because he would not settle for less.

I wondered if anyone was aware of my age when inquiries about the job were made. What did these people know about me? Whatever the case, I was honored by the trust and responsibility my employer was willing to invest in me. I looked forward to this new venture.

Within an hour, I experienced my first uncomfortable situation by not being able to speak Japanese. Mr. S. had left the room when Mr. Ito looked at me and said something in Japanese. In a moment of desperation, seeing Mr. S.'s *boekoe pienter* lying on his desk, I was tempted to grab it, but then realized I had no idea how to use it or what to look for. Noticing my helplessness, Mr. Ito repeated his question, only this time he applied hand gestures. I could now make out that he and Mr. Sato wanted to welcome me. I nodded and thanked him. They both smiled at me.

I could not comprehend how Mr. S. used his book of smarts. He explained his system, but finding the right expressions to suit the occasions still seemed cumbersome to me. I knew then that I had to find a way to communicate, but at the same time realized that even the simplest way might not make it easier without an expanded vocabulary.

My first day on the job, filled with introductions and new friendships, ended pleasantly. I was already looking forward to the next work day. Before closing time, I decided to go see Captain Matoba to thank him for helping me get the job. Surprised and happy to see me in such high spirits, he asked about my family. I told him that my father, too, had found a job and was happy to be working. He wished me luck and asked that I give his regards to my parents and especially to the "little woman."

"Tell her also that I miss the fresh vegetables she produced."

I dreaded the thought of having to walk all the way home, but when Mr. S. realized where I lived, he arranged a ride for me.

That evening at home was a memorable one, too. I answered all the questions my family had about my new job, my bosses, and coworkers. We drank the family's favorite drink of coconut juice and bits of young coconut, made especially for the occasion. Delicious! After such a perfect day I had no problem drifting off to sleep.

The next morning, Mr. S. sent me to the police station to find a bicycle among the confiscated ones in storage. It would be my transportation to and from work.

"Maybe I'll find my own bike!" I said to him.

"You very well may," he replied. "What brand is it, Rick?"

"A Fongers, sir. When we were in Holland on furlough in 1937, my father bought himself, my brother Ronald, and me each a Fongers bicycle." Mentioning my father reminded me that he also had a long walk to work. Perhaps his bike was in storage as well. Without hesitation, I asked, "Could I get my father's bicycle, too, if it's there?"

He grinned. "You ask a lot, my boy! I don't like to display favoritism, but in your case, Rick, I will make an exception."

I had the urge to give him a big hug and a kiss on the cheek, but I restrained myself. With a note from him and a stamp of approval by one of my Japanese bosses, I went to see the Police Commissioner. He took me to the rusty, old bikes in storage. There were bicycles galore, but I wanted none of them. I had the feeling that my bike was there somewhere. Then a pile of bikes—in better condition than the others, covered with canvas for protection against the weather and chained together—caught my eye. I pulled away the canvas, and there they were—the two Fongers bicycles I wanted, my father's and my own. Two police officers were summoned to unchain them. As I suspected, both bikes were still registered in our names. I signed a receipt and returned to the office with them. I was a very happy kid.

Now, how would I get two bikes home? Riding one while holding on to the other one would be tricky, but I was determined to do it. I couldn't wait to see my father's face. The first part of the ride was no trouble until I had to go uphill. Concentrating on pedaling steadily to maintain balance on one bike while keeping the other from sliding away from me was not easy. It was hard work, but I made it home.

When I rode up to the house, the first to notice me were Ronald and René, playing in the front yard. They loudly announced my arrival and within seconds Mommie, Poppie, and Tante Suus came running out of the house. Poppie immediately recognized his bike and took it from me. "How in heaven's name did you manage this?" he asked, walking around and around the bicycle in a state of disbelief. He ran his hands carefully over it and examined it for scratches. "It's my old bike. I don't believe my eyes!"

He hugged me tightly. "Thank you for this enormous, unbelievable surprise. I love it!"

"You're welcome. There was nothing to it, Pop," I said jokingly.

Again, he carefully examined his precious bike and asked how I had managed to bring it home. I told them the whole story. I believe that the manner in which I handled myself that day, getting the bikes on my own, gave my parents and Tante Suus the assurance that I was able to fend for myself.

Before I went to bed, they complimented me again on my initiative in seeing Captain Matoba. "You have made us proud parents, Rick," Poppie teased.

"And your aunt is very proud of you, too, dear," Tante Suus added.

Chapter 16

A family pastry-on-order business and an occasional sale of homegrown vegetables seemed to be the answers to our money problem. These necessary measures followed as a consequence of insufficient income to provide for a family of six.

Mommie and Tante Suus shared the baking. Tante Suus made the deliveries to the customers in person and thus carried the brunt of the workload. In addition to that, she tended the vegetable garden. Sometimes, in order to reach her faraway customers, she had to walk quite a distance. On rainy days, she took a *dogkar*. The two-wheeled horse-drawn carriage was a privilege and luxury she could not afford too often.

A completely different atmosphere prevailed for me at work: an atmosphere of learning. Mr. Ito taught me a few common expressions in Japanese: good morning, good afternoon, good evening, and a few others. I was able to greet someone in Japanese, offer that person a seat, and ask, *"Ogenki desu ka?* How are you?" It wasn't much, but it was a beginning. I looked forward to more of Mr. Ito's tutoring. I knew he would help me, because the inability to converse with me seemed to bother him as much as it did me.

As time passed, the teaching sessions occurred on a daily basis. We soon realized that the only sensible way to communicate was to make drawings on paper, then elaborate on them. Hand movements were often needed for clarification, and most of the time, we eventually arrived at what we were trying to say. In general, Mr. Ito repeated a word or phrase, I wrote it down in my notebook as he pronounced it, and then I added the definition in Dutch. These language sessions were always entertaining and at times even amusing. My success encouraged me to persevere.

Things got even better when a brochure from the new government crossed my desk. It told about an upcoming plan to start a course in the Japanese language. Nobody was as happy with the news or as eager to participate as I was. I went to the registrar's office and signed up right away. My name was the first on an empty registration list.

Back at the office, I approached my boss. "Mr. S., I just came back from signing up for the Japanese course," I announced.

"What are you talking about? I haven't heard anything about it!"

"Well, I've signed up for a course in Japanese, and I'm the first one on the list."

"That doesn't surprise me at all, knowing how it annoys you not to be able to converse with Mr. Ito and Mr. Sato. Congratulations and good luck!"

"And there's another reason why you should be happy

to see the course start soon," I teased. "You'll be able to throw out your book of smarts and lean on me."

Information about the course stated that a written exam would be conducted every three months. Those who passed the test would receive a certificate, a color-coded pin to distinguish the level of the course completed, and a note guaranteeing the bearer an increase in pay. The entire process would be repeated every three months until the course was completed. After a year, students could be expected to adequately speak, write, and read Japanese.

I had no doubt that I wanted to participate. The prospect of being able to carry on a civilized conversation with my Japanese employers without using a kindergarten approach appealed to me. I was excited about it and couldn't wait for classes to begin. At the same time, I couldn't help but wonder if I would be able to finish the course. The uncertainty of not knowing when we would be uprooted again came and went. I was determined to start learning Japanese and I just had to wait and see how far I could get. Every part of learning the language was worth it to me.

Our teacher, an officer in the Japanese army, spoke exclusively Japanese. I was the only Dutch student and the youngest among mostly married Indonesian government employees. I was afraid I couldn't keep up with them, but the pressures of going to school, holding a regular job, and managing homework and family turned out to be too much for many of them to handle. Some dropped out after only a few weeks. I was determined that that was not going to happen to me.

The lessons in our workbooks were in the Indonesian

language and accompanied by translations into Japanese. Although I spoke Indonesian, I had never read anything in that language. I quickly discovered that I had to do some translating between the Indonesian and Dutch languages before I could determine what to do. It was quite an experience, but I overcame it in a relatively short time. After all, Indonesian was a close second language for me, Dutch being the first.

Almost immediately, we were taught to write *katakana*, the most popular and easiest of the Japanese writing styles to learn because it was phonetic. Mr. Ito, again realizing my eagerness to learn, took time to teach me the intricacies of writing the characters. He showed me how to create them by using the common writing utensils of the Japanese, a brush and india ink. He demonstrated how to hold the brush, where to start, and how to move. Watching him paint elegant strokes with such precision and artistic flair was fascinating. The intense concentration of every move he made on the paper sometimes made me hold my breath.

The writing portion of the course was not easy. Writing the Japanese way was extremely difficult because it had nothing in common with our kind of writing. I took my homework assignments very seriously; I devoted practically every waking moment to practicing and perfecting my letters.

Halfway into the course, we learned to write a combination of phonetic script and Chinese characters: the *hiragana*. Toward the end, we were familiarized with the system of fancy lettering based on borrowed or modified Chinese characters called *kanji*. The latter two were the more difficult and sophisticated styles used in letter writing.

Documents, magazines, and newspapers usually exhibit a combination of the three styles.

Another aspect of the course that intrigued me was the way reading material, as in a newspaper, was displayed. The writing started at the top right-hand corner and continued down. Each following line continued to the left of the previous one. In other words, one had to read the paper from top to bottom, right to left.

My bosses frequently inquired how the Japanese class was going. Little by little, I tried to impress them with things I had learned. My enthusiasm contributed to their generous assistance with my studies, and their encouragement was an important factor in helping me reach my goal. I passed my first exam three months later.

In the meantime, my job responsibilities began to increase. Occasional trips to the bank in an armored car to deposit or withdraw large amounts of money were added. On those days, I felt extremely privileged. What other thirteen-year-old had that kind of responsibility? It was extraordinary! As time went by, those trips to and from the bank developed into a permanent part of my daily duties.

Despite the enjoyment of carrying my own weight at the office, I wondered to myself many times how my superiors had come to trust me to handle such an exceptional task. My coworkers were aware of my added duties, but not one of them ever said or did anything to indicate that they were envious of my position.

I worked hard on my Japanese whenever I could, at the office as well as at home. Two days after my first exam, I received the official announcement that I had passed with high grades. The first pin of distinction, a certificate, and a note that entitled me to a pay increase arrived. I was happy to share that moment with everyone who had made it possible. What a feeling of accomplishment that was.

At that point, I was able to converse with my Japanese bosses in a reasonable manner. An improvised dictionary had been provided with the course, so I was now in a better position to look for the right words to use in my conversations. Mr. S. was impressed with the progress I had made, and so were my Japanese employers. They suggested that we not use the drawing pad as often, so I would be forced to use my newly acquired language skills. I tried to oblige, but to play it safe, I kept the drawing pad and notebook close by.

When I showed the certificate to my father, he twirled me around and around on the wobbly floor boards of our house. My mother and Tante Suus weren't nearly as dramatic, but they were equally proud. Ronald and René had no idea what the commotion was all about. I don't even think they cared, but it didn't matter.

That week, Mr. Ito invited me to his house for a party. I believed the invitation to be genuine but requested time to talk it over with my family. They urged me to go to keep people from becoming suspicious.

Promptly on time, Mr. Ito's car arrived to pick me up. When I arrived at the house, he greeted me at the door. Like Captain Matoba at the dinner with my family a few months before, he, too, was dressed in a beautiful silk kimono and wearing straw slippers. I took off my shoes and he ushered me into the party room.

The guests had traded their military uniforms for colorful kimonos. After an exchange of bows, my host asked me to take a seat opposite him at the other end of the long, low table. When I saw the seating arrangements, I was prepared to suffer through an entire evening sitting cross-legged on the floor. Lowering myself, I decided to make the best of it.

Looking around, I recognized a few of the guests from crossing paths with them during office hours, but I had never seen them in civilian clothing. A nod of recognition was exchanged here and there.

Mr. Ito started his introduction. "Gentlemen, our guest of honor has arrived. This young Dutch boy, my friends, is currently employed in my office. His name is Rick la Fontaine and he is thirteen years old."

He told the group how I had come into his life and that I had attended the first course in Japanese offered for the benefit of office workers. "Rick is the only Dutch boy in the class. He is the youngest, had perfect attendance, and earned the highest grade on the exam."

Although it was embarrassing to hear my boss's praises, I felt appreciated. He was genuinely proud of my efforts and progress, and the guests applauded enthusiastically. He told them about the times we had tried to communicate in the office by using our hands and drawing silly pictures on a pad. "That's what made this boy take the initiative to attend the course and persist with determination to learn Japanese. Sato-san and I are grateful for his effort."

"*Banzai! Banzai! Banzai!* Hoorah! Hoorah! Hoorah!" they all cheered.

Mr. Ito admitted to his guests that the closeness of working side-by-side with me made him often think of his grandson in Japan. Catching himself in a vulnerable moment of nostalgia, he quickly recovered his composure. It was an honorable tribute, and I felt inadequate in expressing my thanks. All I was comfortable saying in Japanese was, *"Domo arigato gozaimasu, Ito-San, Sato-san.* Thank you very much, Mr. Ito, Mr. Sato."* I made a few extra bows to emphasize my gratitude, hoping the gesture came across with the intended sincerity. They all applauded.

Then, out from behind a beaded curtain came women dressed in kimonos. Their backs were slightly arched as they moved about, taking tiny steps. They never lifted their heads to look up, nor did they speak a word unless spoken to. Even then, they would not look at the speaker, but remained humble and responded in a soft, barely audible voice. Looking up was a gesture of disrespect, I learned. When the women reached the table, they went down on their knees and served cups of warm *sake,* Japanese rice wine, to each guest. Then they left, showing the same submissive posture they'd used when entering the room.

The host and his guests, including me, toasted several times. I joined them by raising my cup to touch my lips while making sure the contents never reached my mouth. At a signal from the host, the servers again entered the dining room, this time carrying large platters with freshly cut vegetables, raw fish, and other necessary ingredients to prepare a dish. The next trip produced a wok, cooking utensils, and a hibachi, which was placed on a protective mat on the table in front of the host. Japanese tradition dictated that the host do the cooking. *Sukiyaki* was on the menu.

While Mr. Ito prepared the *sukiyaki,* each guest received a bowl of steamed rice and a set of chopsticks. I looked around to learn how to use them. I knew it would not be long before I lost my patience and gave up. I had tried it before without success. My request for a fork and spoon did not go unnoticed by the guests. The jokes they made about it totally eluded me, but the food tasted much better, and I was sure that every bite would at least reach my mouth instead of landing in my lap.

Up to that point there had not been much conversation between me and the other guests because of the language barrier. Then two of the quieter guests came out of their shells and began to talk to me in a combination of English and Indonesian. They empathized with my language problem and told me I was doing well as a beginning speaker of Japanese. They admitted that, although they spoke two foreign languages, I spoke theirs better. Their honesty made me feel good because they were keenly aware of what I was going through. The rest of the evening progressed smoothly and I became more relaxed. The two guests and I occasionally consulted one another for correct translations of conversations, sometimes causing hilarious moments for all.

The party ended with Japanese tea and a sing-along. Not knowing the lyrics, I hummed the ones that sounded familiar. The guest next to me seemed surprised to hear me hum and asked where I had learned the songs. I pointed in the direction of the schoolhouse, which was visible from where we were sitting. I told him about the two parties I had attended while still imprisoned, and explained that I had learned a few Japanese songs at those parties. "I played the accordion to entertain the guests," I added.

"You played a musical instrument and entertained the commandant and his guests?"

"Yes, sir, I did," I answered affirmatively.

"Where is the instrument?" he then asked.

"I don't know, sir, but the last time I played it was at the quarters of Captain Matoba, the commandant of our camp."

Addressing Mr. Ito, he then said with admiration, "You have found yourself a jewel of a boy, Ito-san."

At midnight, I was driven home in Mr. Ito's car. During the ride, I thought about how lucky I was to have experienced all this. I compared the evening with the two parties in the camp. What a difference! I hadn't wanted this party to end because I really had fun. There had been no misbehavior, and I had not felt jeopardized for a moment during the entire evening. My pretense as a boy became second nature and lived out to the fullest.

As I expected, Mommie, Poppie, and Tante Suus were awaiting my homecoming. I prepared myself for their barrage of questions. Looking at them, I knew that hearing about the success of the evening and how I enjoyed myself pleased them. They were proud to hear that I was the guest of honor. I told them that despite my age, I had received genuine respect and admiration.

In bed, I relived the entire evening. I still couldn't believe I had been the guest of honor, but it was true. Something else that seemed unbelievable was that my enemies had honored and celebrated me tonight. I decided that they were not my enemies; they were my friends, just as Captain Matoba had been a friend to a camp of women and children at one time.

Chapter 17

After months of studying hard, I passed the second Japanese exam. The family pastry business was flourishing, providing us with a comfortable additional income. We were a happy, content family and everything seemed to be going our way. Then, tragedy struck.

I arrived home from work one day in May to an odd, lingering stillness in the house. Entering through the back door like any other day, I saw my father at the bench cleaning and filling up the kerosene lamps. It was a daily event and nothing new to me. What concerned me, however, was that he seemed preoccupied, not himself, and even worried. Instinctively, I knew that his behavior and the stillness had something to do with my mother. My heart pounded in my throat. I was afraid to ask where she was and dreaded his answer even more. Instead, I asked, "Where's Tante Suus?"

"She is delivering an order of pastries and is planning to visit the Schooks at the Heights. She might come home a little later than usual," he informed me. "The boys are playing somewhere in the neighborhood," he added, speaking softly, pretending to concentrate on cleaning the lamps to avoid having to look at me.

"Pop, why are you whispering? Where's Mommie? Why isn't she cooking?" I asked, knowing that something was seriously wrong.

"She's in bed. She isn't feeling well."

I became panic-stricken, knowing that my mother was not a healthy woman. What worried me more than anything else was knowing that since before the war broke out, and during our captivity in the schoolhouse, she hadn't seen a physician. We hadn't had a family doctor since moving to Djambi, although my parents had contacted one, Dr. Sambiono, just in case.

I tiptoed into the bedroom and saw my mother lying on her side. I kissed her on the temple and was alarmed at the coolness of her skin. She didn't move at all. I waited for her eyes to open, trying to decide if I should touch her again to let her know that I was home. She finally opened her eyes, and I was relieved. Secretly, I had harbored a deep fear that she would not wake up.

Recognizing me, she smiled faintly. I bent down so that she could see me better. A peacefulness surrounded her. I smiled and held her hand tightly in mine, kissing the tops of her fingers a few times. I had difficulty holding back tears. I felt powerless and sad, but I didn't want her to see how worried I was. She squeezed my hand softly for a few seconds. I gently touched the skin of her hand with my lips again and whispered, "How are you, Mom? How are you feeling?"

"I don't know, dear," she responded wearily, before closing her eyes again.

As I sat on the edge of the bed, still holding her hand, I knew she was suffering from something more than just "not feeling well." Occasionally she stirred, but in general, her body seemed lifeless.

I didn't know what had happened, if anything at all, before I came home that evening. From the expression on my father's face and the way he acted, I could only conclude that he must have been aware that it was something more serious. He must have been extremely afraid, knowing he was unable to help her. This was probably the reason that he concentrated on his daily routine more intensely than ever, instead of sitting with her. Most troubling to me was that Tante Suus was not home. She was the only one familiar with my mother's care and medical background. Without her to attend to his sick wife, my father must have felt even more lost until I came home.

Still holding my mother's hand and squeezing it occasionally, I let her know I was still with her. Although her eyes remained closed, she gripped my fingers tightly. Perspiration beaded on her forehead. Using a hand towel, I wiped her face with soft strokes. Then I laid the towel across her bare arm.

Moments later, she indicated a desire to turn over onto her other side. It took great effort to bring it about, but she managed. She was now facing the wall and away from me. I moved the towel to her upper arm and stayed with her, wishing with all my being that Tante Suus would change her mind and come home. She would know what to do. I leaned over my mother and gently placed another soft kiss on her temple. Suddenly, I heard her voice. It was almost impossible to hear what she was saying. She lifted a hand

and moved it around a few times, as if she wanted to emphasize something. Looking at her hand, she asked, "Don't my hands look old? Do I look pale?"

I looked at her hands and then at her face and saw that she did indeed look pale.

"Yes, Mommie, you look a little bit pale, but . . ." I never finished the sentence because at that moment her hand fell back limply and she started to throw up. I jerked the towel off her arm but not fast enough to catch the vomit. She lay still as if she were dead. The sight of her frightened me. I wiped her mouth with the towel. I wanted her to pull in her tongue and open her eyes, but that didn't happen. I was numb and unable to think. Seconds passed before it occurred to me that she might have stopped breathing. To reassure myself, I held a finger under her nose. There was absolutely no breath. My mother wasn't breathing! I realized then that she was dead.

The silence around me and the tranquil look on her face overwhelmed me with a tremendous sense of loss. Tears rolled down my face. A sudden and urgent need to be with my father made me call out for him. My outcry must have given him the clue of what he feared would happen. His cry, intermingled with loud, wrenching sobs coming from deep within him, tore me apart. It was such an unnatural sound to hear. My father's incoherent sounds of grief became too much for me to bear. I blocked my ears and ran out of the house into the woods.

I ran deeper and deeper into unfamiliar surroundings while the tears streamed down my face. I had no idea where I was going or how long I had been running, but I finally slumped against a tree trunk. Still crying, I felt a terrible emptiness, as if my heart had been ripped open. The tranquillity of the tall trees and the soothing sounds of leaves rustling in the light breeze relaxed me. After a while, recovered from the shock, I remembered leaving my father alone at the house and decided to return to console him.

When I reentered the house, he was slumped over my mother's lifeless body and the truth hit me all over again. My mother, my friend, had left me. She would no longer be there for me, to sing with me, to give me moral support, and to make me feel lucky to have her as my mother. So many conflicting emotions welled up within me. Why was this happening to me? I needed her. The world seemed empty, my mother's death meaningless, and the air heavy and dark.

Together in each other's arms, my father and I wept and wept. We remained in an embrace, needing each other's support and strength as never before. Some time passed before we were able to compose ourselves. We decided that I would go fetch Tante Suus. He agreed to look for the boys in the neighborhood and call the doctor.

My task was particularly difficult because to get to the Schooks' place I had to ride uphill on my bike. The trip took about forty-five minutes one way. That by itself was not too bad, but I dreaded what was to come after I arrived there. I had to confront Tante Suus and ask her to come home without revealing the real reason. I couldn't tell her the truth. She might become over-emotional and faint. I had to remain calm.

I arrived at the Schooks' gasping for breath. Tante Suus, Maggie Schook, and her mother (whom we kids called Oma) were sipping iced tea on the front porch.

"Rick, you look like you've been chased by a ghost," Mrs. Schook announced.

"It was the uphill ride, Mrs. Schook. I'm all right."

She offered me a cool drink, but before I could answer, Tante Suus interjected, "Is something wrong with your mother?"

Trying hard to sound as casual as possible, I explained that my father wanted her to come home because my mother wasn't feeling well and he didn't know what to do. Waiting for Tante Suus to get ready to go, I made sure to stay at a distance because I didn't want my eyes or face to reveal what had happened. I wanted so desperately to be truthful with all of them, but I just couldn't.

Reappearing from the inside of the house, Tante Suus turned to her friends, "Maggie, Oma, *tot ziens!* Until we meet again!"

To me, she said indignantly, "You should have found me a *dogkar*."

Fortunately, the ride back home was mostly downhill. The added weight and Tante Suus's arms around my waist hindered my pedaling. I felt like a horse wearing a cinch pulling a loaded wagon. She had many questions during the ride, but I managed to deflect them with the excuse that I needed my energy to pedal. My carefully worded answers avoided the real issue.

Everything seemed to be in control until we got close to home. I recognized the Indonesian doctor my parents had become acquainted with before the war, pushing his bike up the hill ahead of us. Tante Suus noticed him, too. She started to shake me and pull at me, bombarding me with questions. It became impossible to maintain my balance, and I was forced to stop pedaling. We walked the rest of the way up the hill.

As we walked, Tante Suus's suspicions intensified. She screamed at me, trying to find out what was going on. When I didn't offer a satisfying answer, she burst out, "The doctor is on his way to the house to see Paula. Isn't that true?"

I tried to stay calm. "It is possible that Poppie called the doctor."

When we finally reached the house, she ran to the door. My father met her and barred her way, hoping to prepare her for what she would find inside. She lunged at him, speaking gibberish and acting like a crazed woman, totally out of control. My father kept her in his grip, whispering in her ear, trying to calm her down, which seemed to work.

They broke their embrace and walked through the front door hand in hand. The doctor was still in the bedroom, finalizing the death certificate.

I heard Tante Suus say, "Oh, my Lord," and then there was a primeval wail so unearthly it gave me goose bumps. When she touched my mother's body, she cried out, "She's warm to the touch, Vic. She couldn't be . . . She's asleep. That's all it is. She's asleep. Tell me she's not gone, Vic."

Tante Suus fainted. My father and the doctor carried her to her own bed, where they stayed until she regained consciousness. The doctor gave her a sedative and left. Neighbors and people we didn't even know quietly gathered outside to pay their respects.

It was one of the most difficult nights for all of us. My mother had always been in ill health, but we never thought for a moment that we might lose her, and at such a young age. She was only forty-one. Everything had happened so fast. Less than two hours before, she had been alive, talking to me, and whispering her last few words.

Looking at her as she lay on the bed, quiet and lifeless, I thought I saw a smile on her face. She seemed to be at peace and happy now. Because she had died quickly, I consoled myself with the belief that she could not have suffered any discomfort. The more I looked at her, the more beautiful she appeared. My mind took me back to the many good times we had shared. In my memory, we laughed, we joked, we sang, we talked, we hugged, and we kissed. Now I had to face the future without her.

When Tante Suus regained consciousness, she was confused, and Mrs. van Zanten helped her sit up. Seeing her sister lying lifeless a few steps away brought it all back. "Why couldn't it have been me?" she wailed. "Why did Paula leave us? The children are so young and need their mother." She sobbed and sobbed.

Trying to console her, Mrs. van Zanten reminded Tante Suus that the family had the recent opportunity to spend many happy months together after a long separation. "Paula must have had a premonition of what was ahead, inspiring her to make every minute count with her loving family. Spared from a life of ill health and perhaps facing death under less favorable circumstances, she has now entered a better world."

Mrs. van Zanten took my aunt's face in her hands and brought up a very sensitive point, one that we couldn't ignore. "Paula was happy the last few months, Suus."

It was Mrs. van Zanten who took pity on Tante Suus and took her to her house for a cup of coffee. We had supper at Mrs. Rijken's that evening, and a mutual decision was made to keep my aunt there overnight.

Because of the high humidity, the burial had to take place within twenty-four hours. As neighbor women bathed and prepared my mother's body for burial, their husbands worked all through the night to construct a coffin. With the bright lights, hammering, sawing, and loud talk in the front yard, it was impossible to sleep.

Chapter 18

The following morning, my father approached me. "Since you are familiar in dealing with the authorities," he said, "I would appreciate it if you would make the necessary arrangements for your mother's funeral." He hesitated for a second and then with an uneasy look on his face, added, "I feel awkward asking you to do what is actually my responsibility, but I know you will have better results than I would. Don't you agree, dear?"

I knew nothing about burials, but I told my father that I'd take care of things, and that I would stop by his office to notify them that he wouldn't be in to work that day. I gave him a quick kiss on the cheek and stepped toward my bike. I had the feeling there was something more on my father's mind. "Is there anything more you'd care to have me do, Pop?"

He hesitated, but finally expressed his wish. "Yes, there is something special I hope you can get done. Do you think you could get a priest to perform the burial ceremony?"

I was almost certain I could arrange it, but I didn't want my father to get his hopes up, so I just said I would try.

First I went to his place of work to tell them about my mother's passing. Then I went to the police station to report her death and to request transportation to and from the cemetery. A truck was scheduled to arrive at the house at two that afternoon.

My final stop for the day was Mr. S. He expressed sympathy when he heard the reason for my being late. I gathered the courage to ask him if it would be appropriate to request a priest to perform the burial ceremony. He talked to Mr. Sato and Mr. Ito about it. They gave him a name to call. At the end of the phone conversation, I heard Mr. S. say, "*Hai! Hai!* Yes! Yes! *Domo arigato gozaimasu, Osawa-san.* Thank you very much, Mr. Osawa." We had a priest, and he would arrive at the house with the truck that afternoon.

I couldn't believe how easy it was to get things done. I could understand even less why everyone was going out of their way to help me. Who was I? Did I really deserve all this courtesy? It was overwhelming to think that I, an impostor, a girl in disguise, was given such privileges. Wasn't I the enemy? No matter how I viewed my disguise, it was a strange situation, but one that began to fascinate me more and more. Despite it all, overwhelmed and appreciative, I was unable to think of a way to express my true thanks. The best I could do under the circumstances was to bow extra deeply, more often than usual. Perhaps I overdid it, but I felt that as a boy I was supposed to act like a little gentlemen and not show my emotions, so I didn't.

Before I left the government building to return home, I felt obligated to personally notify Captain Matoba of my mother's death. I didn't want him to hear about it from another source, knowing how he had admired her. Deeply shocked and saddened by the news, he seemed touched by the courtesy I had shown him. He asked if he could help in any way. I told him what I had arranged for the burial. After he expressed his admiration about my mature approach, he promised to be there as well, "as a tribute to a great lady I have always admired." Again, I had that strange feeling of not knowing how to appropriately express myself for his kindness.

Back at the house, Mmes. van Zanten and Rijken were with my family. The coffin was still open to allow us to say good-bye. When I saw my mother lying there, washed and smelling of soap and her hair neatly combed, I knew she was at peace and in a better world. Serenity veiled her face. I wept in silence. Supported by her friends, even Tante Suus had an air of calmness about her. She, too, said her last farewell to her sister in a rain of tears. After Ronald and René had said theirs and had kissed her, I followed. My father requested privacy for his last words with her.

In the meantime, the truck with the priest arrived. I was not sure if it was fate or mere coincidence, but the priest was our good friend Father Koevoets. He greeted us with a solemn look, said a prayer in the name of the family and friends, and offered a benediction. At the sound of the hammering of nails into the coffin, we all realized we would never again see my mother. That moment was too much for Tante Suus to bear; she fainted again. Poppie thought it best that she not come to the cemetery with us.

The mourners gathered outside. My Japanese employers, Mr. S., and Mr. Tamboenan were there along with Captain Osawa, who had provided the priest. Captain Matoba and the Chief of Police were also present. The guards accompanying the priest and the officers stood at attention while friends and neighbors carried my mother's coffin out of the house to the truck.

Guards led my family to a car and Father Koevoets to the truck. Waiting for the procession to begin, the two leading officers were in deep conversation. At a command by one of them, the guard on the truck and Father Koevoets jumped off and got into the car with us. In the guard's presence, the conversation between the priest and the rest of us was light rather than solemn. Father Koevoets explained how the event had gone for him.

"I could not believe my ears when I was told to get ready for a funeral. 'What funeral?' I asked. The guard told me not to ask any questions and to be ready for a trip outside the jailhouse. It shocked me to finally be told that it was your wife who had died," the priest said, looking at my father. He pulled a handkerchief out of his habit and rubbed his hands.

At the cemetery, the priest performed his duty. In his eulogy he spoke with tenderness and compassion of my mother as a faithful wife, a caring and loving mother and sister, and a considerate, generous friend. It was a good thing Tante Suus was not there. It would have been too much for her.

The trip home was unbelievably sad. It was quiet in the car. We could almost hear each other's melancholy thoughts. The house had been tidied during our absence. It was restored to its usual state, but it now seemed empty and unhappy. The soft humming and whistling sounds that usually came from anywhere in the house where my mother would be were no longer there. She had been a high-spirited woman despite bouts of pain, but now there was nothing left but silence, and the soft fragrance of Coty body powder that always surrounded her. We all had a hard time facing the emptiness. That night my brothers and I went to bed at the usual time, while my father and Tante Suus stayed up and talked deep into the night. The dim light of a kerosene lamp was the only witness to the heartfelt devastation of two people who had lost a dear loved one.

Lying in bed, letting my mind roam freely, I remembered words my mother had spoken, telling us that the little shack we lived in was not much of a house but that we should think of it as our special place. For a short time, it had indeed been paradise. The few months that we were together were a bonus, a gift, fate, or whatever one cared to call it, particularly to my mother. I believed she knew her time was up and that the strength of something beyond her own power made her live the last days of her life in pure happiness and contentment.

My thoughts went further and further into the past. I remembered the laughs we had, the singing sessions, sitting on old musty trunks in the sparsely lit storeroom. I also remembered frequent doctor's visits to the house, the whispering voices between the physician, my father, and my aunt. I was too young then to understand what was wrong.

One particular episode stood out in my mind. As a daily routine after school, before I did anything else, I always visited my mother at her bedside and spent time with her. I was nine years old. On that particular day, as I reached the door to her bedroom, ready to knock, Tante

Suus opened it simultaneously from the inside. She picked up a white bowl from the floor. It contained a bloody substance with something floating in it.

"Close the door, Rita," she ordered, "and follow me into the bathroom."

"I want to visit with Mommie."

"You may do that later," she said. I closed the door behind me and followed her into the bathroom. From the basin she took out a small jellylike mass, careful not to have it slip out of her hands. "This is the beginning of what could have been a baby brother or sister," she explained.

I stared at the substance cupped in her hands. I was stunned. How could that be? I wondered. Tanta Suus prepared the little body for burial. She suggested burying it in the yard between the two banana trees against the back wall. Later that afternoon, Ronald and I, with the help of our gardener, dug a small hole. Then Tante Suus carried out a small box containing the miscarried child, placed it in the hole, and covered it with dirt. We prayed together and sprinkled the tiny grave with rose petals. Ronald and I visited the grave every day and played close by to keep it company.

Despite her poor health, my mother had always been happy and radiated energy. She had a vibrant personality. She seemed to possess a magical power to make people around her forget their own problems or difficulties. She was able to find a story to tell or something to say to make people laugh and feel good again. The days after her death were full of sorrow and difficult adjustments.

On the seventh day, as is customary in the Indonesian

culture, we planned a family visit to her grave. I took the day off from my job to devote it solely to the memory of my mother. My father arranged the same. Just before we were about to leave for the cemetery, the *Kempetai* drove up. Before the officer spoke a word, I had a strange feeling that bad news had arrived. The officer, one we had never seen before, stepped out of the truck and in perfect English addressed my father directly. "Sir, pack your belongings and come with us."

"Pack my things and come with you?" my father repeated in disbelief. "No, sir, I am not coming with you. Not today."

"Those are my orders," the officer insisted. "You and your countrymen are to be returned to jail, sir."

"What! What did we do?" my father asked, almost in tears, thinking of our plan to visit the grave.

"You did nothing, sir, but you all have to return to jail," the officer answered with admirable patience.

My father struggled to compose himself. "Sir, I beg of you. I lost my wife a week ago. Exactly one week ago. My sister-in-law, my children, and I had plans to visit the graveyard this afternoon. Would you allow me to go? I'll report to you as soon as I have returned. I want to say good-bye to her one more time."

"I cannot allow you that privilege," the officer said. "Go inside and start packing. I'll wait for you."

My father pleaded with the officer for a last chance to visit my mother's grave, but to no avail. That unexpected development affected him more than any of us. He reacted as if he had lost his bearings. I felt so sad for him.

The officer took charge. "Mr. la Fontaine, did you hear what I just said to you?"

"Yes, sir, I did, but . . . I promised my children we would visit their mother's grave today. She died exactly seven days ago, you know," he repeated. It broke my heart to witness my father resisting the officer. He was in a state of total confusion. "I don't understand why you won't let me go to the graveyard. It would be a matter of an hour or two," my father pleaded.

At that moment, Tante Suus, acting stronger than I had ever seen her, came to his rescue and led him into the house. While she packed his things, she explained the situation to him as carefully and as clearly as she could. My father just sat on the edge of the bed staring into space. He didn't say a word. When Tante Suus finished packing, she took my father's arm and led him outside to the officer.

The *Kempetai* officer waited while my father said good-bye to us. It was a very sad good-bye. First Poppie hugged and kissed Ronald and René and told them to take care of Tante Suus. Next he walked over to my aunt. She did most of the talking, though she was barely able to speak. "Take care of yourself, Vic," she advised at the end, "and don't worry about us." She sobbed and so did my father.

He then turned to me and said with a warm, tender voice, "You are the one I count on to take my place."

I tried to be brave and strong, and promised that I would do what he expected of me. A terrible fear that I would never see my father again enveloped me. I looked up at him and through my tears I saw a broad smile on his face. I couldn't smile back because my tears prevented it. Instead, we hugged in a last embrace. Then the truck drove away with my father.

Tante Suus, Ronald, René, and I stuck to our plan and visited my mother's grave. We prayed and asked God to watch over my father and all the other men and their families who were undergoing the same fate.

Chapter 19

Now orphans had it not been for the blessing of having an aunt to care for us, Ronald, René, and I had to adjust to life without parents. Tante Suus had to give up the family baking business and only accepted an occasional special order. She took the boys with her on deliveries. The rest of her time was devoted to caring for us, the house, and our vegetable garden.

Coping with the loss of my mother and the absence of my father was difficult for me, but I tried to be strong. Blocking all negative thoughts from my mind, I went full speed ahead and studied hard for my upcoming exam in the Japanese course. Since I was now the sole breadwinner, the benefits that came with passing the exam were more important than ever.

Since the men were returned to camp, the Japanese government began distributing food rations to families left behind. The extra food was a welcome commodity, especially for families with small children and no means of income. In our case, the rations supplemented our reserves because I was adequately provided for through my job.

One day when I came home from work, Tante Suus gave me the news that a busload of women and children had arrived in town. Some were the families from the gold mines located deep in the interior of the island and in hard-to-reach mountainous areas. They had believed themselves safe from Japanese infiltration. Thus, with none of the worries of those living closer to towns and cities, they had made no effort to hide. They had continued living comfortably in their homes—that is, until the Japanese authorities found them.

Also in the group were two families who had been in the convoy that came to our house to evacuate us at the start of the war. The Japanese had captured them just before they boarded a ship that would have taken them to one of the offshore islands. They were held captive until the enemy decided to return them to Djambi, their starting point. They told us that several missionary nuns riding in a separate bus had joined them for a time. However, when they arrived in town, they discovered that the nuns were not with them and nobody could say what had happened to them.

From the two families, we learned that earlier rumors about the Djambi refugees being on a boat that was bombed and sunk were not true. One boat sank, but the Djambi group was not on it, as we had originally heard.

Then a horrible thought chilled me. If Tante Suus, Ronald, René, and I had evacuated with this group and returned with them now, we would never have seen my mother or father again. I silently thanked God for the months of love and happiness we had enjoyed as a family, despite the tragic ending.

Days went by with no further developments. Then one evening around midnight, our peaceful existence was rudely interrupted. The roar of a military vehicle awakened us. Its motor stopped, and through the quietness a sharp voice barked instructions in Japanese.

Tante Suus was calm. She got out of bed and dressed quickly. Seconds later, our house was surrounded by men running in heavy boots. It seemed as if an entire army was about to burst into the house. Flashlight beams flicked in all directions. Voices shouted orders, but I couldn't make out what they said. Then came a heavy pounding on the front door. We didn't dare to breathe. The same barking voice, this time in Indonesian, ordered us to open up. When Tante Suus opened the door, the officer pushed his way in, flashed a light into her face, and bluntly accused her of harboring a criminal.

The bully then stomped through the rooms, flashing his light over and under the beds, behind chairs, and everywhere else he thought someone could be hiding. "Come out and show your face!" he yelled. "I know you are hiding somewhere. Come on out! It's no use hiding! We'll find you!" He repeatedly whacked surfaces all around him with a short, heavy club to force out the culprit. He kept yelling the same words over and over.

Tante Suus followed the officer. "Who are you trying to find in my house, sir?" she demanded to know. "I live here with three children; nobody else lives here."

Turning to her in anger, the man shouted, "Don't lie to me! Where is he?" He pushed her aside and strode into the bedroom where Ronald, René, and I were cowering. He flashed his light over us again, then went to the back of the house for a second look under the bench and in the makeshift lavatory. He found nobody, of course.

As the officer left, he mouthed a brief, insincere apology. Shaken by what had happened, it took a while before we were able to go back to sleep. The incident left us wondering. Who were they looking for? And why was our house targeted for the search? The following day we learned that no other household in the area had experienced that kind of harassment.

Two nights later, a second search party came by. Even though this group was less intimidating than the first, they were just as fastidious in their mission to find someone they had labeled an escaped murderer. They told us that a few days earlier a murderer had escaped from a jail located less than a mile from our home. They believed a woman was supplying him with food.

Tante Suus was furious. "You believe that woman to be *me*?" Her voice rose high in pitch as she shouted words of disbelief.

Her outburst surprised the officer and he stuttered a bit. "This house is the closest to the woods. Witnesses say that you and the boys enter the woods on a daily basis. Is that not true?"

Tante Suus explained the trips into the woods. "We go there to look for edible vegetation to stay alive! I have four mouths to feed and cannot afford to buy much food. With the children's father back in camp and their mother deceased, I am responsible for them. Now, do you really think I would jeopardize our lives by doing something stupid like harboring a murderer?" Her entire body shook so badly that she had to sit down. Tears of bafflement, anger, and fear erupted, and her lips trembled from sheer frustration and intimidation. At last convinced we were in no way involved in the escape, the officer and his entourage departed.

After that last invasion on our privacy, Tante Suus and I agreed we would either move out of the neighborhood or take in a male friend for protection. The latter was discarded almost immediately. We knew no man well enough to share our house or, more important, to share the secret of my identity.

Tante Suus began a search for a more secure place and succeeded in finding an apartment. Although it was smaller, it was livable. The rent was affordable, and it was located in friendlier surroundings. The area was hilly, but it made us again feel like part of civilization rather than like bush people.

Our move to higher ground was hard on Mrs. van Zanten and Mrs. Rijken. They didn't want us to move away, but they understood. I personally missed the serenade by the native children who welcomed me home after work every day. As soon as they saw me coming, they would start singing one particular song and not stop until I had entered the house. They had started doing that when we first moved in. I never found out what the lyrics of the song were or why they sang the song only when I came home. Why only for me? My family discussed the matter on several occasions, but they, too, were at a loss for an answer.

The move had a positive effect on all of us and brought us closer to the Schooks. One neighbor, Mrs. Lazare, was an eccentric who didn't care much for children, but she tolerated us. Although I had to ride my bike uphill to get home from work, I didn't mind. I looked forward to being home and spending time with my family. The boys found friends to play with, and Tante Suus became involved in neighborhood activities. We were happier in the apartment, felt safer, and were more relaxed. We shared bits of news and happenings of the day at the dinner table. All too often our thoughts and conversation revolved around my parents.

My job challenges continued. I passed the third Japanese exam and earned the benefits associated with it. Pleased with my progress, my bosses showered me with gifts of extra food rations. With the abundance of provisions, Tante Suus was able to be generous again. She prepared dishes to share with families who were less fortunate. Ronald and René were her delivery boys.

Chapter 20

One day Ronald came home with news that he and his friend Paul, both ten, were offered jobs in a Japanese household. A red light went on in my head. I remembered my father telling me about what could happen to young boys hired as domestic helpers in Japanese houses.

According to Ronald, they would assist the Chinese cook in his capacity as housekeeper during the day. Their duties would be to set the table, make beds, polish boots, and help in the kitchen. Ronald wanted the job simply because he could have Chinese food for breakfast, lunch, and dinner.

The job description sounded innocent enough, but Tante Suus and I were skeptical that it might not end there. However, considering that the place was only steps from our back door and the boys had each other as companions, we decided to allow it with certain rules. Ronald could work days only and had to be home before nightfall. We made sure he understood that the slightest fluctuation would end his career. Ronald agreed triumphantly. He came over to me and whispered in my ear. "You are tough, but you are fair. I think I like you as my big brother!"

Ronald and Paul enjoyed their work. The tasty Chinese dishes the cook turned out guaranteed them to be customers for life. Ronald sometimes came home with a dish of leftovers, which we all gratefully feasted on.

Then one day, through Ronald, one of the three Japanese officers living in the house invited me there for an evening. Tante Suus frowned at the thought and threw a suspicious glance my way. I needed to know the circumstances surrounding the invitation before I could answer.

"How did that come about, Ronald?" I calmly asked my little brother.

"The officer came home early and started to talk to Paul and me. He speaks very little Indonesian and uses his hands a lot." I could just picture that conversation, remembering my own experiences before I spoke the Japanese language.

Ronald continued, "So when he asked about my family, I told him I had an older brother who worked downtown and could speak Japanese." Ronald suddenly stopped and, with doubt in his eyes, said, "That was all right, wasn't it? Did I say something I shouldn't have?" He was afraid he might have said something to give away my identity, but I assured him he did fine.

He continued: "When the officer heard I had a big brother, he asked me to invite him—meaning you—to the house Tuesday evening. He wants to get to know you. So what do I tell him?" Ronald seemed rather uncomfortable with his predicament as the middle man.

Tante Suus and I quizzed him more about the officer, but Ronald didn't have much to add. Hearing that he had not given away my true identity as a girl relieved us both. Tante Suus admitted she didn't feel comfortable with the invitation. I didn't ask her what her objections were, because at that point I thought they were the usual ones concerning my disguise.

Tuesday evening came and I went to the house. A young Japanese man in his twenties opened the front door and welcomed me. He was of medium height and, even with closely cropped hair, was rather good-looking. He wore a colorful kimono and straw slippers.

After the traditional ceremonial greetings at the door, he invited me straight into the living room without asking me to take off my shoes. Two glasses of Orange Crush soda, a dish of Chinese appetizers, and a family album were awaiting us on the table.

He asked about my knowledge of Japanese and seemed genuinely impressed when I told him why I decided to learn to speak it. He confessed that he spoke a little Indonesian but preferred to speak Japanese to me.

"I am happy to speak your language," I said, "because it would be good practice for me, but may I ask you to correct me when I make mistakes or fill in the words that will not come to mind?"

He obliged, and on several occasions he gave me help and the confidence to continue. I began to enjoy the evening and his company. We nibbled on the snacks and chatted casually.

During a lull in our conversation, he said he had something to show me. "Come!" he beckoned, heading for a closed door, presumably his bedroom. That gave me an uneasy feeling.

"Can't you bring it out here? I'd rather stay where I am," I said. Possibilities whirled in my mind. Was it his intention to lure me into the room behind the door? How should I act? Was I to handle myself as a boy with no experience, or as a girl in distress? The latter was appropriate on one hand, but on the other, he didn't know I was a girl. Or did he suspect? The more I thought, the more alarmed I became. My innocent mind was unable to answer the questions whirling in my head. I told myself there was nothing to fear. I tried to stay calm and alert. My instinctive curiosity told me to play the game and see what developed. I knew it was risky, but I couldn't let him see how nervous I was.

"No!" he snapped. "I can't do that. So, come. Now!" Then, as if realizing he wouldn't gain anything by forcing me, his voice softened. "I just want to show you something, but it's too big to bring out here. Hurry! My roommate will be home shortly." He reached for my hand and gently pulled me out of my seat in the direction of the closed door. At the threshold of the room, he gallantly invited me in. Hesitating, I glanced inside.

The room was small and sparsely illuminated. It was furnished with a table between two easy chairs in front of a bed. A desk was in the far corner and a room divider in the other. There were two closed windows, one of them barred.

My host placed his left hand on my back and gently but forcefully guided me into the room. He walked me to one of the chairs and sat me down. My heart was pounding in my throat. A feeling of dread came over me. I looked up at him and he seemed to have transformed into a totally different person. The look in his eyes predicted menace. I knew I was facing an unknown danger. Why didn't I run away? Perhaps I was spurred on by the challenge of the unknown and my love of adventure. I had always been one to explore and take risks.

He handed me a photo album, then recited names and described events associated with the snapshots. He told me that he, lived with his parents, a younger brother, and an older sister in a small town in suburban Tokyo before becoming a soldier. I sensed a state of mental anguish and I became genuinely concerned. What did he have in mind? I wanted out. I was too nervous to think.

Halfway through the album, probably thinking he had put me at ease, he got up, excused himself and disappeared behind the room divider. I looked around for an escape, should it become necessary. Dazed, I kept turning the pages of the album, asking questions about the pictures. The answers he gave me from behind the screen sounded unsteady, making me wonder what he was doing back there, but I didn't dare ask. Whatever it was required his attention.

What occurred next happened so fast that the details are a haze. I continued turning the pages. Since I was looking down, the first things to indicate that he was in front of me were his legs. They were bare. Raising my eyes, I saw that he was without clothing. I had seen my little brothers naked before, but never a man. The sight, so unexpected, frightened me terribly.

Trying to stand up, I dropped the album to the floor. He pushed me back down, ordering me to take off my pants. I refused. I tried to get up again; he pushed me down. When I finally managed to break away, he shoved me around, pulled at my pants with one hand and held me bent forward with the other. I fought him with all my might. Angry, enraged, and helpless, I yelled, "What's the matter with you? Let me go!"

I was undoubtedly fighting a madman. He panted and gasped, "I want you! Please, I need you!"

I managed to turn around and face him. "No, you don't!" I screamed. I fought him furiously, slapping him and spitting in his face.

He grabbed my arms, shook me, and shouted, "Don't you know that two men can have as much fun together as a man and a woman?"

I didn't understand what he expected me to do. Desperate, I shouted, "Find somebody else! I don't want to play your game!" I broke his grip. He lost his balance and fell to the side. I bolted toward the door, but he caught me. I struggled with him again, my mind still working on an escape route. He grabbed my shoulders, dragged me to the bed and pushed me onto it, determined to get what he wanted. Just as he tried to jump on top of me, I lifted my legs and kicked him as hard as I could, right in the groin. He grabbed his crotch and dropped to the floor.

I ran to the door again, but it was locked. I headed for the unbarred window, but had to step over the man to get to it. Not knowing whether or not he was conscious, I took a quick giant step and got by him. I opened the window and jumped out into complete darkness. I stumbled for a moment, trying to get my bearings. When my eyes adjusted to the night, I raced down the street, tripping over obstacles in my way. When I finally reached home, out of breath and in tears, I told Tante Suus about the horrifying experience.

My cries woke up Ronald and René, who went back to sleep when Tante Suus assured them I was all right.

My aunt and I had a long talk. She reproached herself for not having told me about what she had been afraid of, namely homosexuality. "I didn't know how to tell you about it," she cried. "I'm so sorry. Oh, how I wish Paula and Vic were here to handle such things."

Poor Auntie had a tremendous sense of guilt. I tried to console her. "With what I saw at the parties, I thought I was prepared for anything," I admitted. "Now I know better."

That night, sleep didn't come easily. The incident replayed in my mind again and again. It dawned on me that I could have hurt him badly with the kick. I remembered needing to step over him to reach the window. Why hadn't he gotten up before I jumped out? Was he unconscious? Was he in pain or . . . could he possibly be dead? Hadn't the officer been familiar with the rules for the wartime treatment of prisoners? If not, why not? Why did he have to pick me?

When I finally dozed off, I dreamed that I was being interrogated by the Japanese and had to reveal my true identity. I woke up in a cold sweat several times that night.

A knock on our door came early the next morning. Tante Suus opened the door and stood face-to-face with the young officer himself. He spoke in Japanese. When I heard him ask to talk to me, I appeared in the hallway. He immediately bowed humbly and begged for forgiveness, keeping his head and eyes down.

As glad as I was that I hadn't accidently killed him, I couldn't stand the sight of him, in his humble pose, beads of sweat across his forehead. He pleaded with me not to report his behavior to the authorities. I wanted to punch him in the nose. He began to make excuses—in Japanese, of course, which Tante Suus didn't understand. He said things I didn't want to hear and was too embarrassed to translate. "I haven't been with anyone in a long time," he confessed. "Your fresh appearance at my door made me desire you, and I knew I wanted you. I should have known better. I wasn't thinking. I apologize, Rick-san."

The officer bowed repeatedly to emphasize how sincere he was. He was a pitiful sight, pleading and crying. How different he was from the lecherous host of the night before.

Feeling strong and in control, I asked if I had caused him any injury with the kick. He suffered only a bump on his head from the fall, assuring me that he deserved whatever I had done to him. His roommate had found him unconscious on the floor.

I told him to go home and that my aunt and I would consider his request. He left, defeated, recognizing that his future—maybe even his life—was now in my hands. Tante Suus and I decided not to report the incident for fear that doing so might compromise my disguise and jeopardize my life. We decided that an appropriate and deserving punishment for the officer was to keep silent, therefore keeping him wondering.

We sat Ronald down and gave him the news that he could no longer work in that Japanese household. The news did not seem too hard to take, but he had no intention of giving up the meals. "Can I visit Chen at lunchtime once in a while for some Chinese food?" he asked.

After the incident with the young Japanese officer, life returned to normal for the four of us. I doubt that the same could be said for the young offender. He never knew I had no intention of reporting him to his superiors. We kept him wondering. My identity was secure and my family safe.

Almost a year had passed since we left the school prison camp. Despite those rather tense and disruptive last days, I managed to study and pass my final exam in Japanese. With the certificate, I became my bosses' full-fledged interpreter. My coworkers demonstrated their appreciation by carrying me around the office on their shoulders. They made much noise, letting everyone know why they were celebrating. I allowed myself to enjoy every second of the attention they showered on me.

That afternoon I took a walk outside the office building past the schoolhouse. It was abandoned. The discovery was so unexpected that I had to look again to make sure that what I saw was reality. It was indeed empty! The doors were closed, the gate wide open, the guardhouse unoccupied. Where were the women? And Norma and Peter? When and where had they gone? The move must have taken place during the night; of that I was certain.

From that moment, my day was ruined and my accomplishments suddenly didn't mean anything. I was very unhappy. What should I do? Should I ask my Japanese bosses what happened to the camp? No; I was so anxious that I couldn't even bring myself to discuss the matter with Mr. S. I considered asking Captain Matoba, but changed my mind about that as well. I was afraid of the answer. I wasn't ready to hear him say that the same would soon happen to us.

Late that afternoon, I was sitting at my desk and, from across the room, Mr. Ito asked kindly, "Is something bothering you? Can I help in any way?"

His concern was so genuine that it gave me the courage to ask him what had happened to the prisoners. An unsettled look came across his face. He answered evasively, but there was a hint in what he said: "It's much easier to have all prisoners in one location rather than scattered all over the island. Don't you agree, Rick? I think that is what happened." To avoid more questions and to set my mind at ease, he added, "You shouldn't worry about it."

How could I not worry? Unable to put the probability of being returned to prison camp out of my mind, I asked, "Do you think my family and all the others will be picked up and taken to the same camp, Ito-san?"

"That most probably won't happen, but if it does, you and everyone else would do best to obey the order." He paused. "I want you to know that Sato-san and I would certainly not welcome the idea of letting you go because it would mean losing a friend and our best interpreter. I mean that in all sincerity, but, as I said before, orders are orders. I am very sorry."

Mr. Ito was kind but not at all encouraging. To me the possibility of being returned to a prison camp wasn't far away. That evening, I told Tante Suus about the empty school. She, too, came to the inevitable conclusion: How much longer until our freedom would be taken away again?

The dreaded call came into the office three weeks later. Mr. Sato picked up the telephone. At the time, I didn't know how significant it was or how drastically it would change my life, but the few words I overheard during the conversation alarmed me. Not wanting my boss to know, I didn't react or show any emotion, but envisioned our future in a flash.

After that call, Mr. S. and both my Japanese bosses engaged in a long conversation. A hush-hush atmosphere surrounded the three until Mr. S. walked into the back room. He returned with an envelope, which he handed to Mr. Sato. I was then asked to join them. The serious expressions on their faces indicated that I was in for unpleasant news.

"Rick," Mr. Sato said, swallowing hard. "We have received the orders you and Mr. Ito talked about not long ago. Regretfully, the time has come for us to dismiss you. You and your family will have to leave tomorrow evening."

"Tomorrow," I repeated in disbelief. "That doesn't give us much time."

Mr. Sato nervously fumbled and rotated the envelope by its four corners, trying to find the appropriate words to say good-bye. Other workers from the back room had joined us in the meantime.

"There is no time to buy you a gift so we did the next best thing," Mr. Sato said, holding the envelope out to me. "This envelope contains your paycheck and a little extra from all of us with our very best wishes."

Reaching for a second envelope on his desk and handing it to me, he said, "The contents of this envelope will certainly make the commandant of the camp very happy and us envious of him. I think he will want to hire you after he reads what we say about you." He stopped momentarily to look at me. "Are you listening, Rick?" he asked.

I was, of course. He continued, "We have described every aspect of your duties and responsibilities. We have included a review of your performance as a clerk, and we have specifically emphasized your knowledge of the Japanese language and described how valuable you have been to us as an interpreter."

I was too dazed to realize the significance of what he said and presented to me. Mr. Sato could tell I was distracted, so he made it clearer. "The contents of the second envelope may secure your future as well. It contains a letter of recommendation addressed to the commandant of the new camp. I am sure he will be only too happy to hire you after he has read it."

I was overwhelmed by their praise to the point of embarrassment. Deeply touched by the friendship these grown men had shown me, I felt like crying. I said goodbye with a heavy heart.

On the way home I wondered, would they have treated me the same way had they known I was a girl? I would never know the answer, but I did know that as a boy, I succeeded in impressing my superiors.

At home, Tante Suus told me that she and everyone else had received orders to be ready to leave. We started packing. The news about the trip ahead didn't upset Ronald and René. They regarded it simply as any other adventure. Tante Suus and I, on the other hand, knew better and were not at all looking forward to it.

That evening, a young, married Indonesian neighbor, Martinah, who had heard the news, came by with a specially prepared good-bye meal for us. She returned the following morning, too, and gave us snacks to take with us. In return, Tante Suus let Martinah take anything from our apartment that she wanted.

I went out early the next morning to sell my bike, as I had my father's before. On my walk home, I decided to make one last visit to my mother's grave. Not surprisingly, I found Tante Suus already there. Tante Suus admitted that she felt stronger after every visit to her sister's grave. Standing side by side, we both realized that this visit might be the last. We had to say good-bye for an indefinite time, maybe even forever.

Promptly at seven that evening, a truck stopped in front of the house to take us and others to the police station downtown. Our names were called off and checked against a list. We were then assigned to one of three buses lined up and ready for the trip.

"You may carry on one small piece of luggage and place it under your seat. The rest of the suitcases will be tied onto the roof," a police officer instructed. "You may keep the bus windows open now because it is nighttime. However, you must keep them closed when traveling in daytime. Is that understood? That is all! Have a good trip."

"Why do we have to ride in this stinking bus with the windows closed in this muggy weather?" someone protested.

"I'm just following orders, ma'am, and you people had

better obey these orders, too, because you would not like the consequences," the officer snapped.

We assumed closed windows were necessary to maintain secrecy, although it didn't make any sense. Who would notice us driving through the jungles of Sumatra, anyway?

Questions about our destiny and how long the trip would take were apparently unworthy of an answer; they were totally ignored, leaving us to our own imaginations.

After everyone was situated on the buses, an older Indonesian police officer entered and, in fluent Dutch, gave us the last instructions. "The buses will stop at predesignated points along the way for refueling, meal distribution, bathroom, and washing purposes. No extra stops will be allowed for any reason."

At nine o'clock that evening—after a two-hour delay—a shout to the drivers and guards got us underway. We drove off into the darkness of a tropical night, heading for a yet undisclosed destination. Seated in the back of the bus, I was able to determine that our bus was last in the convoy of three buses carrying the women and children, followed by an equal number of sedans occupied by officers and guards.

After a while, I noticed that we had reached the outskirts of Djambi. Beyond that point there was nothing but harsh jungle, and the road was not a highway by any means. Plain and simple, it was a dirt road with enormous potholes, causing the bus to shake on all of its hinges. The trip promised to be a very uncomfortable and tiresome one. So far, the journey had taken us through a pitch-black, threatening, mysterious, solid mass of darkness. Our only visibility came from the tiny beams of the headlights. We were the only traffic on this road, driving and winding through the forsaken, threatening jungle.

Occasionally, my attention would be diverted by two bright spots in the distance when the eyes of an animal suddenly appeared. Not knowing what kind of animal the eyes might belong to, I was happy to be sitting high and dry in a bus instead of down below on the road.

Crowded in the back and unable to move, I felt like a sardine in a can. I hit my head against the ceiling every time the bus went over a bump in the road. All I could do was look out the window, allowing my mind to wander freely, remembering pleasant events from the past. A refreshing breeze helped me doze off a few times, but real sleep in a sitting position was virtually impossible. Awkwardly squeezed between piles of luggage, I became doubly aware of the lack of working shock absorbers. My brothers, on the other hand, had it made. Tante Suus provided them with all the comforts they needed to enjoy a sound sleep. The bus's shaking and wobbling merely rocked them to sleep.

My attention was piqued by a sign in the distance, a dead giveaway of our destination. By the headlights of the bus, I read PALEMBANG. The city was located well south of Djambi. I knew the trip would last a few days more, allowing for breakdowns or other mishaps.

Chapter 22

Sometime during the night I, too, fell asleep. I awoke to a beautiful sunny morning. A gentle haze lazily floated in the forest and was warmed by the sun's rays. It seemed to playfully penetrate the solid leaf cover of the tall slender trees. Multicolored rays, reaching down to the forest floor, formed an eerie scene. It took my breath away. I fantasized that tiny angels from heaven were sliding down the rays, coming to earth to play. I pretended to be part of that fairy world, tiptoeing through the mist, captivated by the mystique of the surroundings. I took in as much as I could and held on to the good feeling of the daydream, knowing the precious moments would soon evaporate. I left my fantasy world to return to one that was neither beautiful nor gentle.

Gradually, others in the bus awoke. The driver ordered the windows closed. That was the moment we found out that the window panes were solid plywood instead of glass. People on the outside were unable to see us, and vice versa. Riding in the unventilated bus in the heat and humidity caused great discomfort. Someone asked the driver when we would make our first stop. His answer was curt: "Soon!"

That first stop was the highlight of our day. Sounds of softly splashing water in the distance welcomed us when we exited the bus. Riding on the last vehicle in the convoy, our group had to wait our turn. The station was devoid of inhabitants, an out-of-the-way place selected for secretive missions. The buses were refueled and new drivers and guards took over. Our new driver was an older Japanese soldier.

When it was our turn to go down to the creek, a guard led the way. No lavatories were in sight. We were to use the creek as a bathroom as well as to wash up. Fortunately, there were large rocks behind which I could hide and go to the bathroom. It was the first time since my disguise that I had been in such a situation and had to take precautionary measures to guard my identity. We were hungry, but the food would not be distributed until the next stop.

Back on the road, we jostled past several tiny villages. Small crowds of sparsely clothed, poor people gathered along the road, waving at the buses. I could see the people through the windshield as we approached. Most of them were children who reminded me of the ones in our neighborhood near the woods in Djambi. Although they couldn't see us, they acted as if they could, waving and screaming with enthusiasm. Traffic in those regions was nonexistent, so it was natural that they would come out, alerted by the sounds of approaching vehicles.

To kill time, the women on the bus read, crocheted, or chatted. Some were content to daydream or to just stare into space. Ultimately, the poor mechanical condition of the buses became the main topic of conversation. Everyone feared the vehicles would fall apart before reaching their final destination. One woman joked about it: "What would happen if this bus broke down and left us all stranded on the side of the road?"

"Stop it! Don't even talk that way," another woman wailed.

As if the words were said to a deaf person's ear, the first woman continued: "I'll tell you what would happen. We'd have to walk to the prison camp, wherever that is."

The idea of being dumped in the middle of the jungle was simply unthinkable. The awful prospect didn't go over well and was quickly dismissed.

Despite being deprived of daylight and fresh air, we continued our journey with surprisingly few complaints. Considering that they were unable to move around or play, the children behaved well. The situation was under control, but it was, after all, just the first day of travel. There were several children in the other buses, but our bus had only six, including the three of us.

Later that morning, the buses in front of us turned onto a very narrow dirt road. After about a mile and a half, they all came to a screeching halt. An officer emerged from one of the cars and was immediately surrounded by the bus drivers. Hand gyrations indicated that the lead bus had taken a wrong turn and we had to turn around. Considering the size of the buses and the narrow road, turning around seemed impossible. Eventually, however, all three buses were facing in the right direction to continue the ride.

Back on the main road and now led by one of the sedans, we traveled about half an hour and then made another turn. This dirt road showed obvious signs of daily heavy use. At this point we passengers were impatient and anxious to reach the food. In the distance ahead, we saw an open barn and a setup of long tables displaying leaf packages of food and bottles of refreshments.

After being last again and waiting outside the bus, one of the officers gave us a sign: It was finally our turn. First he took us down to the stream to wash up. The cool rippling water looked so inviting and sounded like crystals blowing in the wind as it flowed over large and small rocks. The children, including Ronald and René, walked straight into the water and started playing before anyone could say or do anything to stop them. In no time at all, they were splashing one another and having great fun. While all this was going on, I took advantage of the situation to wash my face, neck, and arms.

A signal sounded to indicate that wash-up time was over. We formed a line and marched to the barn. Ronald and René were soaking wet. Tante Suus and I wrung out their clothes and they put them back on. The damp clothes would help the boys withstand the heat in the bus later in the day.

At the barn, we picked up the day's provisions—two heavy food packages wrapped in banana leaves and a bottle of what looked like tea but tasted worse than anything I had ever drunk. In the packages were boiled rice, two pieces of *ikan asin* (dried, salted fish), and *sajoer* (a vegetable/meat soup). Each package was held together by picks carefully woven through the leaves, similar to staples.

Midafternoon, the hot tropical sun reached its climax, causing the humidity to soar and the degree of discomfort to increase to the point where we felt faint. The heat in the bus became unbearable, despite the wash-up in the creek a few hours earlier.

Desperate for fresh air, a woman sneakily cracked open the window beside her, but it didn't help at all. The outside air was as saturated with humidity as the air inside the bus. The children moaned and whined. Ronald and René leaned listlessly against Tante Suus, suffering like the others.

No matter how many complaints the driver received about the plight of his passengers, he was unable to do anything about it. "In a little while the sun will be going down. The evening will be cooler and the windows can be opened and remain open all night. So, ladies, please be patient for just a bit longer. I am suffering as much as you are."

On the second day of the journey, we went through the same routine of refueling, driver exchange, meal stops, bathroom use, and wash-up. Some of the women showed visible signs of tiring of the drive and sitting in the same position on uncomfortably hard seats in an overheated bus. They couldn't even muster the energy to keep themselves occupied. The children, too tired, too weak, and too hungry to act up, slept most of the time, which was fortunate for their mothers. We had a hard time remaining in good spirits. We prayed for the ordeal to end soon.

News that we would reach our new camp by morning rejuvenated us. We were unable to think about anything but the prospect of ending our miserable bus ride through the South Sumatran jungle. After sundown, I allowed the wind that blew through the open window to freely play with my hair as I breathed in the fresh air. Despite the knowledge of a future as a prisoner in another prison camp,

I was ready to face the new challenge. We were destined for it, and there was not anything anyone could do to change it for the better. So, what was left but to go along peacefully?

When I opened my eyes at dawn, I noticed that the bus in front of us was not the same one of the day before, and looking through the rear window, I noticed an unfamiliar bus there as well. Where had those vehicles and their passengers come from? Were we all heading to the same destination?

Since the morning stop involved more buses and more people, the wait for our turn took considerably longer. We were instructed not to contact or mingle with the new group, so the guarding was more intense. We were unable to learn anything about the newcomers.

Back in the bus, we had no idea how much longer it would take to reach the camp. Looking straight ahead through the front windshield, I observed that we were driving through a more populous area. We drove past a palm oil plantation and several rubber plantations on the outskirts of the city of Palembang. The area looked more civilized. We drove past a hospital, *Charitas Ziekenhuis,* with its name visible on a sign out front.

Presumably to avoid traffic and curious eyes, the buses entered a narrow street off the main road. We passed a cemetery and maneuvered through winding, barely passable streets in slumlike areas. Minutes down the road, however, we noticed improved living conditions. The houses had nicely groomed lawns with Japanese flags flying on poles out front. Just beyond the houses, the buses groaned to a full stop. The driver told us to stay seated.

After a long, hot wait, it was finally our turn to get off.

We grabbed our belongings and stumbled in the direction of the entrance to the Palembang prisoner-of-war camp. A committee of women prisoners greeted us. Registration went smoothly while our baggage was thoroughly inspected by the Japanese guard. We were assigned a place in one of the four barracks. Volunteers walked us there and assisted us in settling in. Some of the women already living there told us they were former residents of the city of Palembang who had been confined in regular housing since the outbreak of the war before being transferred to this camp. There was also a group of nuns, led by their Mother Superior. Later that afternoon, coffee and cookies were served in the *pendopo,* an open hut in the center of the camp. The women and children crowded around us, eager to hear news from the outside world.

Mother Superior, the oldest of the blue-robed missionary sisters, and the camp's interpreter, Mrs. Mulder, accompanied by the Japanese lieutenant of the guard, entered the *pendopo* and called us to attention. Mrs. Mulder introduced the officer, who was also the military physician, and translated his welcome. Lieutenant Takahashi welcomed us and apologized for the commandant's absence, but promised that he would meet with us in a few days.

We spent the remainder of the afternoon getting acquainted with our new friends. Exhausted from our three-day trip in a rickety bus, we barely had the energy to make our beds or have a well-deserved wash before turning in for a good night's sleep. The thin, military mattresses already laid out on the primitive *balé balé* (bamboo platforms), along the walls felt heavenly to our tortured bodies.

PART IV

NOVEMBER 1943–SEPTEMBER 1944

Chapter 23

Our camp in Palembang was the former men's camp. The men had been relocated to Muntok, a seaport on the island of Bangka.

The Palembang camp was about the size of a football field. It had a courtyard with a *pendopo* in the center. The barracks were crudely built out of bamboo-plaited walls called *gedèk,* and palm-frond roofs. A *balé balé* stretched along the walls. Each one accommodated fifty people and provided everyone with a *tempat,* a place to call our own. On our *tempat,* about five feet long and twenty inches deep, we slept, ate, and spent leisure time. An overhead shelf running along the entire length of the wall provided storage for personal belongings. Larger items could be stored under the *balé balé.*

We newcomers were asked to gather in the *pendopo* the next day. We were instructed that each barrack had a set of unwritten rules and regulations, and we were made to understand the importance of abiding by them. We were then assigned various duties and chores, but because of the long trip, we were exempt from work that day. We received the basics to start our new life and were provided with pails, tableware, tin plates, and cups. Tante Suus learned that occasional private cooking was permitted, so she requested and received a chafing dish and a wok.

Like everyone else, we received a ration of sugar, corn kernels, palm oil, coffee, tea, salt, and pepper. Some of those products were not in the pure state we were used to. The sugar, for example, was in chunks or clusters, like lumps of crystals. Until those clusters—less sweet than regular sugar—were crushed in a steel stamper, we were unable to use them.

The corn kernels were unfit for human consumption. Before they could be used in cooking, they had to be crushed into flour or soaked overnight to tenderize. The unrefined palm oil was the most curious of all. It was a thick orange-colored substance, resembling a concoction of margarine and ketchup. Everything fried in the oil turned orange and could not get as crisp as when fried in regular oil.

What impressed me the most was the camp's size. Walking around it, I realized that the school camp in Djambi, with a handful of women and five children, was a chicken coop in comparison. I observed three different orders of nuns: the white-robed sisters (hospital), the blue-robed sisters (missionaries), and the light-blue-stripe-robed sisters (education).

In a community of nearly seven hundred women and children of different nationalities there was an obvious need to divide the camp into sectors, categorically known as the Dutch side and the English side.

Accommodations in the barracks were not ideal but were better than sleeping on the cold, hard floor. The four barracks, each divided into two sections, held one hundred people per section. Lying side by side like sardines in a can, privacy of any kind was nearly impossible unless one hung a sheet or a sarong between the *tempats*. The easiest solution, however, was to ignore the situation altogether and adjust to the current living arrangement. For some that was not an easy thing to do.

Once enlisted for camp duty, I became much more aware of the unfavorable aspects of life in a prison camp of this size. It was a matter of getting used to keeping house together and volunteering for community duties. Everyone had to do her share to make life workable and successful on a daily basis. Teamwork was essential.

The kitchen, by far the most important part of our existence, needed volunteers daily. One group hauled water from the wells to the central kitchen. The vegetable-cleaning group sawed through vegetables, cutting them and removing the decayed leaves. The group responsible for cleaning the rice had the toughest job in the kitchen. They had to carefully look for and remove glass, stones, dead beetles, maggots, and other undesirables.

Then there were the volunteers who cleaned the bathrooms and scrubbed the concrete floor on their hands and knees. They had to work with very little water and no disinfectants, brooms, or brushes. The least desirable duty of all, however, was emptying the latrine. It was the most humiliating and the riskiest job at the camp. Every other day, two women scooped the fecal matter out of the drain into containers, which were then removed by a local service.

During my walk around the camp, I became aware of the physical condition of the women and children. Women who had once been healthy and robust were now thin, stalky, and pale, obvious signs of a prolonged imprisonment. They were hungry and had trouble keeping up their spirits. To divert their hunger pangs, many women scribbled on small pieces of paper new food ideas such as special sauces, fancy desserts, and recipes. They exchanged them with others. Talking about food had a hidden meaning for these women. Every imagined meal became an important lifeline for many, and it seemed that this same spirit turned depressed minds into more optimistic ones.

The women's way of life had changed so drastically that diversion was needed to bond them. Creating a recipe was therapy, and the believers in that kind of therapy claimed it helped them appreciate what they had on their plates at mealtime. Non-believers insisted that it worked the opposite way.

Tante Suus and I strolled along the grounds and did more exploring. We met up with the Djambi group from our first camp, who sympathized with us about our agonizing bus trip. They wanted to hear everything we had to tell them about our time outside the camp. They were sad about my mother's death. Helen, the Scottish nurse who had been my friend before anyone else, was ecstatic to see me again, and so was I to see her. The first thing she asked was, "How is your foot? Show me." She checked it and noticed the scar the wound had left.

The reunion with Helen brought back many memories, some good, some bad. I told her about the parties and how the situation during the second party made me run out of the restaurant. She turned red in the face when she heard about it. I gave Helen a full account of how we lived in poverty among natives in the woods after leaving the camp. I told her about my mother's death and my father's return to prison camp exactly a week later. I told her about the nightly searches for an escaped murderer and other insults we had endured. I even told her about the episode with the homosexual Japanese officer.

She listened quietly and was in awe, realizing how grown-up I sounded and had acted throughout. I could see it in her eyes.

"You are a brave, courageous, and strong little girl. You are the pride of your family."

Before nightfall, we were instructed to fill our pails with well water for our morning wash. It was a precautionary measure to make sure things ran in an orderly fashion between then and roll call.

After a good night's rest, my second day in camp started with new discoveries. Promptly at six-thirty in the morning, a strident whistle penetrated the early, quiet hours. The sun was just peeking over the horizon, sending its first rays out to warm the atmosphere. I was awake long before that time.

Turning onto my stomach, I looked out. An amusing scene played out in front of my eyes. The camp came to life. Women and children emerged from their barracks carrying their pails of water for their morning wash, toothbrushes, soap, and towels. Still dressed in their sleepwear, yawning, scratching, wishing they were still in bed, they strolled leisurely to the washroom, only to be met by a long line in front of them. What a sight to behold!

Behind me, in the same barrack, other women were getting dressed. Some feverishly straightened their *tempats*, folded mosquito nets out of sight, rolled up mattresses, and stacked the pillows neatly up against the wall. Several places had covers thrown over them to give a neat appearance.

Entering the communal bathroom at its busiest time embarrassed me. Women stood naked in elbow-poking proximity to one another around a large, rectangular basin. Everyone was rationed five liters of well water for the day, about enough for a bird bath. That morning I learned to skillfully use the precious little water in my pail and not to waste one drop of it.

Exactly half an hour after the first whistle, a second one sounded. It was time for *tenko*. Like ants out of an ant hill, the prisoners swarmed to their place in line outside their barracks. At the same time, Mother Superior, Mrs. Mulder, and Lieutenant Takahashi left the guardhouse for their rounds and the day's count.

Lieutenant Takahashi was the young officer who had first welcomed us into the camp. He had dimples, rosy lips, and was considered cute by many of the women. He had a pleasant personality and a sweet disposition, but he was painfully shy. The women adored him. He walked with a kind of hop, which gave the women a reason to tease him. Easily embarrassed and excessively aware of being observed, he sometimes acted clumsily, which usually had a charming effect.

Seven-thirty was breakfast time. A typical breakfast was either rice or flour porridge, if the blob on one's plate could be called porridge! The pasty gruel looked uninviting and tasted bland. A neighbor taught us to make it edible by adding a spoonful of the orange palm oil and a dash of salt to enhance the flavor. My brothers emptied their plates without whining.

The first days went by smoothly. Tante Suus and Ronald and René found new acquaintances, but I had not yet found a way to occupy myself and be content.

During roll call on the fourth day, the regular *tenko* trio stopped in front of me. The lieutenant said in Japanese that the commandant had returned and would like to meet with me after breakfast. I responded to the lieutenant in Japanese. Mrs. Mulder was completely thrown off. She hadn't known that I spoke the language. I detected indignation and displeasure in the way she looked at me.

As soon as we were dismissed, I ran into the barracks to check my suitcase and immediately discovered that my papers were missing. I could only assume that they were in the hands of the commandant, the man we hadn't yet officially met. The possibility to be working again secretly excited me. Tante Suus was not pleased, however. The realization that I could be exposed to unpleasant situations again, just when she thought that everything was behind us, was troubling to her.

After breakfast I reported to Lieutenant Takahashi, who walked out of the camp with me onto the road leading around the barracks. We conversed in Japanese.

"How do you like it here?" he asked.

"It's all right," I answered. "This camp is certainly a real one compared with the three-room school building in Djambi. That one was only a chicken coop," I joked.

The officer laughed, then asked, "Where did you learn to speak Japanese?"

I explained everything to him as we walked. He was shocked that I had been working as a clerk. We reached the house. I noted that directly on the other side of the tall wooden fence behind the house was the camp kitchen. I could even hear women's voices and those of children playing nearby.

"The house has been converted into office space, where the commandant has his place of business," Lieutenant Takahashi pointed out. He entered an office to announce my presence, after which I was asked to enter.

The man behind the desk was in his fifties, short, and a bit heavy, the fatherly type. He struck me as a kind man. I bowed and introduced myself, as did he. He was Captain Yamamoto.

My answer to his first question, as to how old I was, caused an expression of surprise. "It is true then that the person I have been reading about in this introduction"—he held up the letter of recommendation—"the one so highly praised and having all the credentials I have been looking for, is a thirteen-year-old boy?" He laughed in astonishment.

I didn't know what to make of his reaction. Was he laughing at me? "Those papers are mine, sir," I responded curtly. "I will be fourteen in a few weeks."

He laughed even louder. "This is unbelievable," he said. "When Lieutenant Takahashi informed me that these documents belonged to a young boy, I didn't believe him. I had to see for myself."

He invited me to stay for lunch, which I did. He apologized for removing my papers without my knowledge. Then he asked me which languages I spoke. I told him that my main language was Dutch, that I spoke Indonesian to the servants, but knew very little English. "And you must be the judge of my Japanese," I added shyly.

We discussed my first prison-camp experience in Djambi and life outside the camp thereafter. I described in detail my job as a clerk in the Department of Finance. Then he gave me the news I was waiting for. "There is a distinct possibility for a job," he said. "These papers and our little meeting today took care of everything I need to know about you. I will work out the details and let you know when I have come to a decision."

I thanked him for lunch and went back to the camp. Despite Tante Suus's apprehension about my working again, she was happy for me and wanted to hear all about my visit with the commandant. A second interview happened two days later.

Chapter 24

Captain Yamamoto, Mrs. Mulder, and two unfamiliar officers were waiting in the office. It was clear that something
special was brewing. The captain announced that Mrs.
Mulder and I would take a language test. The two officers,
from the men's camp, would assist.

The announcement came as a total surprise, not only to
me but to Mrs. Mulder as well. I had no idea I would be
competing against her for the job of camp interpreter. The
rules were given. The idea was for us to write down a translation of a given order into Dutch, English, Japanese, and
Indonesian. I reminded the commandant that my knowledge of English was insufficient to give an accurate interpretation of an order. Mrs. Mulder quickly interjected that
she had a similar problem with Indonesian. The commandant promised to keep our deficiencies in mind.

He gave the first orders in Japanese to be translated into
Dutch and English. Indonesian was rarely needed, unless
addressing the Indonesian guards. The two visiting officers
had their turn and gave us messages in Dutch, English, and
Indonesion to be translated into Japanese. These messages

could be considered the women's responses or questions to the commandant. I thought that the setup was ingenious and very challenging.

We waited in the next room while the officers graded our test papers. Strangers to each other, Mrs. Mulder and I sat uncomfortably in our chairs. After a few minutes, we began to talk about the test. Anxiety and tension built up during the last few minutes of our wait.

"We have come to a mutual decision," the commandant announced, looking us over. "Rick is the one who came out the favorite." Addressing Mrs. Mulder, he added, "There could only be one winner. I am sorry."

I couldn't believe it. Mrs. Mulder had lived in Japan for several years because of her husband's work. She spoke Japanese and had been the camp's interpreter long before I entered the camp. I was pleased with my victory, but the humiliation on Mrs. Mulder's face filled me with sadness. How mortifying it must have been for her to be defeated by a child and to be informed about it in the presence of strangers.

The question of why the test was so necessary nagged me. Wasn't there a less painful way to dismiss Mrs. Mulder? Couldn't the commandant have offered to keep her on in a different capacity? The more I thought about it, the more annoyed I became. I did not want her to lose her job and benefits because of me.

Mrs. Mulder returned to camp, but I stayed for tea. One of the officers noticed my melancholy mood and tried to distract me with questions about my father. My spirit perked up when he assured me that if my father were in the men's camp he would find him. The officer even offered to say hello to him for me. "The captain has given me permission to contact your father and give him a full report of the day's events."

I was overwhelmed by the kindness of these men. I knew that my father would welcome news about the family, and what better way to get news to him than this officer's suggestion to surprise him with a visit.

Later that afternoon, Captain Yamamoto revealed to me how well I had done on the test by showing me the scores. I showed no enthusiasm. He knew I was upset. "I want you to know that I had to conduct the test," he stated. "I had to do it for personal reasons and out of fairness to Mrs. Mulder and to you."

Mrs. Mulder's look of dejection was still clearly imprinted in my mind, preventing me from showing any emotional response to the captain's explanation.

"You aren't happy with my reasoning, nor with the final results, are you, Rick?"

"I am not happy with what you have done to Mrs. Mulder," I confessed. "Did you have to let her go?"

He did not respond nor did he look at me. I felt I had displeased him. Had I overstepped the line? Was I too forward, too outspoken? I decided that I had acted inappropriately by disputing his final decision. While I was questioning my behavior, his expression changed. In an apologetic manner he repeated his reasons for doing what he did, but in a different way. He never actually revealed the *real* reason for his decision, and I did not think it was my place to ask any more questions.

Then a frightening thought entered my mind. "How do you think the women will receive me as Mrs. Mulder's replacement, sir?" I asked worriedly. "They have known her since the beginning."

I got no satisfactory answer, but that afternoon I stood beside him in my official capacity as interpreter. Since this was his first appearance after returning from his trip, he addressed the newcomers by introducing himself to them. After a few words of welcome, he came to the main topic: Mrs. Mulder's dismissal. He looked in the direction of where she was standing and, as if speaking directly to her, said, "Mrs. Mulder, as I have mentioned before, don't think too seriously about retiring. The need to reinstate you is still a possibility."

He resumed his speech and announced my appointment. While I translated his message to the crowd, a look of pride came over him. It was an expression to assure me that I had no reason to doubt how the prisoners would feel toward me. The long, loud applause surprised me. Despite the outburst of acceptance and the rapid heartbeat it caused in my chest, I was certain that it was not genuine from all.

Before the captain left, he suggested that I mingle with the women to give them the chance to get to know me. I felt awkward but knew it was a good idea. Many women came by to talk. The Djambi group, in particular, showed pride, because I was one of them. The majority of the women were unimpressed with the new structure. They simply turned and walked away. I knew I would have to prove that despite my age, I was mature enough to handle the responsibilities. I mentally prepared myself to deal with all situations. One confronted me almost immediately.

Mother Superior approached to offer her congratulations.

Her high position in the community obligated her to represent the committee, but I detected a coolness and resentment in her voice, as if she'd rather not say the words to celebrate the moment. She tainted my beautiful moment of triumph and glory and made me feel inadequate. The few words she spoke did not come from the heart and were therefore meaningless.

Looking around, it dawned on me that I had to work with a committee of mature, adult women: mothers, grandmothers, teachers, nuns, and housewives. The idea of it caused me to panic. I had no idea what to do to establish a healthy and happy working relationship, one with room for understanding and that was free of hostility.

With a heavy heart, I hurried to find Tante Suus in the crowd. She saw me coming. We embraced and she swayed me back and forth in a loving gesture. Her warm, compassionate voice whispered, "I am so proud of you, darling. My heart swelled like a balloon when you translated the commandant's words of praise. I felt like shouting to the world, 'He is mine! He is my boy!'"

I acknowledged my fear of working with committee members who were so much older. If they refused to cooperate, because in their eyes I was only a child, what would I do?

I wanted to spare Tante Suus from knowing about my less than pleasant encounter with Mother Superior, but under the circumstances I thought it best to tell her. The events of the last few days had taught me to speak up. More important, they helped me overcome the barrier of shyness and allowed me to enter a life of self-preservation with an increase of self-esteem. I was certain that I had taken the first step into the world of grown-ups, despite my age, size, and inexperience.

After supper, I decided to go see Mother Superior. I was intimidated by her sternness, but I stated the purpose of my visit and asked, "Mother, have I done something to displease you?"

"What makes you think I'm displeased?" she responded, upset.

With a lump in my throat, I explained that I didn't think her words of congratulations had come from the heart. To my great surprise, she admitted that Mrs. Mulder's dismissal had deeply upset her. "I cannot understand how he could appoint a thirteen-year-old boy to a position of such importance," she said vehemently. "He has placed the burden of the prisoners on your shoulders. Can you do better than a grown woman?"

Her response was chilling. It was as if she blamed me for what had happened. I told her about the test and my talk with Captain Yamamoto. "I can't predict that, Mother, but I'll do my best. I'm not happy with the outcome either. I tried to prevent what happened."

Speaking for the entire committee, Mother Superior told me, "Out of fairness to Mrs. Mulder, I cannot accept your assignment." I was devastated and reiterated that I had not asked for the job.

Silence fell. We had nothing else to say to each other. Then the thought of revealing my identity came to mind. Could it be the tool to clear up the hostility between us? I wanted it to be, but didn't know how Mother Superior would receive the news. I was quite nervous and my palms were sweaty, but I decided to go through with it. "Mother, I have a secret to tell you. You know me as Rick, but my real name is Rita," I said softly. Then I told her all about my disguise.

Her mouth fell open. She brought her hands to her face, covering her cheeks, and in a whisper said, "You are a girl? I don't believe it!"

She stared at me, whispering the words repeatedly as if to convince herself that what I had told her was the truth. "You are a girl?"

I told her about my life before coming to this camp. Not once did she interrupt me. I could see that what I was telling her gradually painted a better picture of me. "After all you have told me," she said when I finished, "I see that you are not a brave little boy but a courageous young girl." She raised her eyes toward heaven.

I urged her not to reveal my identity to anyone. She promised that she would not.

It was getting late and almost time for her to join her sisters in their hour of prayer. Just as I was getting up to leave, she said, "The committee will stand behind you one-hundred percent. I'll see to that! And . . . my nuns and I will pray for your safekeeping."

"Thank you, Mother."

Chapter 25

Before seven-thirty the next morning, although accompanied by a guard, I was thrilled to be walking on a road outside the camp, on my way to work. I felt as if I were on my way to a surprise party. When we arrived at the house, the officer said, "Wait here. Captain Yamamoto will be coming soon to open the door." Then he turned around and walked away.

In total disbelief to find myself without a guard, I called out after him, "Don't I need to be guarded?"

"No," he responded. "Captain Yamamoto will join you momentarily. Just wait there."

I sat down on the stone wall of the front porch. It felt strange to be sitting there alone and, even stranger yet—I felt free! A few minutes later I saw Captain Yamamoto climb over the low stone wall of the house next door.

"*Ohayo gozaimasu*, Rick-san," he greeted cheerfully.

"*Ohayo gozaimasu*, Yamamoto-san."

He unlocked the door and we walked into a partially furnished room with a desk and a swivel chair. "This is your office," he said. "Do you like it?"

Indeed I did. I had never had my own office before. A few minutes later a guard carried in a Royal typewriter and placed it on my desk. The Royal typewriter must have been popular because this was the second one I had in a year.

Sitting proudly in my chair, I arranged things around me to create a comfortable workplace and contemplated what else I needed. The guard showed me the supply room, and I provided myself with all the office necessities. I was busy all morning getting settled.

Just before lunch, the commandant came into my office. "Are you ready to work?" he asked, waving a bundle of papers in the air. "These, my boy, are handwritten lists of names of the prisoners in this camp. I want you to set up a card filing system. Verify the data before you enter them on individual cards. I expect the data to be accurate so that the system will be up-to-date." He handed me the lists.

As the clerk, I was allowed to have all my meals at the mess across the street, which was managed by two Dutch-Indonesian women. They kept house and did all the cooking for the commandant and his officers. I was free to cross the street unguarded, at any time and as many times as I wanted during the day. If work at the office was slow, I was to assist the cooks.

For my first lunch hour on the job, I walked down the driveway by myself and stopped at the end. A sudden sense of being free overwhelmed me. Pretending that I was in the middle of a city, I looked both ways. It amazed me to be walking in the street, unguarded. What I was experiencing was most certainly a privilege not enjoyed by anyone else in the camp.

When I reached the mess hall, I heard a woman's voice

speaking Dutch with a heavy Indonesian accent. I couldn't see her from where I stood, but by her tone I knew she was irritated about something. Her words were demanding. Suddenly, we stood face-to-face. She was short and squatty with curly black hair. Her companion was a bit taller and a rather serious type. Both were in their late thirties or early forties.

I introduced myself. The smaller of the two introduced herself as Mien and her coworker as Hetty. She kept working the whole time, not even looking at me. Her attitude made me feel terribly uneasy.

When I told her that it was my first day working in the commandant's office, she finally looked up and for no reason began to insult me. With her hands planted on her hips and a slight smile of superiority, she said, "So, you're assigned to the office of the commandant? That is what you have just told us, right?" She accentuated every word in a most belittling and humiliating manner. "To do what? Sweep the floor? Empty the wastebaskets?"

Mien's attitude was worse than Mother Superior's. Both experiences within twenty-four hours was too much. I'd much rather go without meals than endure such harsh treatment. The thought of starvation was quickly abandoned to make way for a defensive strategy. Why should I allow her to get the best of me? She didn't even know me.

With my head held high, I said to her, "I am the new interpreter."

She stopped working, looked straight at me, and said, "Ah, you're the one everyone in camp is talking about." She moved back a step to take stock of me and, with a bit of irony, added, "Why, you're only a child."

Her taunting challenged me to show that I was old enough to stand my ground. I announced with pride, "I'll be fourteen in a few weeks."

She kept up the banter. "Did you hear that, Hetty? He's going to be fourteen in a few weeks."

The confrontation left me with a taste of unworthiness. She, like Mother Superior before her, didn't think I was old enough to handle the responsibilities, and neither was willing to accept my assignment. Why did they make me feel this way? Why would they humiliate me? I just couldn't see myself working here. It was simply unthinkable. Realizing what I was up against, however, made me more determined to stay and enjoy the privilege of having lunch. As far as I was concerned, Mien simply had a personality problem and needed time to get used to me.

Hetty, in the meantime, observed the situation from a distance. She had been working with Mien from the start and knew her well. When Hetty thought Mien was through with me, she gently pulled me aside.

"Mien isn't as bad as she sounds. Are you familiar with the saying 'Barking dogs don't bite'? Well, that's Mien."

With Hetty on my side, I stayed for lunch. I really liked what was served. I wasn't familiar with the dishes and concluded that they tasted as good as Chinese food, especially when you haven't had any for a long time. After the last of the lunch crowd left, I assisted with the cleanup. We did the dishes and set the table for dinner.

The commandant called me into his office after lunch. He took a key out of his uniform jacket and waved it in front of me. "This opens the back entrance to the camp, the link between camp and the outside world. It's yours. Giving you this key shows my complete trust in you. Guard that trust with all your being."

Totally staggered by the many benefits bestowed on me in such a short time, I began to wonder why this was happening. Why was I so privileged? Nobody else was. What did I have to give in return? As if the day hadn't had enough new developments, one last surprise was still to come.

Just before closing time, Captain Yamamoto called me into his office again. "Rick," he said, "after you have completed the filing system and administration for this camp, I have another project for you to consider."

He smiled, but I detected an ominous undercurrent. He got up from behind his desk, walked to the window and looked out. He was solemn when he turned around to face me. "I want you to be prepared to receive messages from the men's camp."

I was dumbfounded and asked, "What kind of messages, Yamamoto-san?"

He paused, then almost in a whisper, he said, "Death notices." He paused again to catch my reaction. "You know what they are, don't you, Rick?"

I responded affirmatively. A few seconds of silence followed. Noting the somber effect his announcement had on me, I think it occurred to him that perhaps I was too young. Nevertheless, he inhaled deeply and continued. "All information concerning the men, death or otherwise, must remain in this office until I myself make it public knowledge. Is that understood, Rick-san?"

"You can count on me, sir. I will comply with every policy of this office." We showed our mutual respect by bowing to each other.

This was not child's play; this was the real world. Everything was coming down on me all at once. It convinced me that I had to prove myself. That evening, for the first time, I let myself into the camp through the back door with my own key. I walked straight to my *tempat*, crawled inside, and lay down, too tired to even think.

Tante Suus saw me walk through the back gate near the kitchen. Alarmed to find me lying flat on my stomach staring into space, she sat down beside me. Knowing how happy and upbeat I was when I left that morning, she was naturally puzzled to find me in that condition some hours later. "What's the matter, darling?" she asked softly.

Hearing her cheery voice so overwhelmed me that I started to cry and was unable to stop. She rested her cheek on my upper back and held me in a tight embrace. Realizing that I needed to let it all out, she simply held me while I cried. I felt much better afterward and gave her a general account of the day's happenings. Her complete trust, understanding, and compassion made it difficult to tell her what I had to say. Would she understand that my work prevented me from discussing certain matters with her? How could I prepare her for the inevitable distance in our relationship due to the confidentiality of my job?

We talked extensively about my position and its responsibilities. The more we talked about the death notices, the more we realized that until the commandant had informed the survivors of their loss, I would be unable to offer them solace. My heart filled with an indescribable heaviness. I hugged Tante Suus and we both cried.

"It's going to be hard for me," I said, "to know I can't

pour out my heart to you. That privilege has been taken from me."

"We'll make it somehow," she assured me. "Together, we'll be victors in this battle, you and I."

I thanked God for my Tante Suus.

That night in bed I analyzed my situation. Disheartened, I knew I was facing a life in which I had to fight my own battles, make my own decisions and mistakes. It was not the kind of life I looked forward to, but the challenge of making the best of it was still as strong as before. I believed determination could help me live through it and face all obstacles head-on.

After breakfast at the mess hall the following morning, I entered my office just as the commandant poked his head around the corner.

"Two officers from the men's camp will be here," he reported. "I want you to join us when they arrive. You will need to sign a paper in their presence. By signing this piece of paper, you are promising to keep information you receive in this office completely confidential."

When the time came, I signed the document without hesitation or questioning its legality. After the officers left, the commandant and I continued our conversation of the previous afternoon. He wanted to know if I had thought more about the death notices.

"I had a long talk with my aunt," I told him. "I have always regarded her opinion highly. She not only gave me the moral support I needed, but she painted a clearer picture of things for me."

I told him about my mother's death and how Tante Suus automatically had taken over the care of us children and the household.

As days went by, I gradually felt more confident and relaxed in my office, as well as in my domestic duties. I found my way through them with ease, learned to adjust to Mien's outbursts, and equally appreciated her sense of humor. She could be very funny at times, and we had many days of laughter.

The first evening that I ate supper at the mess with her and Hetty was one of genuine camaraderie. After having done the dishes, we put away pots and pans, set the table for the next morning, and cleaned up the kitchen. The left-overs were divided equally among the three of us and we took them home. After that, they often surprised me by slipping an extra portion of home-baked cookies into my container. I felt as if they had adopted me. As the weeks rolled by, I began to appreciate them more and more. As Hetty told me in the beginning, Mien turned out to be tough but generous.

My friendship with the two of them delighted Ronald because of the leftover food I brought home. It reminded him of his working days with the Chinese cook at his first place of employment.

I enjoyed the variety in my life. I worked hard at the office and did my share at the mess. My domestic duties three times a day acquainted me with several of the military personnel, who considered me their friend.

Chapter 26

My chief responsibility as an interpreter was to translate messages from Japanese into Dutch and English and vice versa. Translations into Indonesian were rarely necessary, unless I had to address the Indonesian guards.

Since my knowledge of English was insufficient, Mother Superior or Mrs. Mulder usually passed those translated versions on to the women for me. My shortcomings in that area gradually turned into a burden, interfering with my ability to concentrate on my work. I decided to do something about it. My only experience with and exposure to the English language were my daily conversations with Helen, the Scottish nurse. In those days, I had tried to make myself understood without paying much attention to grammar or correct pronunciation. Sometimes even a single word was enough to determine the context of the subject at hand.

Now, having such an important job and not being able to carry out all facets of it was disconcerting. I decided to learn English. Mother Superior introduced me to one of the school sisters, Sister Bernardine, a former English teacher at the Roman Catholic parochial Dutch-Chinese school in Palembang. She was a short, chubby woman in her early thirties, with a cute little turned-up nose, small piercing eyes, a round, freckled face, and a bubbly personality.

We met and worked out a schedule. I felt as if I were back in school. She explained that she would assign homework. I would read children's stories and write essays about them. She would quiz me about the stories to check my comprehension. The most important aspect of her teaching method was that she spoke English exclusively. It reminded me of my Japanese classes where we spoke only Japanese. With Sister Bernardine, however, I had to learn to speak English from a textbook written in Dutch. "I do not want to hear one word of Dutch during our sessions together!" she repeated.

I tried to interrupt her, but with a wave of her hand, she suggested that I listen and continued, "I don't want you to be afraid or ashamed of making mistakes. After all, there's nobody else around to hear us. If you make mistakes, I'll help you to understand what you said incorrectly and explain why. So please, Rick, relax."

The following days, weeks, and months were consumed by studying. Her promise to be flexible with her time made it easier for me to pay attention to my other obligations. I spent every free moment on my studies and even stole time from work to progress. Despite her bubbly personality and easy teaching style, she was a tough teacher who aimed for nothing less than perfection.

After almost four months of intensive English conversational exercises and written tests, she informed me quite unexpectedly that I was ready to graduate. I couldn't believe it, but when the message finally sank in, I became emotional. I had reached my goal. The pressure was off. I felt as free as a bird. Although I wanted so very much to shout from the highest point in the camp and let everyone know I had graduated, I decided to hold off a little while longer. Tante Suus was the first person I told.

My friends at the mess were not surprised when I finally told them I was done. Mien, who had witnessed my focused studying, felt compelled to comment, "To the point of neglecting your domestic duties!" She had a smile on her face when she said it. I knew that she, too, was happy for me.

My next step was to tell the commandant. Determined to surprise him, I had kept him totally in the dark about my English lessons. The next day after our mutual morning greeting and bowing, he looked at me and said, "The expression on your face tells me that your morning is a happy one. What makes you so cheerful?"

I challenged him to guess what my secret was, but he had no idea. We bantered back and forth, teasing and laughing. "Should I take my whip out to punish you for keeping secrets from me?" he quipped.

Finally I told him. We continued the teasing back and forth for a while longer, but in the end he congratulated me.

The first time I relayed an order in English to the women was an extra-special occasion. Without preparing me for what he intended to do or say, the commandant announced to the prisoners that I had completed a course in English. He made a joke about being kept in the dark about it. The women laughed and nodded in agreement. They knew he was speaking words of pride. It felt strange not to have Mother Superior or Mrs. Mulder behind me as

backup, but I didn't need them anymore. The most embarrassing part was translating the words of praise from the
commandant to the prisoners. The words I had to say com-
mending myself sounded so conceited.

I took a moment to say words of my own to the crowd.
I thanked Sister Bernardine, and I thanked the whole group
for accepting me, despite my age. They loved it and gave a
round of applause. In contrast to a few months ago, Mother
Superior had more meaningful, congratulatory words to
say to me to mark this event. She even joked about having
more time to nap without interruption now that she was no
longer on standby.

As I had busied myself with clerical and domestic
duties, a group of women had been actively rehearsing a
choir in a shed off the kitchen. They had been meeting in
the greatest secrecy. I was completely unaware of their
activities until Tante Suus mentioned there was going to be
a concert. I knew she wasn't speaking of a concert in the
style one would expect, one of shiny, well-tuned instruments played by properly dressed musicians before
groomed patrons. She was talking about prisoners giving a
musical performance of their voices for other prisoners.

The day before the concert, a torrential downpour
caused small waterfalls to pour through the barracks' palm-
frond roof. Puddles formed in the aisles and, as we walked
to and from our *tempat*s, mud squished between our toes.
Fortunately, the weather was better on concert day.

I came home early that day to be a witness to the preparation of the event. Observing the frenzy of activity, I wondered how it was possible to organize an event of this
nature. It was well known that the Japanese did not allow

crowds. Gatherings of more than ten people at a time were against camp rules.

That afternoon at four-thirty, the courtyard began to fill up with prisoners dressed in their most festive attire. The boys were well groomed, and some of the girls had ribbons in their hair. The women wore dresses saved for a special occasion. Some even wore rouge and lipstick they had found among their meager possessions.

When it was time to begin, a group of thirty women walked in single file from the kitchen to the *pendopo*. Each carried a small stool in one hand and sheets of paper in the other. They certainly didn't look like musicians. They were a sorry sight. Wearing faded shorts and halter tops or mended faded cotton dresses shortened at the hem, most of them were barefoot. Some wore sandals made of odd pieces of wood with strips of material as straps. Some had bandaged tropical sores on their legs and ankles. Most of them hobbled and limped to the concert. Some women had straight, stringy hair; some had cut theirs short; others had pulled the strands back into ponytails. Their appearance was a clear indication of what toll the war had taken on them.

There were no musical instruments. A wooden box placed on bricks in the *pendopo* functioned as the conductor's podium. The conductor, an English woman and a professional musician, raised her hands. There was total silence. Then, very, very softly, hums floated into the air. They were the first sounds of the largo movement of Dvořák's *New World* Symphony. The volume gradually increased until those thirty voices became one beautiful voice. Then, the volume and intensity of the humming gradually soared into a full crescendo. It sounded magnificent.

I had been to school concerts before, but I was certain I had never heard anything quite so beautiful. The sound was that of a choir of angels. The extraordinary sound came from the heavens and seemed unreal for our squalid surroundings. It was amazing. I had goose bumps.

During the performance, somebody signaled that an angry guard was approaching, but nobody cared. The concert continued. The guard stormed into the crowd, carrying his rifle with a bayonet in place. He screamed and yelled for attention. The women in the audience surrounded him, and because he was so short, he practically disappeared from view. Only the top of his hat was visible. Surrounded by the crowd, his shouting and yelling stopped as well.

The moment the conductor noticed the guard's approach, she encouraged her singers to give it their all for the crescendo. At that moment, she was a towering figure of victory and pride.

Nobody knew what had triggered the guard's rage or what quelled it. Was he overcome by the sweet voices? Or had the women blocked his mouth to prevent him from disturbing the angelic performance? They wouldn't dare do that, would they? Where was his rifle? The guard stayed until the end of the concert. He never reported or disapproved of the gathering.

What was so phenomenal about the concert was that the women had no sheet music. The conductor had written it all from memory. She and others worked on the project for a year, writing the music on scrap paper with bits of charcoal and other makeshift materials. Despite enormous obstacles, the women gave their fellow prisoners a precious gift of beautiful sounds.

After the concert, still enraptured by the beauty of the evening, I once again thought of my mother. She had loved music. I remembered the time we spent in a storage room at home while she reminisced about her adolescent years. We found a songbook in which she had collected her favorite songs as a young girl. Turning the pages of the book, she sang every song with great feeling and told me stories associated with them. Mommie always told wonderful stories. She had a special ability to make each one come to life, especially those about her growing-up years. She was the youngest of eleven children. Her father was very strict and overprotective.

One of the most amusing and poignant stories she told me was about her desperation to learn to dance. She didn't dare ask her father's permission to take lessons, so her best friend agreed to teach her. It had to be done in secrecy, and the only place they could think of was a dried-up ditch. The best time was just before nightfall when there was still enough daylight. The two girls would make their own music by singing and improvising the rhythms and beats of popular tunes. I could clearly visualize my mother and her friend stumbling in the ditch to learn each step, and having great fun doing it.

My mother and I spent hours and hours together playing the gramophone, listening to old songs pouring out of the horn. The melodies became indelibly imprinted in my mind and part of my cherished past. Mommie would have loved the prisoners' concert.

Chapter 27

Life in the Palembang camp was fairly stable and uneventful, until one day our routine was quite unpleasantly disrupted. What ensued was something that the women would not likely forget.

Several loyal Indonesian servants, living outside the camp, clandestinely and occasionally provided their former mistresses with cookies or other edibles, and in some cases money. The parcels were dropped off inside the fence behind the barracks regularly, unseen and unnoticed by the Japanese. One prisoner familiar with the schedule picked up the packages and delivered them to the recipients. The smuggling usually took place at night.

Totally unaware that this was going on, I was surprised when an officer entered my office and announced that he wanted to talk to me about these deliveries. I did not know the man other than having seen him at mealtimes. I didn't much care for him. His beady, penetrating eyes made me uncomfortable.

The women who had known this officer from the beginning called him "the Snake." His reputation of startling and scaring women by suddenly popping up out of the dark had earned him that very appropriate nickname. He moved about with an athletic, flexible, and lean body. Like a snake, he slithered underneath the small tables outside the barracks or hid in dark corners. From those locations, he stalked and observed the women. His strange behavior, often the topic of discussion among the women, made him a mystery.

I told him truthfully that I wasn't aware of any rule violations in the camp. He questioned me repeatedly, and his persistence led me to wonder if something really was going on. If what the Snake suspected was true, it was inevitable that someone might be in grave trouble. I decided to investigate the allegation myself and to repress it to keep the women out of trouble. I approached Tante Suus cautiously and asked her about the smuggling. She looked at me in surprise and asked, "What are you talking about? Where did you hear that rumor?"

From her reaction I read two possibilities: She either truly didn't know about any illegal activity or she was afraid to talk. When I told her about the Snake's suspicions and the danger, she reluctantly mentioned a name. I went to the woman in question. I wanted to warn her and try to deter her from continuing her practice.

She was feisty and quite a talker. With little encouragement, she told me about her nightly trips to the secret entrance, how she picked up the packages at a certain time and made deliveries. I listened quietly while she gave the details of her little smuggling operation, confident and proud of herself. When she realized that she may have said too much, she stopped and turned pale. Looking around to make sure no one was near, she asked, "Why are you, of all people, interested in what I'm doing?" Her voice was trembling.

I told her about my encounter with the Snake. She cringed in horror and fear.

"He's out to catch you," I stressed. "I'm here to warn you and to suggest that you stop what you're doing."

When she didn't respond, I continued. "He's unpredictable. He might punish you for what you did. He might also involve the entire camp in the punishment. I'm certain you wouldn't want that on your conscience."

A few days passed without incident. Then rumors surfaced, claiming new sightings of the Snake slithering through camp. My heart stopped. Had the woman taken my advice? If not, she might walk straight into a trap.

I convinced myself that she had taken my warning to heart. Unfortunately, a few nights later, it became evident that she had not. In the middle of the night, the Snake bellowed my name. It echoed throughout the camp, waking everyone but me. Tante Suus shook me awake.

Still half asleep, I approached the guardhouse. Inside were the Snake, three Indonesian guards, and the woman, who was shaking like a reed and sobbing. The Snake was yelling at her in Japanese and she was yelling back in Dutch, but neither had any idea what the other was saying. It was total chaos.

As soon as I entered the guardhouse, the shouting stopped. For some inexplicable reason, the Snake chose that precise moment to rise from his chair, pull the woman up, and slap her several times. Then he pushed her back into her chair. It was disturbing to witness.

He ordered the woman to explain what she was doing when he caught her. Since I was there to be the interpreter, she told me in Dutch that she had been aware that several packages were lying in the grass behind the barracks. She was afraid that if she did not retrieve them the contents might spoil. As she spoke, she kept glancing at the Snake. I translated for him. When he asked *why* she smuggled, she gave me the most damaging answer imaginable.

"I needed some excitement," she explained, "some adventure to break the monotony of the dull life I'm living in a camp full of women."

I knew that translating her answer word for word would have infuriated the officer and provided him with more ammunition to go after her, so I rephrased what she had said. I replaced *some excitement* and *some adventure* with *something*. When I finished my tame interpretation, the Snake's eyes narrowed. He was furious.

"Tell her she'll have to remain here until morning. I might come up with a healthy dose of *something* for her to think about. Tell her that!"

He paced with his hands clasped behind his back, growing more agitated. He suddenly stopped and turned to face the woman. He stepped up to her, jerked her head back by her hair, and yelled, "Now, are you going to tell me the truth?" I translated rapidly.

"I have told you the truth!" she choked in Dutch, snapping at him. "Let go of my hair. You're hurting me."

I was petrified. I wanted to help but recognized there was nothing I could do to ease the situation. It saddened me that she hadn't taken my warning seriously. Now the

Snake had the satisfaction of taking out his frustration on her and of being the victor.

He returned to his own chair behind the desk. Keeping his gaze fixed on her, he moved his hand to one of the packages. Slowly, he pulled it to himself. Smirking, he stroked it a few times. The woman turned away, but he screamed, "Look at me!" He pointed to his face and slowly lowered his finger to the package, making sure she observed his every move. The tension was palpable.

The Snake passed the box of Chinese cookies around to me and to his men, inviting us to help ourselves. I refused. Then he popped one into his own mouth. He chewed with loud smacking sounds. "This cookie tastes very good," he mocked. "Where did you get it?"

She ignored him and looked away.

"Look at me!" he yelled. "Did you hear what I just asked you?" I translated.

"Yes, I did, but I can't answer you because I don't know where they were purchased."

I realized too late that my refusal to take a cookie would only trigger more anger. He gave me a dirty look and offered a second helping to his men.

"Why didn't you take one, Rick?" he asked, sneering.

"I don't care for sweets, sir," I replied honestly.

My answer wasn't what he wanted to hear. He struck the desk with his fist, making everyone jump. "Is that the real reason, or was it to express your disapproval of how I am treating the prisoner?" Behind his words was a suspicion that I had known of the smuggling operation all along and wanted to protect the woman.

His suggestion offended me and I found myself snapping

back at him, fighting for my dignity and unwilling to give him the satisfaction of a victory. The woman interrupted our screaming match, asking me what our fight was about. I told her. In turn, she insisted that I tell the Snake that I had nothing to do with her activities. I informed her that I had already tried to convince him of that fact, but that he refused to believe me.

The officer demanded a translation of what she and I had just said to each other. I gave it to him. He merely shrugged and asked one of his men to serve him coffee. After the last of the cookies were consumed, the Snake brushed the crumbs and the box onto the floor. With an exaggerated display, he stomped on the box, as if flattening something vile. I hated the sight of him and all of these ill-mannered men.

Assuming the interrogation had ended, I asked to be dismissed. He answered with a decisive, "No!"

He renewed his harassment of the woman. With both boots propped comfortably on the desk and his chair cocked back, he asked, "Who are your accomplices?"

I translated and she answered. Before I had time to translate her words, he snapped, "What is she saying, Rick? Come on! Tell me!"

I translated as quickly as I could. "The prisoner operates on her own, sir. She had offered her services to friends until they realized what was involved. Afraid of the consequences, they asked her to stop, but she ignored them and claims that this would have been the last time. She takes full responsibility for her misconduct."

The explanation seemed to satisfy him, because the questioning stopped. He asked me to convey a message to the Indonesian guardsmen that she was to remain in the guardhouse for the night and was not to be served any food until further notice. Familiar with the Indonesian language, the woman needed no translation to understand his order. There was fear in her eyes. After that, he allowed me to leave. I feared for the woman's safety, but there was nothing more I could do.

Back at the barracks, everyone was still up, awaiting my return. Leaning out from under their mosquito nets, the women wanted to hear about the incident. Instead, I excused myself and crawled into bed. Mentally exhausted yet totally awake, the entire scene played over and over in my mind. A few women kept talking about what had likely happened, speaking loud enough for me to hear, hoping that I would chime in with some corrections or clarifications.

On my way to work the next morning, accompanied by Mien and Hetty, I passed the woman standing against the guardhouse wall. She appeared worn out and looked at me with questioning eyes.

I saw the Snake at breakfast. I had a feeling the case had not ended and that this thing would drag on throughout the day. My suspicions were confirmed when I later found him waiting in my office.

"Has breakfast been served in camp?" he asked.

Looking at my watch, I responded, "It might still be in progress."

"I want you to go in and confirm with the guards of the morning shift that my orders are to remain in effect and be enforced to the letter."

"But I thought she would be released this morning, sir. Didn't you say she was just staying for the night?"

"That doesn't mean she is now free to go, Rick!"

I pleaded with him not to deviate from his original punishment. "Stay out of this!" he yelled. "She needed something other than a dull life. I'm doing my best to oblige her!" A smirk of satisfaction came over his face.

Enraged, I walked to the guardhouse and relayed the order.

I returned to the office, but had trouble concentrating on my work. I grew even more uneasy when I saw the Snake enter the commandant's office and close the door behind him. What was he reporting about the incident? How would he present the facts? And even more important, how would the commandant react?

Unable to stand the suspense, I prepared to go across the street to the mess hall. As I was about to leave, the Snake came out and told me to tell the guards that lunch could be given to the woman.

"But," he added, "after that I want her taken outside to stand in the bright sun. I mean in the sun, not in the shade! I want her to stand with her arms stretched toward the sky, like this!" He held both arms straight up. "She may feel the need to ask for help from someone up there before it is all over." He smirked sadistically.

I pitied the woman, but I also resented her for dragging me into the situation. I was definitely not prepared for such a development and hoped it would soon end. A feeling of helplessness overcame me, but as her mediator, I had a duty to perform.

Dread accompanied me every step of the way to the guardhouse. I relayed the Snake's information. Without looking in the woman's direction, I could feel that she expected me to stay and give her moral support. However, I was at such a low ebb myself that I ignored her pleading eyes. I felt terrible, but I had to leave.

Lunch hadn't been served. I went to our *tempat* to wait until the woman had eaten. Tante Suus, not used to seeing me in the camp at lunchtime, approached me cautiously. The troubled look on my face was undeniable.

"Is it over yet, dear? The smuggling case, I mean."

"No, Auntie, it's not. Let me tell you one thing: I hate being in this predicament. It tears me apart. One side of me wants to support the woman; yet the other side, being totally committed to my responsibilities, prevents me from doing that. When I translate the officer's words of punishment to her, it feels as if I'm the one handing out the penalty. He does it in such a contemptuous manner that it's difficult for me to stay emotionless. I hate to be in the middle of it all. I hate it!"

"You did what you could, darling. I understand that you're frustrated, but don't let it affect you this way. You shouldn't take it personally. It hurts me to see you in pain like this," Tante Suus said, trying to comfort me.

"How can I not take it personally, Auntie? Tell me how," I pleaded. "I'm right in the middle of this mess."

Tante Suus had no definitive answers, but just verbalizing my troubles to her helped me feel a bit better. I collected myself and walked slowly toward the guardhouse to see if the prisoner had finished her lunch. On the way, Mother Superior beckoned me for an update on the smuggling case. I gave her the details, including what had happened before the woman was arrested, and lingered on to talk. We both agreed that the officer's behavior was deliberately sadistic. Like Tante Suus, Mother Superior counseled me not to blame myself.

When I returned to the guardhouse, the woman was waiting for the next instructions. I led her to a spot in the sun. "Do I really have to stand in the hot blazing sun, Rick?" she cried. "Please! Have mercy!"

My voice began to quiver as I snapped, "You should have thought of it beforehand. It's much too late now. Please do as I tell you, and don't make it harder for either of us by resisting!"

"How long do I have to stand here?"

"Until the officer comes to release you."

"When is that?"

"Don't ask any more questions. The situation is already precarious enough. Please, just do what I said." I left her standing in the bright sun with her arms stretched up toward the sky.

"Rick!" she screamed as loudly as she could. "You can't do this to me!" I walked away with teardrops rolling down my cheeks.

Back at the office, I washed my face, trying to remove all traces of my emotional outbreak before resuming work. I wondered what had brought on the alteration in the woman's punishment. What had the Snake told the commandant? Had he been truthful? Did the commandant approve the punishment?

Thinking of the woman standing in the sun at the hottest time of day, my stomach tightened. I hoped she wouldn't suffer harmful aftereffects. My mind kept wandering off in various directions. Why had she been involved in smuggling? Why would she risk her life? Was it really worth it? An even more nagging question entered my mind. Why had she ignored my warning? Maybe she didn't want to disappoint the prisoners who had been looking forward to receiving the packages. Or, knowing that a delivery had been made, perhaps she felt obligated to make one last trip to retrieve the parcels.

About two hours later, the Snake burst into my office and insisted that I come with him. The wild look on his face frightened me. As we walked through the back door into the camp, we could see the guardhouse ahead of us. The woman was not there.

"You said you carried out the order," he snarled. "So where is she?" He gave me another evil look.

"I don't know, sir. Something must have happened."

As we approached, a nun came out of the hospital barrack to meet us. Addressing me, she said, "The woman collapsed from standing in the hot sun. The doctor diagnosed a mild case of sunstroke but has assured us that she will be fine."

The nun led us to the patient. The Snake looked down at her and sneered, "Have you had enough excitement this time around?"

The woman said nothing; she merely looked at him with hate in her eyes. As tears ran down both sides of her face, a look of triumph came over the officer's face. "I have my answer!" he said.

On the way out, he told me to call the prisoners together. "I want to make something clear to all the women. Sound the whistle for a meeting!"

In my heart I welcomed his suggestion, because I never ever wanted to find myself in that kind of situation again.

In the Snake's address to the women, he confessed that he had been waiting to apprehend this particular person for quite some time. Now that he had, he wanted to impress upon the women the importance of obeying his rules and never underestimating his power.

I continued the translation: "Your fellow prisoner told me she needed something to bring excitement into her dull existence in a place full of women. Well, I gave her a dose of that something, although I don't think it was what she had in mind. I deliberately frustrated her by keeping her in suspense about the punishment and by altering it several times. I think I succeeded."

He paused in his lecture and looked over the crowd, apparently seeking signs of respect or approval. Nothing happened. He continued: "Ladies, I have ways of finding out whatever I want to know, so I suggest that you follow all our rules very carefully. You are forewarned, and you have witnessed the consequences of breaking the rules and getting caught, especially when I'm the one who catches you."

Total silence hung over the crowd. The incident of torture, along with the Snake's lecture, had made a big impression on the women. The Snake wasn't done yet. "Before I adjourn this meeting," he said, "there are other things I would like to bring to your attention. First, I've decided to acquit the prisoner from her punishment. I have to add, however, that it was not my intention to go easy on her. This young man, here"—he placed his hand on my shoulder—"he is the reason I changed my mind. He deserves a medal for the fight he put up to defend one of his own."

The prisoners clapped spontaneously. The Snake

continued: "Without realizing it, the woman placed Rick in a very difficult position. I respect him for his courage to do what he did. He defended her as a little, determined lawyer would. You all are in good hands. You may certainly consider him an asset to your community. I want you all to know that. Thank you!"

After dinner at the mess hall, the Snake called me aside. Before he had the chance to say a word, I thanked him for the praise he had given me. Words that, admittedly, I had never thought he would say about me.

"I know you don't particularly care for me, Rick, but I had to give credit where credit was due. You deserved it. You should become a lawyer," he joked. "My compliments for your brilliant defense tactics!"

As for the smuggler, what had happened to her opened her eyes. It taught her to accept life in prison just as everyone else had. The Snake's thirst for revenge had quenched her desire for excitement and adventure.

Chapter 28

A time of tranquillity—to the point of monotony—
returned to camp life after the traumatic smuggling incident. Busy at work one day, my concentration was broken
by the loud roar of a motorcycle interrupting the quiet
neighborhood atmosphere. Seconds later, a military courier
entered the office. He handed me a duffel bag and a letter
and asked me to sign for them. I took both items to the
commandant. "Sir, a messenger left these for you."

"Thank you," he responded in a low, indistinct manner.
He opened the letter before I had a chance to leave his
office. "Wait, Rick! I think I'm going to need your assistance!"

A frown creased his forehead, and a sudden chill of
uneasiness came over me. I looked away. Was the courier
from the men's camp? I quickly abandoned the thought.
Then the commandant spoke. "Do you know where the
messenger came from?"

"No, sir," I admitted, but his question heightened my
suspicion. After reading the letter, he asked me to open the
bag and empty it out on the table so the contents could be

examined. When I saw the personal items in front of me, my worst suspicions were confirmed. The sight made me nauseous. In a flashback, I remembered the commandant preparing me for such a moment. Now that it had arrived, the reality was still difficult to grasp.

The bag held various items that a man would keep in a bureau drawer. They were now only mementos of a happier life, loving memories for a wife he had left behind. My heart pounded, thinking that one day I might open a similar bag to find my father's possessions. *No,* I told myself; I couldn't give in to thoughts like that. I had to concentrate on the matter at hand and be strong.

The commandant and I checked every item on the table against the list that came with it. After we were done, he said, "Hold on to the bag and make a note of it on the woman's card." He handed me the letter with the name of the deceased. "This is our first death notice," he stated. "Do I need to remind you of our talk about the policy in such a matter?"

"No, sir. I confirm: The information is not to leave the office until you have given the order," I stated, and he nodded.

"I had hoped this moment would never come," I admitted with great sadness.

"I understand, Rick, but don't forget that we're in a time of war. Even though there is no fighting here, or bombs dropped, people still do die from natural causes."

I gathered courage for the next obvious question. "When are you planning to notify the widow?"

I never received an answer. He seemed not to have heard me or had no intention of responding. Consequently,

I spent the following days in a state of anxiety, unable to concentrate on my work. I was overcome with sorrow for the widow. I felt a deep sense of grief for a woman who was going through her daily routine, totally unaware that her husband had died. I began to feel uncomfortable being with people. I even hesitated to spend time with Tante Suus. I was afraid I would become emotional and need to explain why. I hoped the commandant wouldn't wait much longer to make the announcement.

More than once, Tante Suus caught me staring off into space. She knew I was fighting an internal battle and ached with me in silence. Knowing I was unable to discuss my problem, she would simply come close and hug me without saying a word. Her quiet presence assured me that I was not alone.

Three days later, the captain announced that he was ready to see the widow. Before I left to fetch her, he stopped me and, in a voice full of compassion, said, "I want you to know how genuinely sorry I am to have to put you through this. It is unfortunate that the man could not be with his family when he left this earth for a better place. However, as I said before, death under any circumstance is part of life in war or peacetime."

At the barracks, I calmly asked the woman to come with me to see the commandant. She never even asked why. Neither of us said much on the way down. I wondered if she suspected the purpose for the call. I was terribly afraid that she would ask me. Although it was a short walk to the back door of the camp, under the circumstances it seemed much longer.

I observed her from the corner of my eye. She seemed

to be lost in thought and in control of her emotions, until she suddenly stopped. She grabbed my wrist gently, making me face her. With tears in her eyes, she gasped, "It's my husband, isn't it?"

Surprised by her suddenness, I was unable to confirm or deny the fact. "That's all right, Rick," she said. "You don't need to say it. I can see it in your eyes." After a moment she continued: "I thank the Lord for taking him. You see, Rick, my husband had a liver problem that needed constant medical attention before the war broke out. The doctors had told us he did not have much time left. I am truly amazed that he held on for so long. I'm sorry—I shouldn't burden you with it."

"I am sorry, ma'am. I'm sorry for your loss."

"Thank you, dear boy. The thing I regret the most is that I wasn't with him to help ease his exit. Other than that, I'm relieved and happy, knowing he will no longer suffer."

At the office, I translated the commandant's message of her husband's death into Dutch and handed her the bag containing his possessions. She cried silently at first. Then she held the unopened bag against her lips, buried her face in it, and cried, her heart breaking. When she began to open the bag, the commandant and I left the room to give her privacy.

I walked back to camp with her and made sure she would not be alone. Back at the office, the commandant asked for a report on the woman's condition. I told him that she was in the care of a friend and that she had entrusted me with her husband's health problems. His death was a blessing for both.

Responding to my unhappy face, the commandant

asked how I was doing. "I've had a few rough days," I confessed, "but I'm hard at work to get back to normal."

"Is there anything I can do?" he asked.

"Well," I said, getting straight to the point, "it would mean a lot to me if you wouldn't wait so long after receiving the death notice to tell the family members."

I explained that it was hard to keep a secret from a woman I saw in camp every day, that it was difficult not to walk up to her and tell her what she was entitled to know. I spoke slowly because it wasn't easy to maintain composure. Finding the right words was a chore because I was afraid the commandant might find my behavior immature, or too compassionate for a boy. I stopped to take a deep breath. "In the meantime," I reported, "I'm barely able to do my work and have experienced sleepless nights. Carrying around such a secret has totally disrupted my concentration."

The commandant seemed overwhelmed by my confession; he left without saying a word. I couldn't understand why he did that. I was disappointed, surprised, even stunned by his reaction. What had I said to displease him? Was that his way of telling me that he wasn't interested in knowing how I felt? But he had asked!

That evening before I left the office to take up my domestic duties, he called me in. "After listening to you, I have to agree that I treated you unfairly. I didn't realize you would take your responsibilities so seriously. I am genuinely sorry to have done this to you," he apologized. "I realize now how great a burden I have placed on your young shoulders. I walked away from our conversation because I was keenly aware and ashamed of what I had done. I disliked myself very much at that moment." He paused, looked me straight in the eye, and added, "From now on, let's call the person in question as soon as *you* have updated the cards. That way, the matter will be dealt with within a short time."

His willingness to understand my point and to meet my request caused me to experience a momentary loss for words. I apologized for having pursued the matter with such determination.

Shortly after that first death notice, rumors spread through camp that I had access to confidential information. Some women asked me to find out about the well-being of family members in the men's camp. Even nuns approached me to check on imprisoned clergymen. Despite my telling them repeatedly that I was not in the position to oblige them, some women kept pressing me. Many called me names and considered me arrogant, snobbish, or a know-it-all. I fully understood their resentment; I probably would have reacted the same way under such circumstances. Despite their ill feelings toward me, I never held a grudge. Only I knew how disappointed I was in myself for having to hurt them, but no one was aware of how much I needed their emotional support.

In time, more bags of personal belongings of deceased men were delivered. I thought my emotional involvement in these events would gradually become easier, but it did not. I disciplined my mind to block out unwanted thoughts. Doing so enabled me to control my own emotions at will, in order to provide moral support to a widow or to a mother who had lost her son.

Then something happened that turned rather ugly.

Three bags of possessions arrived from the men's camp. I located the three women, but as soon as I had gathered them together, I realized I'd made a mistake. Could I handle three at once? Would they ask me the dreaded question? Is it my husband? My father? My son?

While the four of us walked toward the back door, we attracted attention. People along the way stopped what they were doing and watched our small procession. It was unnerving. At any moment, I expected an onlooker to jump out and hit me over the head for being the carrier of bad tidings.

Just before we went inside, the women's angst grew. Two had husbands as well as sons in the men's camp. One grabbed me and said, "Listen, Rick, we all know why we have to see the commandant, but can't you tell us who has died? It would make it so much easier if we knew what to expect. It wouldn't make any difference to you at this stage, right?" She spoke in a slow, deliberate, and demanding way.

"I'm sorry, but I can't say anything. You know that! Why are you doing this to me? I'm just following orders. The commandant will tell you what he wants you to know."

Agitated by my answer, the woman lost total control and screamed, "You goddamned squirt! Who do you think you are?"

I was stunned to hear such language. I pleaded with them to stop asking questions they knew I couldn't answer. The same woman grabbed my arm again and pulled me toward her with a hard jerk. I was so close to her that I could feel her breath in my face. Her eyes were spitting fire

247

and her voice was loud and desperate when she swore again: "Damn it, Rick! What the hell's going on? Which one have I lost? Tell me!"

"I can't do that, ma'am," I reminded her.

She was vexed by my answer. "Make an exception, damn you! Who gave you the right to keep to yourself the news we are entitled to? So, just tell me, which one did I lose?" she shouted.

The other two women surrounded me, their faces expressing the same sentiment and urgency. I managed to break free and find my way to the office where the commandant, aware of the commotion, stepped outside his office and ushered the women in. He offered them a seat and looked me over. "What happened to you, Rick?"

I didn't answer; I didn't want to incriminate the women, but he knew something was wrong. He shook his head in apparent disgust and sat down behind his desk. He looked at the three women and started to call out their names. He handed them each a bag containing personal belongings of the deceased. One woman, the one who swore at me, became hysterical when she saw her husband's possessions. It was too much for her to bear. There was something sinister in the way she looked at me. I wondered what was going through her mind. She moved away from the table and took a few steps in my direction. Standing in front of me, she yelled in my face, "What are you staring at?"

"I'm not staring at you, ma'am," I replied softly.

"Listen to this smooth-talking kid. Hell, yes, you were staring at me!" There was such agony in her eyes. I didn't react to her accusation because an answer would only have worsened her situation.

"You knew about this all along and didn't have the guts to tell me. You heartless little punk!" she jeered. "You feel protected, don't you? With your big boss behind you, what could go wrong? I hate you with a passion!"

Her tongue-lashings were merely the response to the profound loss of her husband, but they were embarrassing. Her cries came from deep within. It hurt me to see the woman in so much pain. It was almost impossible to listen to her cries without becoming emotional myself. Even though I was only fourteen, I could empathize with her. I knew sorrow; I was still grieving for my dead mother.

The woman's sorrow was so intense that she became physical. She started to attack me in a desperate search for justice. She scratched me, pulled my shirt, shook me, and pounded on me wherever she could. I tried to protect myself by throwing up my arms. The commandant and the two other women jumped to my rescue, but the blows and scratches had already left their marks.

I, too, cried. I cried tears of sympathy for the woman, for her husband, for myself. I understood so well her sense of loss, and for that reason I did not fight back.

The commandant had the guard return all three women to camp. The last one to leave whispered words of regret. "I'm sorry for what happened, Rick."

I freshened up and returned to my desk. Moments later, a face poked around my office door and a voice asked, "Are you all right, Rick?"

"Yes, thank you, sir, I am," I responded.

He walked in and seated himself on the other side of my desk. "How old are you? Thirteen?"

"I turned fourteen two months ago," I said proudly.

"Oh, is that a fact?" he said, with a twinkle in his eyes and a big smile on his face. "I would have thought you were much older than that. Say, fourteen going on forty." We both laughed. We talked awhile about the incident.

The commandant commended my behavior. "I'm moved by the way you defended yourself, or should I say by the way you did *not* defend yourself. You never lifted a finger to fight back the blows the woman landed on you. You just stood there. You, my little friend, you never cease to amaze me."

We continued to talk for a while longer. The commandant was easy to talk with and was virtually the only person I could confide in about anything associated with my work.

At day's end, I locked up and reported to work at the mess hall. Mien, the cook, asked about the scratches on my arms and face. "What the hell happened to you? Must have been quite a fight with your girlfriend, huh?"

"One of the women did this," I confessed. Mien, indignant at my response, asked other questions, but I chose to say nothing more.

When I went home that evening, Tante Suus already knew about the unfortunate encounter in the office. Mother Superior had told her. The three women had gone straight to Mother Superior to report what had happened and, concerned about me, she didn't want to pass judgment until she had a chance to talk with me.

Physically as well as mentally exhausted, I promised Tante Suus I'd go see Mother Superior the next morning. As I crawled under the mosquito netting, ready to retire, I heard the voice of the woman who had attacked me.

She wanted to speak with me. Tante Suus told her I had already gone to bed, emphasizing that I had had a very emotional day.

"That's why I'm here," she replied. "I feel so ashamed. I did him a great, great injustice and took out my frustrations on him. Suus, please let me talk to him. I won't be able to sleep until I do."

I peeked out from under the netting. The moment she saw the scratches on my face, she became emotional all over again. "Rick! Rick! Dear boy, I came to apologize for what I did to you this afternoon. I can't imagine what came over me. I didn't mean anything I said about you in the office. Those were words of anger, frustration, anguish— call it anything you want. I feel terrible. Please forgive me. I'm so ashamed." She rambled on until Tante Suus tactfully ended the visit. The woman left in total despair.

Before going to work the next morning, I went over to the nuns to give Mother Superior my version of what had happened. I showed her my scratches.

That evening, Tante Suus told me that last night's visitor had stopped in during the day to invite me over to set things straight between us. She and Tante Suus had had a long chat. I decided to go see her, mainly to put her at ease concerning her feelings of guilt.

"My talk with your aunt increased my regard for you," she said. "I learned about your position, about what you stand for and how you represent us, your fellow inmates. I would never want to stand in your shoes. I hope that you can forgive me for my outburst and my misbehavior." She embraced me and kissed me lightly on my forehead.

The rest of the evening was spent in a friendly get-acquainted atmosphere. She told me about her deceased husband and her life with him. At times, she became emotional, but that was to be expected. It was quite late when I left her.

Chapter 29

One sultry evening after a hard day's work, Tante Suus and I sat down to enjoy a few minutes of relaxation. Friendship became the topic of conversation. I was surprised when Tante Suus brought it up. She thought it would be good for me to have a friend my own age. "Do you have someone in mind?" I asked.

She did—Tina, a girl who lived with and was being cared for by the white-robed hospital nuns. Tina had received training in the medical field while working in the nuns' hospital before the war broke out.

"Does Tina know I'm not a boy?"

"She does. Mother Superior has made all the nuns of all three orders aware of your identity. The secret is safe with them," she assured me.

I was skeptical of Tante Suus's idea of my building a friendship with a girl, but the more we talked about it, the more it appealed to me. Having someone my age to share confidences with might be nice.

I was nervous about meeting Tina, but was looking forward to it. Admittedly wrapped up in commitments and responsibilities from a very young age, I had never allowed myself to find ways to relax with others. Now I had to learn to socialize. I worried about what to do, how to act, or what to say when I met her face-to-face. I never had many friends, and the more I thought about it, the more I realized that I preferred to live a solitary life. I never wanted to be bothered with things that would complicate it. I wanted my life the way I wanted to live it. My studies, my work, and my family were my life.

When I went to the hospital barrack to meet Tina, a nun told me that she was with a patient. Standing outside the ward looking in, I watched Tina prepare a little boy for the night. She leaned over and kissed him on the forehead. I liked her right away.

Tina was a few years older than I. She wore glasses and had a head of thick, heavy, dark brown hair that hung down to her shoulders. She was five feet, five inches tall and weighed 135 pounds. She stepped outside the hospital ward and introduced herself to me. She told me about her patient, an eight-year-old Dutch boy who had polio. He was in the hospital when war broke out. When the nuns were captured and interned, they brought him, Tina, and three other foster girls with them. At the boy's request, Tina became his private nurse, and their relationship grew into a very special friendship.

Tina's and my first meeting went smoothly. She told me about her life before the war. She and her brother were orphans and taken in by an aunt, their only known relative. The aunt's age became a handicap in bringing up teenagers, so Tina's brother was placed in a foster home and Tina herself ended up living with the nuns.

Tina and I instantly took a liking to each other. "I have to admit . . . uh, Rick," she said my name with hesitancy, knowing that I was a girl, "I've been planning to come and see you, but I know your days are very full and demanding. I felt a visit might be imposing, so I watched you from a distance, but I hoped we'd become friends. Now, here we are. What do you think?"

"I think it's great," I responded.

"It's so strange to call you *Rick*," she said softly, quickly adding, "but don't worry! Your secret is safe with me, and with everyone else in our barrack who knows about your disguise."

Tina was an excellent listener. From the start, she understood my need to talk about simple matters, and she was perceptively aware that some topics were impossible for me to discuss. One day out of the blue, she asked, "How do you hide your period?"

"My what?" I asked, forgetting all about that female matter of inconvenience.

"Your period. Your menstruation, you know . . . ?"

"Oh, that," I stammered, "I had it twice before the war, but it stopped when we entered the first prison camp in Djambi. I've not had any sign of it since."

"Lucky you," Tina grumbled. "It's such a nuisance."

Our conversations were limited to topics we knew about from living in confinement. They didn't include boys, dates, shopping for new clothes, or anything else that teenagers would normally talk about. After all, we were living under extremely abnormal circumstances. In spite of it all, however, our friendship flourished and we were even able to tell jokes and have a few good laughs.

255

If I wasn't too tired, visiting Tina for a couple of hours before the lights-out sign was a certainty. We would exchange information about anything that came to mind. What I valued the most in our friendship was that she always gave me a free hand in choosing the subjects to discuss. She understood my limitations in the choice because of my work.

Walking back to my barrack one moonlit evening after visiting Tina, I saw the shadows of two people in the *pendopo*. I assumed two women were having a private conversation. But as I approached, I saw that one was a man. The couple was standing close together, too close to be having a conversation. The situation piqued my curiosity and held me captive.

Were they kissing? Who was the man? The only men were the Indonesian guards and Japanese officers, and they were forbidden to have physical contact with the women prisoners. So, what was going on? My brain worked overtime. Another possibility came to mind. Maybe what looked like a man was a woman with a man's haircut. Several women in the camp had mannish cuts. That idea seemed incredible until I remembered the conversation with Tante Suus about homosexuality a year or so ago.

Confused and coming closer to the couple, I began to hear sounds, as if one was enjoying something very pleasing. From the corner of my eye, I could see the couple engaged in a rhythmic movement. As the cadence increased, so did the sounds. The couple was apparently totally oblivious to their surroundings and my approach.

I became more nervous with every step. I didn't want to attract their attention. My heart pounded in my throat from the excitement of witnessing something I'd never seen before. I was close enough now to be sure that a man was involved, although I didn't recognize him. A military cap gave him away. It was a guard, but which one? I prayed that what was happening would not be the cause for another confrontation with authorities.

I arrived at our *tempat* and went straight to bed. In those days, young people knew very little about lovemaking. I was unable to tell what it was all about. Reliving what I had seen kept me awake most of the night. I tried to understand what the two were doing. I had seen them kissing and heard the sounds they made. Despite my innocence regarding lovemaking, I was convinced that these two people had overstepped the boundaries.

After putting my brothers to bed the next evening, Tante Suus left to visit a sick friend. Sitting in the dark at our table, I was able to overlook the entire camp. I wanted to find out who the woman was and warn her about the danger of being discovered.

"Why are you sitting in the dark, dear?" Tante Suus asked when she returned.

"No particular reason," I replied. "I'm not sleepy."

"Well, I am. Good night," she said, and kissed me. I stayed up, waiting. An incredible scene unfolded before my eyes. After lights-out, a young English-Eurasian woman came out of a barrack across from ours. From a distance, even under the dim lights of the hospital and the guard-house, I could see that she was nicely dressed. She began to flaunt herself by pacing back and forth close to the *pendopo*, apparently wanting to be noticed by someone in the guard-house. Her long black hair was done up in a fancy hairdo, and I knew she was the woman I had seen outlined in the shadow the night before. I kept watching. I needed to find out which guard she had been with. At the same time, I questioned myself. What would I do once I knew the identity of the man? Would it be proper for me to get involved?

The camp was in darkness except for some scattered luminous points. It was late, but I could not let myself retire. The young woman was still awaiting her date, and I was anxiously anticipating the next stage of this affair. Then, slowly and inconspicuously, a guard left the guardhouse. He took a detour, as if he wanted to assure himself that it was safe to approach the *pendopo*. It was obvious that this was a prearranged encounter. The distance and the darkness prevented further observation, so I decided to go to bed. Good sense told me not to get more involved.

Surely I couldn't be the only witness to this affair. It was unthinkable that something like that would go unnoticed. Someone else must have seen what I saw. If so, why had that person not done anything to stop it? If the affair was unknown to others, what could I do to prevent it from escalating into something worse? The thought of approaching the young lady to ask her questions, and then warning her to discontinue her escapades, even for her own safety, seemed bizarre. She might become offended and tell me that it was none of my business. No matter where I turned, I found myself against a brick wall.

A few weeks later, unexpectedly, their trysts came to an end. I was optimistic that everything was going to turn out well and that somebody might have talked some sense into them. Little did I know.

One day the commandant entered my office and blurted

out, "I have reason to believe that one of the prisoners had an intimate relationship with one of my men. Are you aware of any such relationship, Rick, or have you heard rumors about it?" He was highly agitated.

I faked surprise and denied any knowledge of it. At the same time, I felt guilty. Should I have aggressively tried to prevent the incident from coming to this?

"I've been told the woman is pregnant," he continued. "Pregnant! Damn! I don't understand how it could have happened." He swore heavily in Japanese. "I don't know which guard is responsible for this, but I shall find out!" He slammed the door on his way out.

I had never seen him so furious. What I had feared before was now reality. It was out in the open, and the truth would have to come out.

On the telephone for most of the morning, he came out of his office in a state of rage. He waved his arms in the air, ordering me to fetch Mother Superior and a certain young lady by the name of Diana Hanson, the allegedly pregnant young woman.

Minutes later in the office, I translated into English the captain's words about Diana's affair. Mother Superior heard the story for the first time and she was shocked. Diana's face was heavy with guilt. "Are you having an affair?" the commandant asked her bluntly.

Diana did not answer.

"Who is your partner?"

Diana still didn't answer. The commandant pelted her with more questions, but each one either remained unanswered or was flatly denied. Mother Superior talked to the young woman between questionings, attempting to make her see that if it were true, she should come out and admit it. "You can't keep it a secret for long if you are indeed pregnant, Diana. Tell the truth to help yourself get out of this."

"What will happen to me if I do tell the truth?" she asked tearfully.

"I don't know, but not saying anything won't make it go away," Mother Superior explained, trying to talk sense into the young woman.

The commandant jumped out of his chair in a terrible rage and shouted, "I want answers to my questions! If I don't get them, we'll repeat this meeting two months from now. Then it will be harder for you to deny the pregnancy, and I can guarantee you that the consequences will be far greater then, too. Do I get the answers I want?" he asked, looking her straight in the eyes. "Or do we postpone the meeting for two months?"

Diana shivered fearfully when I translated his message to her. She answered the questions and admitted having an affair and that she might be pregnant, but she refused to reveal the man's name.

"You need not protect your lover!" he shouted. "He has humiliated me in my capacity as the commandant of this prisoner-of-war camp, and even worse, he has brought dishonor to his country. He is about to take you down with him. Is that what you want? Do you really want to protect such a man?" The commandant was out of control. "The guard knew the consequences of treason and deserves severe punishment!" Rolling his eyes in disgust, he asked Diana, "Do you even know the definition of treason? Let me tell you: treason is the betrayal of one's country by consciously and purposely aiding the enemy, which both of you did."

He was so enraged that I feared he might become physically abusive.

Hammering at Diana to reveal which guard she was involved with, he slapped her soundly in the face. She broke down in tears, but instead of answering the question, she responded with a question of her own. "What will the military do to him?" Her question infuriated the commandant even more.

I admired her strength and feisty spirit, but I couldn't believe my ears when I heard her concern about the possible consequences for the guard. Was she crazy? She ought to have been worrying about herself! I was simply too young to understand, but it bothered me that she was so adamantly protecting the man who had caused the crisis.

Stubbornly, Diana kept refusing to name her partner. Mother Superior and I became frightened at the commandant's continued fury. Finally, he walked away, but shortly returned to announce a more effective approach to the matter. He ordered all off-duty Japanese guards into his office. When Diana saw the men walk in one by one, she became distraught. The commandant yelled in her face, "Which one? Which one of these men is it?"

Diana avoided looking at him or the men and, with her head down, was still unwilling to answer the question. Her refusal to cooperate was an open invitation for drastic measures. The commandant took a step toward her and forcefully lifted her chin. He made her look at the men in the lineup. Still holding her face, he pointed at them and repeated what he wanted her to do. "Identify the man!"

Big tears rolled down Diana's face, but she gave no response. The commandant released her chin, and she dropped her head again. Then, exhibiting ultimate rage and intolerance, he squeezed her face around the jaw with one hand and slapped her twice with the other, yelling and screaming all the while. He didn't even give me enough time to translate.

I watched the men. One reacted ever so slightly when the commandant slapped Diana. His reaction was so barely perceptible I wasn't certain it had actually occurred. Mother Superior whispered encouraging words to Diana to end the ordeal, but to no avail.

The commandant hurled insults at Diana. "You little tramp!" he shouted, his face red, eyes bulging, the veins in his neck enlarged. "I'll give you one more chance. Be quick about it! My patience has run out."

He grasped Diana's hair with one hand, with the other he held her arm behind her back in a tight grip. He maneuvered her slowly but roughly toward the men, forcing her to look them straight in the face. As they stopped in front of each man, Captain Yamamoto gave her a little jerk to remind her that he expected an answer. He concentrated intensely on any sign of recognition. When they reached the guilty party, Diana became visibly emotional. She had unwittingly identified her lover. It was the same man I had seen blink his eyes for just a second when the commandant hit her.

The man was one of the least good-looking of the guards. I could even characterize him as ugly. He had a homely, flat face, a square jaw, and big ears. Diana's loneliness must have drawn her to him, because his looks alone wouldn't have done it. To me, the pair resembled the Beauty and the Beast.

Diana and Mother Superior returned to camp. Captain Yamamoto took the guard into his office. Their loud arguing blasted through the wall into my office. There were harsh, demanding words of reprimand. Then the slamming of a door ended the meeting. The guard left the building and was taken away by the *Kempetai* later that afternoon. Although the incident was never mentioned again, the tension remained.

Two days later, it was my duty to tell Diana to pack her bags and report to the commandant's office. Mother Superior became extremely upset when she heard the news. Diana, on the other hand, remained composed up to the last minute. I could clearly see, however, that saying good-bye to her mother, also a prisoner, was the hardest thing she had to do. She left the camp a lonely, lost, and very ashamed young woman. Information regarding her destination was never revealed.

A couple of weeks later I came across a memo addressed to Captain Yamamoto. Out of curiosity, and not thinking for a moment that I could significantly decipher the words written in Japanese, I glanced over it. I discovered that by putting bits and pieces together as in a puzzle, I was able to partially decipher its contents. I gleaned that it concerned the guilty guard. Lack of time prevented me from determining the entire message about his fate.

Chapter 30

A terrible drought had been plaguing the camp, and the heat became unbearable. The dry season had made its entrance in full force. We experienced low water pressure and were immediately rationed only one gallon a day per person. Our meager ration had to take care of laundry, dishes, and personal washing. Daily baths were prohibited, and punishable if the bather were caught. It soon became evident that the water supply had to come from elsewhere.

The commandant instructed me to round up women volunteers and their children to tote water from an outside hydrant down the street. I instructed them to bring along pails and all available containers. A sizable group of volunteers assembled.

I translated for the captain. "Ladies, thank you for volunteering. We are experiencing a severe shortage, forcing us to replenish our water supply. The only way to accomplish this is to carry it in from the outside. I realize that it is an inconvenience, but as a team, and with so many of you, the work should not be too hard."

Guards would be posted along the route to lead the women to the hydrants, where they could fill their containers. "The kitchen and hospital drums have priority. After the camp's need is satisfied, I expect you to do the same for the mess hall, the office, and my quarters. Are there any questions?" There were none. "Walking in this heat will not be easy. Take your time, walk slowly, and keep your eyes on the road. Considering the size of the group, you may not have to make many round-trips," he said with encouragement and genuine concern. "Cover your heads from the blazing sun, and protect your feet by looking where you step. The drought is affecting us all, so I shall therefore expect everyone to participate."

From my office, I was able to see the first group of volunteers toting their buckets. The women and children were pale and bony and walked slowly under the weight of their load. With little strength and endurance left, they moved slowly up the hill, taking mincing steps. They had to be careful placing their feet on the pebbled road because it was covered with chunks and pieces of chipped asphalt. Stepping into the cracks could easily cause injury.

From a distance, the children resembled little old men and women. They were carrying their own small contributions of precious water. Those children had lost their childhood, and now their innocent faces were frozen in fear as they passed guards posted along the way. Swaying rifles with bayonets in place and shouts in Japanese kept the line of prisoners moving.

As I was about to turn away from the window to get back to work, Tante Suus, Ronald, and René appeared over the hill. They were heading toward my office but were diverted along the way. They looked in my direction, but I made sure to stay out of sight. It bothered me to see my family toting water in the hot sun while I was spared the chore.

While I stood hidden and observed the procession, my mind wandered. It was hard to imagine that before the war these skin-over-bone skeletons had been vibrant members of a civilized society. As prisoners, the women had become slaves and pawns. Their individuality crushed and trodden to pieces, they now resembled zombies, showing no resistance or opposition.

That night back in camp, Ronald told me he had looked everywhere to find me. "Where were you? Did you see us?" he asked dejectedly.

"I'm sorry, Ronald. I was too busy to look out," I lied, then added truthfully, "but I'm very proud that you and René helped." That was all it took to make things right again with him. I wished every problem was that easily solved.

Another brigade of water carriers was requested the next day. When the commandant and I entered the camp to check on the attendance, we faced a considerably smaller group than before. "Is this all we have today?" he asked, visibly disappointed with the skimpy turnout of volunteers.

Agitated, he walked into the camp. I followed. We came to two women involved in an intense conversation. They didn't even notice us until it was too late. Through me, the commandant asked them why they were chit-chatting instead of volunteering for the water detail.

Naturally, the women were in no position to give an excusable answer. Wide-eyed, they picked up their pails and bolted to the back door, where the volunteers were gathering for the march to the hydrants. On their way, the two persuaded others to follow them.

To prevent another volunteer no-show incident, the commandant promised extra rations to those who signed up. Although the water situation remained critical for a week, no further problems surfaced.

Then the rains came with such a frequency and ferocity that the camp virtually turned into a mud hole. The deluge played havoc with the barracks. With a roof made of layers of palm leaves, it wasn't surprising that the aisles inside the barracks turned into muddy, slippery paths. Walking was not recommended, unless one liked mud to squirt up between the toes, making sucking noises with every step. The downpours created even worse damage. Mattresses, suitcases, and boxes with precious belongings were water-logged.

Right away the barracks turned into a parking lot for pots, pans, and other empty containers to catch the down-pour from heaven. Mother Nature had done it again. But this time it was too much of a good thing. Where was she weeks earlier when we had *needed* water?

Most outside activities were canceled. Children played in the rain to their hearts' content after the long drought and the many days without being able to take a bath. They were ecstatic, rolling around in the mud, making them-selves look like little mud monsters. It did us all good to see the children having fun again in such a simple manner.

Chapter 31

One day, a sedan drove up the driveway. A Japanese officer and a young woman stepped out and walked into Captain Yamamoto's office. I caught a glimpse of them, but did not recognize the woman. Suddenly, like lightning, a vision of Diana flashed through my mind. Could that woman be Diana? It had been months since pregnant Diana had left the camp. Nobody knew where she was or how she was doing.

The woman who walked into the commandant's office that day was a pathetic sight. As radiant and attractive as she had looked before her departure, she was now the opposite: pale, thin, and forlorn. She had no makeup on, her hair hung loose, and her clothes floated around her body because of her weight loss. She was the most depressed young woman I had ever seen.

Minutes later, the office door opened and the captain, accompanied by Diana, appeared. "Rick," he said, "you remember Diana, don't you? She's back with us. Would you please walk her to her mother?"

The walk to Diana's former barrack was short. We didn't talk much other than to exchange a few cordial words. Her mother was seated quietly in thought on a bench outside the barrack, unaware of her daughter's return. At the sound of our footsteps, she slowly turned and saw us. It was a wonderful, joyous reunion. Mother and daughter became entangled in a long, loving embrace. Both sobbed and repeatedly expressed how much they had missed each other, and how God had answered a mother's prayer. I left. They needed to be alone.

Diana's barrack was near the hospital ward, so Tina and I visited her often. After we got to know her better, she confessed her apprehension at being reunited with her mother.

"I've been such a disappointment to my mother," Diana claimed. "I never listened to her and always thought she was trying to rule my life rather than protect me. I should have known better. Away from here, I had time to think and to realize what I did to her. I thought I knew what I was doing. Obviously, I didn't."

Diana described her ordeal away from camp. She had lived in town in a military household as a housekeeper and performed strenuous work scrubbing floors, doing laundry, and cleaning bathrooms. The officers, totally ignoring her pregnancy, subjected her to fits of abuse and mental cruelty. She told us she gave birth to a baby boy but that he had died the next day. "I thank God for taking my baby," she confessed. "In all probability, he would have been shipped off to Japan for a traditional rearing by his father's parents."

With tears streaming down her face, Diana admitted she had contemplated suicide many times during the ordeal. She had been ashamed to face her mother, and she felt she had caused so much grief and embarrassment that her mother would be better off without her. "But," she pointed out, "by taking my life, I would only prove to be a coward and unwilling to face my mistakes. So, here I am." She wiped the tears from her face and smiled faintly.

While tidying up the commandant's desk a few weeks later, I came across a memo from the Department of Prisoners-of-War Affairs. It was a plan to relocate our camp. No reason was mentioned nor was there any hint of a potential relocation site.

The commandant was late for work that morning, which was rare. He skipped the usual bow and greeting, which was also rare. I took the traditional morning tea to him a few minutes later and found him sitting in his chair with a glum look in his eyes. To cheer him up, I playfully imitated a deep voice to make an impression. "Since this is your first offense, sir, you will not be punished for coming in late, but I must warn you not to let this happen again!"

He forced a smile, then told me he had been on the phone with the main office all morning. "I received news yesterday," he announced, placing his hand on the paper I had read. "The camp will be dissolved in the near future." He rose from his chair and paced back and forth.

"Dissolved? What do you mean by that?" I asked.

"This camp is going to be relocated."

"To where?"

"I'd rather not talk about it now," he said.

I finished my cup of tea and returned to my office. An hour went by before I saw him again. He wanted me to help prepare for the move and to organize an orderly relocation of nearly seven hundred women and children, old and young, sick and healthy.

He explained his idea. "Let's compile lists and divide the prisoners into three or four groups. Once these groups are determined, it will be less disruptive to rearrange them later, if it should become necessary. Don't you agree, Rick-san?"

In total agreement with his suggestion, I started thinking about how to work the plan. It challenged my mind and renewed my energy. I realized that this project would require intense concentration and would totally occupy my days. I couldn't wait to start. It turned out to be a more tedious and complicated process than I had expected.

Volunteers, hospital personnel, and kitchen services should play a major role in the structure of each group. These interrelated crews were, in fact, the crucial parts of the entire operation. Giving similar quality, quantity, and balance to each group was essential. The first and last groups were the critical ones.

The first group to leave needed to be able to function right away when it reached the new camp. The work crew should be mentally and physically healthy to set up the camp before the rest of the prisoners arrived. With all services available, they would set up the hospital ward and the cooking facilities.

The last group required the healthiest and the strongest women, for they would do the actual moving, then clean up and close the old camp. In my mind, I saw the women and children as a seven-hundred-piece jigsaw puzzle. Each piece had to interlock perfectly in order to complete the whole picture. It became a brain teaser and a tremendous challenge.

I shuffled, altered, and rearranged my lists to balance the groups. I was obsessed with producing the best arrangement. The assignment kept me going for days. I was reluctant to leave the office to perform my domestic duties because it would take me away from my puzzle. The commandant kept track of my progress and teased me about my dedication.

After a few weeks, I finalized the lists and typed them up. The women were still unaware of the pending move. Finally, official word came. The commandant was summoned to the main office to meet with his superiors. "I'll take with me the lists you have compiled," he said. "Even though I'm not aware of a final proposition or a plan, I can show my readiness by presenting the lists as a guide to get the move organized."

He spoke triumphantly and there was no trace of his earlier discontent. "I hope your plan will work," I said, trying to sound amiable.

"It will. Do not worry. I'll stump my peers and the colonel with what I have in my suitcase." He brimmed with confidence, in anticipation of a successful presentation. Before leaving, he disclosed a secret. "The new prison camp is on Bangka, an island off the east coast of Sumatra."

The day crept by after he left. I thought about the upcoming changes in our lives. I was certainly not looking forward to another agonizing move, the third one for my family. I envisioned a repeat of the crowded bus ride with plywood windows. This time it would also include traveling by boat across the Bangka Strait, probably followed by another bumpy bus ride to the camp site.

The commandant seemed much more relaxed the next morning. "Good morning, Rick," he said cheerfully when I carried in our morning tea.

Anxiously, I asked about the meeting.

"Thanks to you, the meeting was a complete success. Everything went as I had hoped. Sit. Sit down," he commanded. I sat, and he told me all about it.

"Toward the end of the meeting the men's camp commandant and I were asked how we would organize the relocation of an entire camp. I handed the colonel the lists— excuse me, our lists," he corrected quickly.

The commandant took a sip of tea and continued. "The colonel was pleased with my plan and complimented me for taking the initiative to prepare the lists in advance. However, when I told him that the project was the work of a fourteen-year-old, he was surprised to the point of speechlessness." Glowing with pride, Captain Yamamoto also told me that the two officers who had conducted the Japanese language test for Mrs. Mulder and me a few months earlier were also present at the meeting. They had added their own complimentary opinions about the "boy clerk."

The colonel accepted Captain Yamamoto's plan and wanted to use a similar one for the relocation of the men's camp. As a thank-you, the captain invited me to a special dinner at his quarters that evening.

The move was announced to the women the following day. They were surprised but accepted it as inevitable. The lists were circulated and, from then on, meeting after meeting was held during which alterations to the lists and rearrangements of groups were discussed and made. The final product was a perfectly balanced whole.

Amid tears and laughter, the first group to depart went through a time of packing, reminiscing, and saying farewell. The women had mixed feelings. Some were excited and eager, but harbored a fear of the unknown. Some thought that our transfer to an island was to stow us away from the rest of the world. Others were afraid to be moved to a place nobody knew anything about. Friends thought they would never see one another again. Senses of loss, anxiety, and uncertainty tainted the atmosphere throughout the entire camp.

Two days before the group was to leave, the commandant called another public meeting. He wanted to address the departing group and prepare them for their upcoming journey. There would be a truck ride from the camp to the point of crossing, a two-day boat trip, and the final stretch to the new camp by truck. Mrs. Mulder was reinstated as the interpreter of the group.

On the way back to the office, Captain Yamamoto brought me to a halt and abruptly asked, "To which group have you assigned yourself?"

I couldn't resist the temptation to tease the serious expression on his face. "I shall let you guess, Yamamoto-san." He didn't respond but was relieved to hear that I and my family were in the last group.

The night before the first group's departure, we had a last gathering to make sure that everyone was familiar with the travel plans. At the close of the meeting, I thanked everyone for their cooperation and teamwork and for making it easy for me to work with them. I added that I was happy that their animosity toward me at the beginning of my assignment had disappeared.

One woman spoke up. "Rick, at first we didn't like you.

We resented being told by a boy what to do, but we know better now."

Mrs. Mulder spoke next, saying to the group that she regretted being dismissed but that I had impressed her. A spontaneous burst of applause filled the air. Her words and the applause made me feel appreciated. If it were not for the move, I would never have known what she and the others thought of me. It was as if the prospect of a separation made us all realize how strong the bond was that had united us during our life together in confinement.

Shortly after midnight, the trucks arrived and volunteers busied themselves loading up. The women worked tirelessly throughout the night, stowing equipment and pieces of luggage onto the first two trucks. Next, the hospital patients were carried out and placed on the trucks. Some remained on stretchers; others had to sit up. Then that group's women and children were boarded. After the final farewells and hand kisses, the trucks moved out and disappeared into the dark night.

When I left for work the next morning, I saw women sitting in groups in deep thought about those who had gone. Some wondered whether they would ever see their friends again. There was no *tenko* that day; everything was out of routine.

Two weeks later, we ushered off the second group. With their departure, the camp looked bare and deserted, almost like a ghost town.

Finally, it was time for the third and last group — mine — to go. Once again I had to leave familiar surroundings. On our final day at the Palembang camp, there was no breakfast or coffee as we had served all other groups before us. At precisely four o'clock in the morning, we were ready. The back canvas flap was lowered, and our journey began. As I glanced back through the fluttering canvas cover, I saw only a dark emptiness. An imprint of the deserted camp was etched in my mind forever.

Chapter 32

We drove through a section of town that might have been a former Dutch community. The fluttering truck covers allowed me to catch only short glimpses of the areas we drove through. Since I had not lived in Palembang before the war, I had no idea where we were. After a while, the truck ride was less smooth. We were no longer riding on a paved road. We were driving through the outskirts of town, and the scenery gradually became more wooded. In the meantime, it had started to rain, causing the unpaved road to become muddy and slippery under the truck's big tires.

We drove deeper and deeper into the woods. The truck began to swish and sway from side to side. We were not at all enjoying the ride. It made me wonder how the patients and the elderly of earlier transports had fared. It must have been an ordeal for them, too. The fear of slipping into a ditch or crashing into a tree was on everyone's mind. A steady downpour added to the gloom of an already hazardous situation.

We had to crowd together on the floor in the back of the truck. Our bodies were pressed tightly against the person beside or behind us or were slammed against the truck itself by every jolt it made. Many women complained about aching bottoms from sitting on the hard surface. Since the canvas flaps were not secured, torrents of rain blew in, drenching us to the skin. The convoy stopped in the early morning at a designated area where we were allowed to relieve ourselves. To get to the creek, we had to slosh through ankle-deep, soaked leaves. Re-entering the truck, we received a small package of food for the day.

Before the canvas flaps were lowered to resume the trip, I noticed lush, moss-bearded trees with leafy inlays. Under the gloomy weather conditions, the ferns, appropriately, appeared like lacy parasols. The tall trees, with their canopies partly hidden in a cloud of the misty forest, represented soaring monuments of the jungle.

Later that afternoon, we drove through a section of rain forest where the trees had dense, low-hanging branches. It was as if we were driving through a tunnel. The only sounds we could hear were tires slipping and the engine grinding. It was eerie. The farther we drove into the woods, the more deteriorated the roads became. These roads were probably constructed for the sole purpose of allowing convoys like ours to escape.

After hours of driving, the trucks came to a halt and the canvas covers were lifted. After being bounced around for hours, we felt as if our bodies had been put through a wringer. We were ordered to stand by and gather our things. Happy to stretch my legs, I jumped off the truck and looked around. The Japanese guards were strangers to me. I asked one of them in Japanese where the commandant and his staff were.

"Yamamoto-san and his staff are traveling over water," he informed, "and should be at the boat by now. We are responsible for getting all of you to this point."

I was surprised to receive such an informative answer. Perhaps he was equally surprised by my question in his language.

Since our truck was the last one in the convoy, our walk down to the pier took longer. We followed a path through a densely wooded, heavily soaked, muddy area where walking and holding on to our possessions became an immense problem. It was not only difficult to take a step; it was almost impossible to keep footwear on one's feet because of the suction of the saturated ground.

After we struggled to get through, we caught sight of a waterway in the distance and the contours of a freighter. We had arrived at the banks of the Moesi River. An improvised pier led down to the water. We eventually reunited with the rest of the women who had been traveling ahead of us. They were already comfortably settled in, scattered over two levels of the ship.

I had barely set foot on deck when my name was called over the loudspeaker. I was ordered to report to the bridge, where Captain Yamamoto introduced me to the ship's Indonesian captain and several of his officers. I instantly became the interpreter for the group because neither the ship's captain nor any of his crew spoke Japanese.

Handing me a list, the captain asked me to make certain that everyone was on board. Checking off passengers who had scattered about and were roaming over two decks was a chore, but once that was accomplished, the signal to cast off was given and our voyage began.

From the bridge, I saw the mooring lines being hoisted and knew the moment the ship began to inch away. The distance between the pier and the ship slowly widened, and we floated effortlessly down the river. As we glided past the trees along the riverbank, I saw native women doing their laundry. The surface of the water was mirror-smooth. Downstream, the river widened into an inlet that ultimately fed into open ocean. We had reached the Bangka Strait.

By this time, the sun was upon us, welcoming us on our first day at sea. I decided to go below and join Tante Suus and my brothers. I found them in the long line to the only bathroom on our deck. We all had the same need. Waiting my turn, I stood at the railing and looked out over the rippling waves and the far horizon. I daydreamed, imagining myself swimming around with the fish and flying away with the birds, free to go in any direction I wanted. A call over the loudspeaker interrupted my thoughts. I was invited to breakfast with the commandant and the ship's captain.

The Indonesian captain told us what the passengers would be served for breakfast. It didn't sound at all appetizing. I felt guilty as I sat at the cloth-covered table eating a plateful of scrumptious food. I didn't dare waste one bite. We had a cordial conversation about the voyage. The captain said, "You're lucky that we have such calm weather. With so few bathrooms and so many passengers, seasickness could create an enormous problem."

Later that day, Captain Yamamoto decided to make rounds to check on the prisoners. As crowded as the decks were, the women showed no dissatisfaction about the conditions. We passed groups involved in card games or friendly chats, while others were reading.

Boredom and the gentle motion of the ship lulled many passengers into comforting naps or spells of daydreaming. The sky became cloudy and a soft drizzle began to fall. Toward evening we received blankets, snacks, and containers filled with a liquid someone had the nerve to call tea. Taking advantage of free time, I played a few hands of cards with Ronald, René, and Tante Suus.

Despite the cloudiness, the open space over the body of water was serene and very soothing to the eye. I silently prayed for a safe crossing. That evening, I did some exploring. To my surprise, even on this overcrowded vessel, I was able to find a spot where I could be by myself, alone with my thoughts. I became keenly aware that traveling by boat was something I enjoyed. It gave me a profound sense of freedom. The darkness and the rhythmic heaving and falling of the vessel made me feel like I was floating in space. The monotonous drone of the engines and the waves splashing against the ship's hull were soothing. The smell of the salty sea engulfed my body and spirit, and the warm breeze cradled me, lulling me into a tranquilizing sleep.

The blazing sun was my alarm clock much too early the next morning. After breakfast, the commandant asked me to announce that we would reach the island late in the afternoon. At hearing the news, the entire ship came to life. It stimulated the passengers to compete to be the first to see land. A dark strip on the horizon became the point of discovery. An air of excitement rose from the boat. Soon we were close enough to recognize the different trees along the coast, but we saw no sign of life on the beach. There was a long pier. That was all!

The engines stopped and the anchor dropped. For a little while, we were able to enjoy the sight of the crystal-clear water and the beautiful surroundings. For the second time in as many days, I imagined myself darting in all directions with thousands of fish, exploring the bottom of the sea, discovering beautiful new areas in the coral reefs. Then I heard the call to come to the bridge for instructions.

We had to get ready to disembark but were ordered to stay quiet and out of sight until that time. The commandant went ashore with two of his officers and returned within the hour. Minutes later, we felt the vibration as the engines restarted and heard the anchor being lifted. The ship slowly and smoothly floated toward the pier. From the bridge, with a handheld microphone, I directed the disembarking group.

The women left the ship in an orderly fashion and walked to trucks waiting at the end of the long pier. The trucks had red crosses painted on them and were manned by Japanese and Indonesian personnel wearing military uniforms.

Because the trucks were displaying a red cross, there was no reason for me to be suspicious, but I was. The moving process was going smoothly until one of the Indonesian attendants showed impatience. He shoved and pulled and hustled the women along, ignoring the fact that many had difficulty walking. His insensitivity upset me. Captain Yamamoto, standing beside me, observed the bad behavior.

"Aren't you going to do anything about it, Rick?" he asked.

"Me? It isn't my place to give him an order." I was indignant.

"Why not? You're the coordinator of this operation and . . . you're standing next to me."

"But I don't *give* orders; I *translate* them," I responded defensively.

"You have the authority to act on my behalf. Make that clear to the attendant!" he argued. "Go on! You may be surprised by the results."

We both left the bridge and walked down to the pier.

"Could you be more sensitive to the situation and take the condition of the women you assist into account?" I asked the attendant politely.

He looked at me and said, "Get lost, kid! You're in my way!"

His response didn't surprise me. I hoped the commandant would help me, but instead he stood to the side, urging me on. "Show your power!" he kept saying.

I didn't know what to do. The commandant wanted me to do something more drastic, but I felt powerless. The attendant placed himself in front of me and gave me a very dirty look. "If you don't get out of my way," he snarled, "I'll . . ."

The look didn't scare me; if anything, it made me angrier. My mental state was such that I was unable to think of an acceptable retort. I swallowed a few times and repeated my request with more emphasis. He glared at me. If the commandant hadn't been present, he probably would have struck me. This was the ultimate challenge! Unwilling to lose face, I repeated the order as loudly as I could, which impressed everyone else but him. He didn't even flinch, just sauntered away.

A little while later, farther down the pier, I noticed a bit of a stir. A woman needed help at one of the trucks. She had walked the entire length of the long pier with great difficulty and was now too weak to boost herself onto the truck. She made several attempts but, even with the help of a friend, was still unable to climb on.

The same attendant I had just reprimanded reached the woman. In a crude, disrespectful way, he placed his hands underneath her and gave her a push onto the truck. Women on the truck caught her and, thankfully, she was not hurt.

It was Captain Yamamoto who lost his cool at that moment. He grabbed the man's arm and yelled, "Haven't you heard the boy's order? Look at me when I am talking to you! Didn't the boy ask you politely to be more gentle with these fragile prisoners?"

I translated the captain's reprimand, but the attendant had the audacity to justify his act by saying, "She needed a helping hand and I gave it to her!"

Captain Yamamoto's face took on the same fury it had with the pregnant Diana, months earlier. The offensive man realized he was in no position to argue. Nevertheless, he stood erect and said insincerely, "You don't approve of my help? I'll leave!" He squared his shoulders, turned around, and walked away.

The commandant called after him, "I do not want to see you in my presence ever again! I will report you to your superiors— you can count on that!" The man didn't even bother to wait for a translation, which infuriated the commandant even more. The seriousness of the situation was immediately perceived and the treatment of the prisoners by the team of attendants became much more acceptable. The women thanked me for standing up for them and bowed in the direction of the commandant to express their gratitude for his intervention.

The time came for the sun to set. The last rays of light threw a glow of mystery over the island as we finished disembarking. When we were finally ready to leave, the moon was shining. The trucks motored along a beach road lined with coconut trees. Inland, I recognized mango, banana, and papaya trees. Except for a few primitive native carriages, there was no traffic. The road was narrow, forcing oncoming carriages to pull to the side and give way to our trucks. The moonlight created a shadowy glow over the beautifully layered corn and rice fields that grew against the hills. I wanted to believe we were in paradise.

PART V

SEPTEMBER 1944—MARCH 1945

We entered the Muntok camp that evening, welcomed and cheered on by friends we hadn't seen for more than a month. This camp was much larger than the old one, and the barracks were newly built. There were six barracks and they were more spread out, set up side-by-side over a larger area. My family had about twice as much living space on this *balé balé* than in the Palembang camp.

One of the six barracks was divided into two sections: a communal bathroom and toilets, and a kitchen, now staffed by Dutch, British, and Australian women. Another barrack at the end of the row was the hospital. Not too far from that stood an empty shed. Like the barracks, it was built with *gedèk* walls and an *atap* roof. I found out later that the shed was the mortuary. In this camp, too, water was drawn from wells and there was no electricity.

Sitting cross-legged on our *tempat,* I tried to digest this new environment. A sudden weird feeling came over me. Goose bumps rose up on my arms. I had no clue what brought on the feeling. Later, I talked about it with Tante Suus. To my surprise, she described the same uneasiness and she, too, wondered what it could be.

Tante Suus learned that afternoon that the entire camp was built on a Chinese graveyard. Knowing Indonesian superstitions, she predicted devastating consequences. The living would be punished for violation of something held so sacred. I was too young to understand what it all meant, other than what I had heard people say about it.

Mother Superior and Mrs. Mulder were the first to greet me on my first day back at the office. They brought me up to date with regard to the improvements in living conditions and provisions. The camp had been receiving plenty of fish, fresh vegetables, and a variety of fresh fruits. Comparing the old and the current camp, they sounded very optimistic about the future. The two also talked about the availability of land that could easily be divided and converted into a vegetable garden and sports field.

The day went by without any word from the commandant. The last time I saw him, we were riding away from the pier in the back of a truck.

I began to think about the structure of the Japanese administration of this camp. How was it managed? Except for the team of guards brought in for duty every day, there was only a small contingent of leadership. The camp stood by itself on top of a hill and, as far as we could see, there were no other buildings nearby.

I was uneasy. I felt stripped of my duties without having been officially dismissed. I needed answers. Two days later, unannounced and unexpected, a sedan drove up to the guardhouse. As I watched from the office, Captain Yamamoto stepped out, followed by two officers. All three were dressed in full military gear and carried long sabers from their hips. Captain Yamamoto entered the office by himself.

I was happy to see him again and welcomed him to the Muntok camp. He seemed uninterested and mumbled something to acknowledge my greeting, but his reaction disappointed me terribly. I had hoped we'd sit down to tea and get to work like old times. But it was not to be.

He glanced around the office with eyes like a camera, mentally snapping everything in sight, yet totally ignoring my presence. His cool attitude offended me. I was unsure how to act, what to say, and, even less, what to do.

Without a word, he left the office as suddenly as he had entered. I was dumbfounded. He rejoined his fellow officers, and the three of them walked into the prison camp. I was not invited to go along. Why was he acting this way?

When the men finished their tour, they joined me in the office. The commandant was more relaxed. Smiling, he introduced Captain Hamada, a short, plump, distinguished man, and his secretary, Lieutenant Mashida.

"Rick," he explained, "these two gentlemen are here to familiarize themselves with the facility. Captain Hamada is the new commandant and your new employer."

Addressing his guest, he said, "Hamada-san, may I introduce to you my protégé, Rick-san. He will keep the camp's administration updated."

The news came down on me like a bucket of cold water. I had to hide my disappointment and accept what was happening. The reason Captain Yamamoto had acted so strangely before was probably because it was difficult for him to end our working relationship. What I had considered insulting behavior was simply his way of keeping his emotions intact.

Captain Hamada smiled in my direction. His penetrating little eyes seemed to puncture my skin. He made me feel self-conscious.

"As the new commandant, I need to tell you a few things for better communication, Rick-san," he began. "I am responsible for the men's camp on this island as well as the women's. I have an office and residence in town, a few miles away. You and I will stay in touch by telephone, making a daily drive unnecessary. Can I count on you to make this arrangement work?"

"Yes, of course, sir!" I replied. Turning to Captain Yamamoto, I asked where he would be going.

"I have no idea, Rick-san. I will report to the mainland headquarters," he explained. He looked away and said, "I am terribly sorry for the blow it must have been for you when I gave you the news of my transfer. Although I knew about it for some time, I couldn't tell you about it until now. I think this is the best way to end a friendship. Short and sweet! I'm genuinely sorry." He sounded very sincere. "Thank you for everything and for being such a good and trustworthy employee. What I want you to do is get acquainted with Captain Hamada and give him the same courtesy and impeccable loyalty you gave me."

"You can count on that, sir, but I want you to know that I'll miss you." I spoke with heartfelt sadness.

Captain Yamamoto turned to my new boss. "Hamada-san," he said, "he is all yours. I envy you. I'm going to miss this little soldier." He tapped me good-naturedly on the shoulder and walked outside.

Captain Hamada and I talked for a while longer. "Carry out your duties as you're used to under Captain Yamamoto. I have no intention of changing the routine."

We joined Captain Yamamoto, who gave a signal to conclude the meeting. "Well, little friend, thank you for having put up with me this past year. I have grown terribly fond of you, and I am certainly going to miss our morning tea and lively conversations," he said with a twinkle. "I hope you and Captain Hamada can be friends. I wish you good luck in all your endeavors wherever life may take you. *Sayonara,* Rick."

"*Sayonara,* Yamamoto-san." We bowed our final bows, and that was the last I saw of him.

In his introductory speech during a meeting with Mother Superior and the committee the next day, Captain Hamada announced, "On days when I am not coming in, Rick will be in charge of the camp. Although I will not be here on a regular basis, he is expected to report to me daily by telephone. So my absence will not indicate that I am uninformed."

After Captain Hamada's takeover and sporadic visits, I had a great deal of free time. Much of it was spent with Mother Superior. We talked about the predicament the prisoners were in and ways to relieve it. One important discussion was about the open field and its multipurpose potential. "Whether the open land is sown with seeds, farmed, or whatever, it will give the women something to do—a purpose," she stated.

"But are they strong enough to do the work, Mother?"

"Some are," she said. "Some are strong enough, interested, and able to start a vegetable garden. It may take a long time to get going, but that doesn't matter."

She knew that the women were becoming increasingly depressed and thought that gardening would be productive and a good distraction. She also suspected that the camp was in the claws of what was called the "Bangka fever." Women who caught the fever suffered high body temperatures for days, lost consciousness, and ultimately died. Malaria, according to Mother Superior, was the most probable culprit. The number of beriberi cases among the prisoners had increased, too, due to the lack of thiamine (one of the B vitamins) in the diet. Women with beriberi became very thin, anemic, and suffered partial paralysis of the limbs.

Mother Superior herself was becoming discouraged. She started to pour out her heart to me as if I were an adult who would understand everything she was talking about. She confessed having the same feelings of defeat and hopelessness experienced by many of the other women. She had worrisome thoughts about reports from the hospital indicating a steady increase of patients being admitted.

"Our situation may consequently become a huge medical problem," she lamented. "It's hard for some to cope with camp life because, I suspect, they have problems that lie deeper than we realize. I see things worsening before improving, Rick. I don't want to scare you, but we must prepare ourselves for bad times."

"What kind of bad times do you mean, Mother?"

"The women, extremely depressed, don't seem to care about anything anymore. They've given up. They don't take care of themselves; they don't even care if they live or die. I want them to have something to do, something to live for. Maybe their negative thoughts will be pushed out and replaced by happier ones."

I thought of my family, little René, and Ronald, and Tante Suus. What if the disease, or whatever was lurking below the surface, touched one of them? What would I do? How could I prevent this unknown threat from catching up with us?

Talks with Mother Superior sometimes made me feel desperate and helpless, too. But at the same time, they opened my eyes to the continuing struggle for life among these women whose morale had steadily declined. They not only seemed depressed but had lost all sense of self-esteem and the will to fight for survival. This had to stop! What could I do to make a difference? Was I mature enough to solve the problem? I wished that Captain Yamamoto were there to help answer the questions. He had been so easy to talk to.

A week after we arrived on the island, as I walked through the camp, it struck me to see women showing signs of weakness, not only in body but also in mind. Never having been involved in the daily life among these women as I was at that moment, my observation may have been inaccurate, but it nevertheless worried me.

The first group must have been gradually affected by this abnormality since the time they had entered this camp more than a month ago. It seemed almost impossible to me for them to have changed that much in such a short time. With the symptoms mounting into proportions not to be ignored, Mother had reason to be worried. It was a frightening situation. What could be the cause? Was it nature-related? Or could it be something else? If so, what?

They performed their chores with heads hanging low and backs bent. They moved slowly. Their bodies were covered with open sores from scratching irritated skin caused by head lice, fleas in their clothes, and vermin living in their bedding. Malaria and dysentery were on the increase. At the outbreak of the war, hunger had been a problem, but what we were experiencing now was far more deplorable. The women had lost hope, and without it they would surely die.

Without my superior working alongside me, I no longer enjoyed certain benefits, such as freedom of movement—and good food. My family and I were now living strictly on camp provisions, just like everyone else. Worse than being unable to provide my family with the extra food was watching how the lack of it affected Ronald and René. They acquired the habit of making the portion and each bite on their plates last by licking tiny bits off each spoonful. Other children even went so far as to tongue-dry their plates, but Tante Suus wouldn't allow this extreme at our table.

"Only doggies do that," she said.

Crumbs, no matter how small, were never overlooked and were picked up by a wet finger. It was understandable. Ronald and René were hungry, as was everyone else. It broke my heart to see them suffer, but there was nothing I could do.

Food became the primary topic of conversation among the prisoners. Some women recounted recipes and compared their favorite dishes. Others spoke of special occasions celebrated in fancy restaurants in days gone by. To me, it seemed so cruel and senseless to do these things to themselves, but Tante Suus assured me that talking about food was good therapy for some.

The nuns instituted numerous activities to try to boost

the women's morale. They organized singing sessions, conversational meetings, Bible readings, and religious discussions. The activities worked for a while to give the women moral support and strengthen their faith. Unfortunately, as health conditions deteriorated, so did attendance at the activity sessions. Soon, there was no point in continuing the programs.

On one of my visits with Mother Superior, she reported the increasing difficulty in getting help in the hospital ward. The volunteers had fallen victim themselves.

"The number of patients is increasing," she said. "New patients are being admitted every day. It scares me to see them lie there waiting for the end. Most of them have lost the will to live. They're tired of being sick. We need milk for the children and medicine for everyone." She pleaded with me to take the matter up with Captain Hamada and make him see how desperately we needed medical supplies and food.

She also told me, cautiously, that many believed the graveyard to be the cause of the current health situation. Superstition said that the angry spirits were taking measures to deal with us, the trespassers. Could it be true? Were the spirits beneath our feet punishing us? As incomprehensible as it may seem, many believed the spirits of the dead were after us.

On returning to the office, I outlined the problems to Captain Hamada over the telephone. I did my best to make him see that it was imperative that something be done—and soon. My pleading must have made an impression on him, because he promised to come.

True to his word, he arrived the next day, accompanied by my first employer, Mr. Sato from Djambi. Mutually surprised and pleased to see each other, Mr. Sato and I greeted each other warmly. He was now in charge of prisoner-of-war affairs and happened to be on the island to inspect both camps. He had been meeting with Captain Hamada when my call came in and decided to come along to observe matters for himself.

At the hospital barracks, Captain Hamada, Mr. Sato, and I were joined by the two camp physicians. Mr. Sato at first suggested that the women were faking or overdramatizing their illnesses. But looking around, he witnessed a scene of great tragedy. It was not fake. The physicians gave a full and alarming report and speculated that a serious and rare combination of malaria and dysentery was attacking the camp.

Back at the office, Captain Hamada immediately petitioned for medical supplies, but had little success. He contacted various military bases and local hospitals on Bangka, but they, too, were experiencing shortages or were in no position to share supplies. Captain Hamada then contacted the mainland for assistance. While he was on the telephone, Mr. Sato and I chatted. I asked him about Mr. Ito and the others in the finance department in Djambi. He knew very little because he hadn't kept in touch with them. "Mr. S. felt lost without you for a long time," he told me. "The new clerk didn't know Japanese. We had to go back to drawing pictures and making hand gestures."

After all the necessary telephone calls had been made, the commandant and his guest were ready to leave. I thanked them for their attempts to find solutions to the medical crisis.

"It seems so very odd that no trace of what is going on here is even mildly present in the men's camp," Captain Hamada reflected.

"It's a mystery, indeed," I heard Mr. Sato say on the way out.

I considered mentioning the superstition to them, but decided to keep quiet. I wasn't sure that I could make them believe in something that I, myself, didn't understand. But the subject intrigued me.

The critical health condition in our camp caused Captain Hamada to visit more frequently. He made thorough rounds, and by the end of the week he came to know several women by their first names. He gave Japanese nicknames to those whose Dutch names he couldn't pronounce. The women liked his personal touch.

Throughout the ordeal, the physicians and their assistants did everything in their power to care for the patients. Despite their tireless and exhaustive efforts, the overall health situation worsened as more joined the sick list. The hospital facility was filled to capacity and the number of casualties mounted.

I observed a burial procession one morning. Pallbearers, mourning friends, and crying children were about to part with a loved one. A group of women, undernourished, lifeless and expressionless, stepped onto a truck that would carry the coffin to its final resting place. Like walking skeletons themselves, the women crept along slowly, step by agonizing step, perhaps wondering if they'd be next. It was a harrowing sight. For some, that walk may well have been their last.

After everything that happened, I should believe that there was truth in the superstitions. Despite the fact that more nourishing dairy products, vegetables, and fruits became available, there were no signs of improvement. A variety of mysterious illnesses, depression, and hunger were rampant, along with a continued shortage of medicines. Many patients were in a state of apathy, unable to express their emotions, or had no comprehension that friends were dying around them. Some of the sick, unwilling to prolong their suffering, refused medication and wouldn't eat. Not even encouraging words from friends and neighbors could persuade them to do what was best for them. Depressed and tired of being sick and of not knowing what the future held, many simply gave up. All they wanted was to end their misery. For them, there was no relief in sight.

This was the first camp where I had observed this drastic change in morale. With nothing to occupy their minds, these once-vital women had only the next meal to look forward to. Although too weak to walk, some were ready to disregard their own discomfort to help their friends in need. They lavished sympathy and compassion on their fellow prisoners by providing tender, loving care. Their mannerisms at a sick friend's bedside were a moving sight to behold. They brought tears to my eyes. Listening to the encouraging words of a friend, a joke, or just plain everyday talk, a patient was momentarily able to forget about herself and her condition. We called those selfless women "the miracle workers." Despite their own suffering, they never ceased their mission of softening the condition of others. These volunteers, appreciated and welcomed by all, had the difficult task of keeping up with the day-by-day demands of the sick. "Miracle workers" was the appropriate title for this heroic group of women.

Chapter 34

Even the smallest delivery of medical supplies was greatly appreciated. Helping patients overcome their illnesses became our daily ritual. One day when Captain Hamada brought another precious box of supplies, he sat me down and said, "I want you to come into town with me and stay at the mansion to work on a special project."

I was so astonished that I was tongue-tied.

"You see, my secretary, Lieutenant Mashida—you've met him—must undergo an operation. He will be out of work for a while. I thought it would be a good time to introduce a new filing system similar to the one you originally set up for this camp."

He had it all planned out. Mrs. Mulder would take over in my absence, although he didn't really know her. I told him what I knew about her qualifications.

Continuing his conversation about my assignment in town, he explained that I was to stay at the mansion, which not only contained the office but also accommodated him and his staff. My quarters would be one of the converted storage rooms, away from the main house. I would have my own bathroom and washing facilities and freedom of movement within the compound.

The prospect of leaving camp for the unknown was fantastic! The moment of departure couldn't come soon enough for me. I was ready for a new experience.

It was rather selfish of me to be excited about the chance to escape the unhealthy conditions in the camp, but orders were orders. There was one thing I wasn't looking forward to, however: telling Tante Suus. As I expected, she was far from pleased.

"It will not only take you away from us; it will take you to an unknown place," she fretted. "How do I know you'll be safe? How do *you* know you'll be safe?"

She was right, of course. How would I know? Would my personal safety be in jeopardy? I had no choice. I'd have to rely on the commandant. I had to trust that he would let no harm come to me.

I had thought about the change of scenery and having new things to explore, but Tante Suus's point of view opened up new prospects. I understood her worries. But there was no chance of changing the course of events. In the end, she reluctantly accepted the inevitable and ended the discussion by saying, "You are, in every respect, your mother's daughter. Paula never seemed to be afraid of anything either. It doesn't mean, however, that I will be free of worry."

I embraced her and whispered in her ear, "I'm sorry to do this to you again, dear, sweet, darling, little aunt, but . . . I seem to have been elected for this special project." Holding her at arm's length, I asked teasingly, "By the way, is it good or bad to be like Mommie?" The look on her face expressed volumes, so I retracted. "Never mind, Tante Suus—don't answer." Bringing back memories of her love for and disagreements with her sister wasn't fair. It was difficult enough for her to accept my assignment.

While Tante Suus packed my things, I went to see Mrs. Mulder and Mother Superior to tell them about my new assignment in town. Both were happy for me, but they, too, spoke of concern for my safety.

Tante Suus and my brothers walked me to the office at noontime, where I met Captain Hamada for the trip downtown. A group of nuns, including my English tutor, Sister Bernardine, had gathered in front of the office to say goodbye. I asked the nuns to look in on my family while I was away. They promised wholeheartedly to do so, and to pray for my safety and protection as well.

Riding along beside Captain Hamada in his sedan was much more pleasurable than being shaken to pieces in a rickety bus or a broken-down truck. I felt important riding in a fancy car in the company of the commandant. I ran my hands back and forth reverently over the car seat to get the feel of the fabric. It was rich and lavish to my caress. I pretended to be Cinderella, riding in a carriage on her way to a fabulous party. I was not Cinderella, however; I was a prisoner of war enjoying a privilege like no other prisoner could imagine.

The first few minutes of the ride were uneventful. The scenery revealed nothing spectacular, and the conversation between us was not at all stimulating. The road gradually started to snake through hilly terrain. An occasional open spot between trees and hills revealed lush scenery in the lower elevations of the island. The more we descended, the more breathtaking the landscape became. I'd never have seen all this beauty if I'd been traveling behind boarded-up windows, fluttering truck covers, or in the dark of night. I recognized a few points along the route that our truck had passed on the way to the camp. I particularly remembered the neatly terraced rice fields against the hills of the island. We descended even lower. It was stunningly beautiful, and I took in every detail through the car window as I traveled in comfort. I could hardly believe I was so privileged.

We entered a community where the streets were lined with European-style homes surrounded by gorgeous gardens. I sat up straight and inhaled deeply, thankful for this opportunity to escape the misery in the camp and to enjoy God's creation for a while. At the same time, I felt terribly guilty, knowing that others were deprived of what I was enjoying at this moment.

Our driver turned onto a wide boulevard with grassy zones along a median strip. The beauty was breathtaking. There were flower beds, budding trees, and lush bushes. It was like a magical fairyland. Endless rows of stately palm trees lined the way, side by side like soldiers at attention. I had never seen anything like it. A lump formed in my throat. I wanted Tante Suus, Ronald, and René to be with me to share the beauty.

The vehicle slowed as it approached an iron gate where a soldier stood guard. He waved us through. We drove up a long, climbing driveway to the front entrance of a mansion. Another guard opened the car door, and we stepped out.

Dazed, I tiptoed up the steps that led to a handsome stone-tiled open veranda. Behind me, a carpet of emerald-green grass stretched down to the gated fence below. In the distance was the beautiful ocean. The mansion itself sat on top of a hill surrounded by lovely well-groomed grounds and fruit trees. It was as if nature were displaying its finest splendor in honor of my arrival. I was simply awestruck. Was this real, or was I dreaming?

A hand on my shoulder brought me back to reality. Captain Hamada wanted me to follow him inside, where we were greeted by several officers in the sitting room. The captain introduced me and explained that I would be a guest for a while. After the introduction, the captain himself escorted me to my quarters. "This will be your room for the duration of your stay," he stated. "It should be adequately comfortable, but if there is anything you need, please ask for it."

My room was one in a row of several connected to, but away from, the main building. This section of single rooms, including a bathroom and laundry facility, would under normal circumstances be servants' quarters. The room was small and rectangular. It had one door, one window, and two sets of three oblong air holes in the back wall, about seven feet off the ground. The room was furnished with a "real" bed, a comfortable mattress, and two pillows. I felt as if I had entered a room in a luxurious hotel. A small table and chair completed the furnishing of my little domain in this beautiful mansion. Linens had been left in the room, so I made up my bed and settled in. Shortly, I decided to explore the grounds and check out the fruit trees I had observed on the way to my room.

A guard standing close by followed me with his eyes as I walked toward the trees: a *sawo* and a *ramboetan* tree.

They bore clusters of ripened fruits. Only a few feet away was a barricade of heavy barbed wire that divided the mansion from the property behind it. I suddenly realized that the barricade and the presence of the guard were clear evidence of the need for heavy security. Was the men's camp right behind the mansion? The scene took on an entirely different aspect, and I became more alert.

I saw young men standing around in the courtyard behind the mansion, staring at me, perhaps wondering what I was doing there or why I was not on their side of the barbed-wire fence. Was that the men's camp? With the guard so near, caution was important, so I sauntered on. I walked toward a *ramboetan* tree. It bore plenty of ripened fruit ready to be picked. I reached out to pluck one that was hanging invitingly low. My mouth watered at the thought of putting my teeth into it.

"Hey, you! Hey, boy!" the guard called out in Japanese. "Go ahead, pick one. It's all right!"

I didn't need a second invitation and quickly tore off one. I managed to thank him before I sank my teeth into the juicy fruit. It was indescribably delicious. Precisely at that moment, Captain Hamada came walking across the lawn. "Well, I see you've found the fruit trees," he commented.

"The guard was kind enough to let me pick one." I wiped my mouth.

Captain Hamada invited me to take all the fruit I wanted, at any time. Such an abundance of fruit instantly made me think of my family. Did I dare ask him? Yes, I dared! "Hamada-san," I said politely, "would you allow me to share some of the fruit with my family?"

He looked at me and smiled. "Sure, why not?" he said.

307

"But I don't want to talk about that now. I am much more interested in what the cook is serving for supper. Are you hungry, Rick?"

I admitted my stomach was growling, and followed him into the dining room. His officers were already there. He greeted them cordially and introduced me to them. All eyes were on me, making me uncomfortably self-conscious as we ate. During and after dinner, I became acquainted with several of the officers, including Mr. Moriyama, an elderly man who immediately acted as my protector and with whom I talked the rest of the evening. He was grandfatherly, plump, and his glasses were too small for his face. He promised to meet me after breakfast the next morning to go over the office routine.

As I lay in bed that night in the dark, thoughts of my father surfaced. I assumed he was in the prison camp behind the mansion—near me at that very moment! I wondered how he was. I thought about my disguise; it had been an ingenious idea. Becoming a boy had made it possible for me to be here in this mansion, to do office work for the enemy, and to live this unusual lifestyle. I never, for one instant, regretted having undergone the transformation, except for the sacrifice of my long brown hair. I felt the pain all over again every time I had to trim it.

The night was balmy and I was unable to sleep. In the stillness, I heard a soft rustle in the bushes outside the back wall of my room. I imagined that someone was moving very slowly and cautiously along the other side of the barbed-wire fence! I heard it again and held my breath. What was going on outside my tiny room? Who was out there? Then something fell onto the floor of my room.

From the soft sound of the drop, I knew it was a small object and that it had come in through one of the air holes. Quietly, without leaving my bed, I felt across the floor with my hand. Where was the guard? Had he heard?

I picked up what seemed to be a small rock wrapped in a wad of cotton. I turned it around in my hands and played with it, trying to analyze the nature of its contents. My mouth was dry, and I became rather nervous in anticipation of what I had found.

I held the foreign object gently in my hands and sat up in bed. Did I dare turn on the light? Unwilling to wait till morning to find out what it was, I turned on the light. In its glow, I unwrapped the object. It was a rock with a note wrapped around it and cotton wrapped around the note, all held together with rubber bands. The note read:

Who are you? Write your name on the back of this note and return it now the same way it came to you. I'll be back tomorrow night.

It was signed *F.S.*

I was shaking from fear as well as excitement. With my heart pounding in my throat, I quickly wrote down *R. la Fontaine* and re-wrapped the package as I had received it. I shut off the light. I took a deep breath, stood close to the wall underneath the air holes, and with the help of a soft moon-glow, I practiced a few times to make sure of my aim before throwing it out. I was in such a nervous state of mind that I probably would have jumped up in the air if someone had knocked on my door at that particular moment.

Back in bed, in the dark, I slowly began to calm down and to consider what I had just done. It had all happened so fast, so unexpectedly. The air was oppressively heavy, almost suffocating. Sleep was impossible. I began to think of what to do when F.S. returned the next evening. I got up out of bed, grabbed a piece of fruit that I had brought into my room, and went outside to eat it.

"Anything wrong, Rick?" came a voice from the dark side of the corridor. It was one of the guards.

"No, nothing is wrong. It's just too hot to sleep," I responded casually.

Chapter 35

I was awake long before sunrise the next morning. It took me a moment to realize where I was. *Too early to get up,* I thought, so I stayed in bed and mulled over in my mind the mystery that had begun just a few hours before. A hard wake-up knock on my door startled me. I got up and prepared to go to work.

Breakfast was at the same table and with the same men as supper had been. I, a fourteen-year-old girl in disguise, ate once again in the company of Japanese military men, none of whom had any idea that I was a girl. Some of the officers started light conversation, but time didn't allow for long dallying. Duty called.

After breakfast, Mr. Moriyama led me into an office, guided me over to the chair behind the desk, and gently pushed me into it. "How does it feel?" he asked.

"Nice, sir. And important," I joked, snuggling myself into the soft material. The chair was really too big for me and we both laughed. He walked over to a small filing cabinet and pulled out a drawer stuffed with registration cards. Placing the drawer on the desk in front of me, he said,

"Here they are, Rick—the cards for you to work on. See what you can do."

He took some time to instruct me about office procedures, showed me where I could find the rest of the cards, wished me a good day, and left. Alone, I searched for and found my father's card. He was definitely in this prison camp. At that moment, knowing he was alive was all that mattered. I was now ready to start my job.

Each card contained information about a prisoner. I made notes of missing data on the cards in that first batch. I worked steadily and without interruption throughout the morning hours until Mr. Moriyama came in to see how I was doing. During lunch, we spoke about my findings and the notes. I talked about my plan for reorganizing the filing system. He was pleased but showed little interest. Then, out of the blue, he asked, "Have you found your father's name?"

I acknowledged that I had. He said nothing more about it, but all through lunch he watched me as if trying to penetrate my mind. I felt uneasy and wished lunch would end.

Back in my room after the workday was over, I made plans for the return of F.S. Knowing that my father was in this camp, I was eager to send him some fruit, but how? Determined to find a way, I pulled the door of my little matchbox room shut behind me for privacy and looked around for inspiration. Seven feet up were the air holes. How could I use them? They were my only outlet for lowering the fruit to the outside.

Lying on my bed, I tried judging the distance between the floor and the holes. I allowed my mind to be creative. I imagined a platform, constructed by placing the chair on the table. It would enable me to reach the holes to make the drop. Maybe I could even communicate in a whisper from that height.

The next step was to find a way to lower the fruit without damaging it. Among my belongings, I found a large handkerchief that Tante Suus had packed. By tying the ends of my shoelaces to the four corners of the handkerchief, it would make a sort of upside-down parachute sturdy enough to hold several pieces of fruit. And by tying my belt onto the parachute, I would be equipped to reach F.S. down below on the other side of the wall. I was ready!

The next day, I excused myself right after supper. It was near twilight and I decided to go for a stroll to be alone, to unwind and relax. I was nervous about the night's upcoming adventure. I took a few deep breaths and inhaled the salty sea air, then headed down the sloping grassy field. Taking in the sights and hearing the thundering waves breaking against the sea wall, I slipped into my own fantasy world.

The sun's dying rays created long shadows on the lawn, forming a captivating air of mystery. I watched the sunset paint a twilight more beautiful than I had ever imagined. When the street lights popped on, bicycle traffic and a few horse-drawn carts became figurines recognizable only by their contours against the dim light.

I reached the lower edge of the yard. Tall, well-trimmed bushes bordered the property. I held on to the steel bars of the gate and watched the moving line of traffic. It was an odd feeling to be just steps away from passersby. I dreamed I was free to ride alongside the bikers. I turned around and looked up at the mansion. Mr. Moriyama was standing at his upstairs bedroom window, looking down in my direction.

He caught me looking up and waved. I waved back. What was it about him that made me feel so uncomfortable?

Slowly I walked back up to the mansion. The evening air had refreshed me, and the cool sea breeze invited me to sit down and enjoy nature from the front steps of the mansion. Crickets chirped in the grass, frogs gave low ribbit calls, and the waves noisily pounded the sea walls. I imagined running along the water's edge, challenging the rolling waves to catch me. The colorful lights of a coastal residential area twinkled in the distance. How could this be a world of war?

Captain Hamada startled me by lowering himself beside me on the front steps. "It's the best place to relax after a hard day's work, don't you agree, Rick?"

"Yes, sir, I do," I responded nervously.

He asked with genuine interest how my first day had gone. We talked about a variety of topics before he suddenly asked, "Have you found out whether your father is in this camp?"

"Yes, sir, I have. He's here."

He then asked about my family. The conversation was warm and sincere, and I felt at ease talking with him. I gathered up the courage to ask him if he would take a small basket of fruit to my aunt on his next visit to the women's camp. I was afraid I was being too forward, but he said, "Of course; consider it pay for your work here."

"Thank you, sir," I said gratefully. I wondered if I should stop there or ask for more.

"Is there more?" he asked, reading my thoughts. "You look as if there's something else on your mind."

At the risk of offending him by my greediness, I blurted out, "Would you be willing to do the same for my father?"

He smiled as if he had been expecting such a request. I knew by the twinkle in his eyes that the answer was yes. "Captain Yamamoto warned me that you're a smooth operator with a diplomatic approach when it comes to getting what you want. He also said your requests were always reasonable and justifiable. Therefore, agreeing with Captain Yamamoto, I will allow you to include your father in this arrangement. However," he was quick to add, "you do understand that I cannot let you slip notes to him. If you promise me that, then I promise you that your father will receive whatever you want him to have."

His words were heavenly music to my ears. He would grant both of my wishes! I could have hugged and kissed him right there on the spot, but we just said good night and went our separate ways.

The day was not quite over for me. I was still expecting F.S. to come by. I was a bundle of nerves, knowing I was going against my promise to Captain Hamada. But since I had already made plans with F.S. regarding my father, I decided to go ahead with them. Even though I was at great risk, somehow I had little fear of the consequences and considered myself invincible.

I took a bath to cool off and relax before turning in. Back in my room, I sat down and wrote a note asking F.S. to give my father the family's greetings and love. After signing it with R., I folded the piece of paper into a small package and placed it with the sawos, ramboetans, and doekoes I had selected to drop.

I went through the plan step by step in my mind. Then I built the platform for the launch. I stood on the chair near the ceiling and peeked through the holes into the men's camp. It was so dark I couldn't distinguish a building from a house or barracks, but it was still exciting. Suddenly feeling skittish, I poked my hand through one of the holes and snapped my fingers under the pretense that F.S. was there. I could not help but laugh about my lighthearted, silly nature.

Everything was ready. I became energized and sat on my bed to calm my nerves. My heart pounded in my throat. What if I lost my balance? What if I got caught? I made myself stop thinking such negative thoughts. I arranged the fruit and the note in the center of the handkerchief and placed it on the chair. I had no idea what time to expect F.S., so I sat on my bed literally biting my nails, which I'd never done before.

Around midnight, I heard the familiar rustling outside my room, followed by a soft peck on the wall. Another soft object dropped into my room. I brazenly flipped on the light switch and read the note.

Your father, Vic, is our gym teacher. He has not been feeling well lately, but there is nothing for you to worry about. He sends his love to you, your aunt, and brothers. He is very proud of you. F.S.

Now it was my turn. Before I turned off the light again, I made sure that everything was ready. I waited a few minutes in the dark, then climbed onto the table and then the chair. I was high enough to whisper and be heard by F.S. I squeezed the handkerchief-wrapped fruit through a hole, snapped my fingers as I had practiced, then swung the bundle back and forth to attract his attention. A voice whispered, "*Oke, zwaai 't naar voren!* Okay, swing it forward!"

I leaned against the wall and stretched my arm out as far as I could. Barely able to hold on to the belt with one hand, I swung the bundle in a few trial swings.

"*Laat 't gaan; ik vang 't op!* Let go; I'll catch it!" he encouraged. "*Een! Twee! Drie! Hup!* One, two, three, go!"

A second passed before I felt the weight of the parachute lessening. He had caught it. Three pulls indicated the mission was successful. After a short audible *"Dankjewel!* Thank you!"* I heard him moving away.

I was exhilarated. I lowered myself from the chair to the table to the floor, careful not to fall or make any noise. I dismantled the makeshift ladder in the dark and restored everything to its original location. Finally, lying in bed, I imagined Poppie eating the fruit and reading my note. It had been challenging and adventurous but also physically and mentally exhausting. Happy that it was over, I went to sleep almost immediately.

The next morning at breakfast, Captain Hamada announced that he was going to the women's camp and suggested that if I had fruit to give to my aunt I should hand deliver it to his driver immediately.

"You may also prepare something for your father," he added. "I'll deliver it when I make rounds of the men's camp later this afternoon." He emphasized two things: One: I couldn't write a note to my father. Two: my delivery would be inspected.

The morning went by quickly. That afternoon I happened to look out the window just as the captain and one of the guards walked through the side door carrying the package I'd prepared for my father. At the end of the day, the captain called me into his office and confirmed the delivery. "Your father seemed to be under the weather, but aside from that he looked well."

"Thank you for telling me, sir. I appreciate what you did for me. I'm very sorry to hear that my father is not well. I hope it isn't serious," I added wistfully.

"I hope so, too, Rick. By the way, a guard will deliver the next package to your father," he said with a smile.

"The next package? Does that mean you're allowing me to send more food to my aunt, as well as to my father?"

"Yes. You can prepare one parcel for your father every other day. The deliveries to your aunt, depending on my trips to the women's camp, may occur more frequently."

Even though I was ecstatic, my real concern was for my father's health. I'd never known him to be sick, not even for a day. What might he be suffering from? I felt especially sad that none of his loved ones were there to care for him, but being able to provide him with fresh fruit was a bit of a comfort.

Now that I could legitimately provide him with fruit, why not try for a little bit more? An occasional package with a few eggs and pieces of dried fish or meat would be a welcome addition to his prison-camp food. Chu, the Chinese cook who knew about the fruit delivery, encouraged me to ask for permission to send more. "Captain Hamada and his officers all like you very much," he said. "I know that for a fact. He'll give his permission. I am sure. Just ask!"

After lunch, back in my office, I heard strange voices

coming from Captain Hamada's office. One voice had a heavy Dutch accent. My heart pounded as I thought about a possible confrontation with the visitor. Who was he? Why was he here? Did he know my father?

Suddenly, the door of my office swung open and Mr. Moriyama entered. He invited me to Captain Hamada's office and suggested I bring along the notes I had gathered from checking the cards. He added, "A man from the camp is here. He will assist you with the project. You will give him a list of the missing data, and he will get the information to update the cards."

Mr. Moriyama introduced me to Karel, a tall, middle-aged, fair-haired Dutch man. He was accompanied by a Japanese interpreter. With all eyes focused on me, I tensed up as I accepted Karel's handshake. The surprised expression on his face was comical. He obviously hadn't expected me to be so young.

Captain Hamada asked me to explain what I had done so far and what I expected in return. I chose every word very carefully. Karel spoke guardedly as well. Conversing in English, I handed Karel the notes to be verified and asked him to complete and return them as soon as possible. I was then dismissed, and shortly thereafter, he and the interpreter left.

My days became routine. Breakfast and dinner were with Captain Hamada and the staff; lunch was with Mr. Moriyama. My evenings were free. I kept myself busy by drawing fancy letters and reading hymns from my prayer book. It was a soothing way to relax after a day jumbled with names, cards, files, and the scrutiny of Japanese officers. On occasion, I spent a quiet evening on the front steps of the mansion taking in the view and daydreaming.

After a visit to the women's camp one day, Captain Hamada reported, "The guard who delivered the fruit to your aunt and brothers says they are well. Your brothers asked when you are coming back to them. They send you their greetings and love."

I was grateful for the message. I had heard nothing from them since I had moved out of the prison camp three months ago. Captain Hamada and I continued to talk. I learned that the health situation in the women's camp had not improved, despite the extra food and medical supplies the Japanese had sent in.

In the meantime, I had started to incorporate into the cards the missing data that Karel supplied. We were almost done. My current good fortune of living like a prince would be coming to an end soon. On one hand, I hated the thought of leaving; I liked eating well, having a private room, and electricity. On the other hand, I didn't really mind returning to camp. Life here was lonely. I missed my family.

Chapter 36

The daily routine and schedule at the mansion went unchanged. The work progressed steadily, bringing me closer to completion of the assignment. My days in the mansion were numbered.

One day an officer crossed my path in the hall. Such an encounter wasn't unusual, but this man looked familiar. He was noticeably pale and walked slowly.

Minutes later, Captain Hamada knocked on my office door and entered with the officer I had seen in the hall. It was Lieutenant Mashida, Captain Hamada's secretary, who had been away for an operation. "Rick-san," Lieutenant Mashida said, "I must apologize for not recognizing you. How are you?"

"I, too, must apologize for not recognizing you, Mashida-san. Are you ready to resume your duties?" I asked.

"Are you getting tired of my job?" he inquired.

"Oh, no, sir. I enjoy my work here . . . but I miss my family."

"We understand all too well what you are saying, Rick," he responded kindly. "Captain Hamada told me that you have done an exceptional job. I will come in soon to acquaint myself with the card system you have set up."

We bowed and he left with Captain Hamada.

Lieutenant Mashida returned the following week to learn the new card system. During the hours I spent with him, I could tell that he was not quite ready to return to work. I suspected he was being pressured to cut short his recovery period following the operation.

Something significant was going on, and it became more evident each day. Meetings behind closed doors became more frequent, as did the comings and goings of military personnel. From the expression on the faces of those I joined at lunchtime, it was obvious there was tension in our workplace. The mood among the officers, including Captain Hamada, was low. I began to feel uneasy and desperately wished to be back with my family.

One particular telephone call was the pivotal point. It came during one of Captain Hamada's hush-hush meetings. When the meeting was adjourned, gloom and doom shadowed the faces of the departing officers. I was, however, unable to find out anything, and everyone was somber and tight-lipped.

Days of uncertainty followed. Just before noon at the end of the week, Captain Hamada called me into his office. Distress showed on his face. I suspected my time of departure had arrived. Not certain how to come to the point, he asked, "How is the work coming along?"

I told him the project was complete and that Lieutenant Mashida knew the card system. The news pleased him, but the distress remained on his face. He forced a smile.

"Is something wrong, sir?" I asked, concerned.

"I'm sorry, Rick, but your job here is done." The words were out. "You must leave as soon as possible, but I want to give you a last chance to get some fruit to take with you for your family and also to prepare a delivery for your father. The last one," he added.

"Thank you for your kindness, sir. I can never repay you for your generosity to me and my family. We are deeply grateful and indebted to you."

That afternoon, I picked and packed up the fruit and said my good-byes. Bidding *sayonara* to Mr. Moriyama was more difficult than I had anticipated. I had come to like him, although at the beginning of my stay I was not sure where I stood with him. I learned later that it was his awkward way of trying to protect me. He had begun to call me his "little friend," so it wasn't surprising that he showed genuine regret when I told him I had to leave.

Captain Hamada took me back to the prison camp the next day. We said little as we rode along in the car. He stared out the window the whole trip. Why was he so quiet? Was he protecting me from something? I dared not ask any questions. He was pondering something very deeply. I could almost hear his mind working, but I had no idea how pressing his thoughts actually were. Neither he nor anyone else had informed me how bad conditions had become in the women's camp.

When we arrived at the camp, he allowed me to take my suitcase and the bag of fruit to my family. "Let your aunt know you're back, then return here instantly." It was a stern order.

It was wonderful to see Tante Suus and feel her arms

around me again. Relieved to see me in good health and high spirits, she hugged me longer than ever. She was overjoyed to hear the news about my father but sad when I told her that he wasn't well. Ronald and René were genuinely happy to see me, too. They immediately pelted me with questions, but since I had to get back to work, I promised them I'd return before they went to bed and tell them all about my adventures.

Captain Hamada heaved a sigh of relief when I walked into the office. "There you are, Rick!" Without a pause, he continued, "We have an explosive situation at hand. I would like to get to it now, but first I want to apologize for keeping the information from you."

Despite his sternness, he seemed uneasy and avoided looking me in the eye. I became upset and vented my frustrations. "I knew you were keeping something from me. I could tell by your actions. Now you demand instant attention to the problems. What problems are you talking about? Tell me!" Captain Hamada was so dejected by my outburst that I apologized, ending by reminding him that I was the link between him and the women and that I was trustworthy.

After an exchange of mutual apologies, Captain Hamada told me that, unofficially, preparations were being made to return to the mainland. "Too many prisoners are sick and dying. It is simply no longer justifiable to remain on this island," he confessed. "A plan is being worked out. You must keep this information confidential for now."

Mrs. Mulder and Sister Katrinia came to the office to update us on the health situation. Mother Superior was unable to attend due to illness. "We cannot understand why the deaths increased with such speed," Mrs. Mulder stated. "It is a mystery to us."

I was furthermore informed that a Japanese medical team had visited the camp during my absence. The doctors had been perplexed as to why the men's camp had none of the symptoms that so severely affected the women's camp. The doctors had also learned of the superstition held by the island's natives. They asked Mrs. Mulder if it could be true that the women and children experienced decimation because their camp was built on a Chinese graveyard. She was unable to respond.

Captain Hamada returned to the mansion and left me with the two women. They continued the report on a more personal level.

"Rick," Mrs. Mulder said, "the doctors talked about further investigations. They suggested we find the true reason for the drastic decline of conditions. I was totally flabbergasted and unable to confirm or deny anything."

Sister Katrinia took over. "That was some visit," she began. "We weren't much help to the doctors. I'm afraid they left without an explanation for the medical mystery." Then she remembered something else. "When I was on rounds with Captain Hamada, he said the camp must be in the grip of a mysterious power. I think he was serious. What about you, Rick—do you believe we're being punished for settling on a graveyard?"

I didn't know what I believed, but I had seen and heard enough to suspect there might be some basis to the superstition. Exhausted, I decided to wait until morning to read the notes Mrs. Mulder had left for me. Wanting desperately to be with my family on my first day back, I locked up earlier than usual.

When I entered the barrack, Ronald, now eleven, and René, seven, were ready for bed. They were waiting for me and wanted to hear all about my days at the mansion. I told them how I had found our father's name among the cards, how F.S. and I made contact, and how I squeezed an upside-down parachute of fruit through a narrow air hole, seven feet up, in my little matchbox room.

Ronald asked, "Weren't you afraid you'd get caught?"

"Of course I was, Ronald, but I wanted to do it for Poppie. Fortunately, I had to do it only once. After that, Captain Hamada allowed me to send packages several times a week."

"What did you send Poppie?" René wanted to know.

"Oh, a lot of fruit and eggs, mainly. If I could get things from the market through the Chinese cook, then I would include those, too."

"Wow! Poppie was lucky, huh?"

"Yes, he was, and so were you. Remember the fruit that was delivered here by the commandant's driver?"

"Mmm. It tasted so good. I'm sorry we won't get anymore," Ronald said.

"I liked the *ramboetan* the best," René claimed.

"Quiet, René, let Rick finish his story," Ronald snapped, smiling at the word *his*. Turning to me, he said, "You get everything done for us. You're a nice brother." He winked.

The boys loved hearing about my adventures and were sorry when I was finished. I summed it all up: "I worked hard and I had a good time living in that mansion with the beautiful view. I'm sorry it's over, but I'm not sorry to be back with the two of you and Tante Suus. Life was pretty lonesome away from all of you."

Both boys kissed me good night and disappeared under the mosquito nets. While I had recounted my stay in the mansion, they were listening to their big brother. However, when they hugged and kissed me good night, I realized they hadn't forgotten that under the boy's clothing they still had a big sister who loved them.

Tante Suus and I chatted longer, mostly about the women's health conditions. It was a precarious situation. My heart was far from content with what I had come home to. I slept fitfully.

My first task the next morning was to locate the lists I had compiled seven or eight months previously for the relocation to this forsaken island. They had to be reworked for the return voyage to the mainland. Next, I perused the notes that Mrs. Mulder had left. They contained the names of those who had died. I needed to update the lists. Her notes were heartbreaking. I was shocked at the number of women and children who had died in the months I was away. I ended up with a much more condensed list.

The first time I went on rounds with Captain Hamada after my return to the prison camp provided me with a visual account of the miserable conditions. At least 99 percent, and probably all, of the women and children suffered from dysentery. Many had experienced terrible hair loss from lack of vitamins and nutritious food or had turned bald as a result of lice infestation. Small wounds, despite daily care, usually became large tropical boils, eating deep into the skin and bleeding constantly. Even bandaged wounds attracted swarms of flies eager to drink the juices of the sores.

Malaria was rampant. The medical staff's efforts to properly care for patients were handicapped by the unavailability of facilities and equipment. No lab was available for diagnosing or determining treatment. Prescriptions for badly needed medical supplies went unfilled.

Malnourished women suffering from edema could barely move their swollen limbs without experiencing excruciating pain. Some of them spent all their time in bed. The lack of wheelchairs prevented them from being taken out for a breath of fresh air. Other patients displayed swollen faces, distended stomachs, and muscle weakness. Wrinkled dry skin, hollow cheeks, and sunken, expressionless eyes turned young mothers into worn-out creatures barely able to take care of themselves. The sight of these thin, empty humans, capable only of limited movements, was terribly heartbreaking.

Those who still had the strength to drag their feet were dressed in oversize, shabby clothing and looked like scarecrows. At one time they had been healthy, robust women; now they resembled skeletons. Many, too sluggish to care, came up with excuses to ignore all rules of basic hygiene. Because more than half the population was down with a health problem, there was no way to properly care for them. The sick not only suffered physically; they also had great emotional difficulty coping with the atmosphere of disease and death surrounding them. The hopelessness was overwhelming. Only a handful of women were well enough to serve at burials and provide care to those unable to care for themselves.

After our rounds, Captain Hamada asked my opinion of what I had observed. There was no need to answer. The grimace on my face could have written volumes. I was so angry for these people. "What is going to happen next, sir?" I asked curtly.

He tried again to explain why he had kept me in the dark about the terrible conditions. "I couldn't possibly bring myself to talk about such despair with a child," he said. "Problems of this magnitude are not to be discussed with a fourteen-year-old. These are adult matters."

He confided that the plans for relocation to the mainland were in the final stages. A suitable site hadn't been found yet, but when it was, the departure date would soon follow. The health problems were too severe to risk staying on the island longer than necessary.

My family was not exempt from the suffering. Ronald, like nearly everyone in the prison camp, contracted malaria, and there was little medicine for his or their treatment. I returned to work, but the nightmarish visions my eyes had encountered during rounds with Captain Hamada wouldn't leave my thoughts.

Chapter 37

Within two weeks, trucks carried the first group of the most severely sick to the pier where a sailing vessel awaited. The guards, officers, and drivers accompanying the convoy were instructed to stay with the group until the ship had set sail. It was a good policy because two patients died before they were carried onboard. Their bodies were returned to camp for burial.

A week later the second group departed, followed by the third and last, which included my family. Nearly everyone in our group suffered from dysentery in addition to their other maladies. The stench of feces and urine deposited on the decks permeated the entire ship. The hot, humid climate intensified the smells. With more than a hundred passengers and just one bathroom, the situation became intolerable.

Heavy rain and high winds added to the misery of the cramped conditions on the freighter. Canvases were draped over each deck in an attempt to protect us, but they proved totally worthless. We were soaked to the bone. Seasickness was rampant as the vessel heaved fore and aft and rolled side to side on the rough seas. Vomit joined the excrement underfoot.

Midway through the voyage, Captain Hamada disclosed our destination: a rubber plantation known as Belalau, on the west coast in the state of Benkulen.

Two days later, we arrived at the same improvised port from which we had departed seven months earlier. As the ship's crew lowered anchor a safe distance offshore, I received an urgent order over the loudspeaker to keep everyone down and out of sight.

After dark, looking out over the water, I spotted an intermittent blinking light on the distant shoreline. Someone was sending a coded message. A blinking light from our ship responded. Shortly thereafter, the ship's engines restarted and the anchor was lifted. Instructions rang out to remain quiet and be prepared to disembark.

We left the ship and boarded three waiting buses. Another never-to-be-forgotten journey began. The rules were the same as on previous trips. Windows had to remain closed during the day and the stops were prearranged at designated locations along the way.

After a full day's ride, we left the wilds of the Sumatran jungle and entered mountainous terrain marked by the change of scenery. We traversed the *Pergunungan Barisan* (Barisan Mountains), their high peaks covered with dense greenery. The view fascinated me despite the drenching rain. I had never seen such rich and varied plant life outside of magazines. The rock formations were breathtaking. The boundary markers of this part of the island had a unique beauty of their own.

Because of the torrential rain, the roads were a slippery

mess. The drivers were forced to pull over to the side often, waiting for the rain to subside. The going was slow and quite treacherous at times. New drivers took over twice a day, for the safety of the drivers as well as the passengers. As the fully-loaded buses groaned laboriously to higher elevations, the road became more twisting. Dangerously deep but beautiful ravines waited for a driver's mistake. I closed my eyes many times and held my breath, praying for a safe passage.

Finally, on the third day, we drove onto the property of the Belalau rubber plantation. We got our first glimpse of it through the tall trees arranged in perfectly straight rows, a characteristic of a rubber plantation. About a mile down the road, we began to notice barracks off in the distance. They had sheet-iron roofs. As we drove through the plantation's gate, I counted five brick houses on a hill.

Many prisoners ran out to meet the buses. We recognized several familiar faces among our jumping greeters. Eager to see us, they pounded on the bus's exterior, impatient for it to come to a halt. When it did and we got off, they showered us with hugs and kisses. It was clear from their pink-tinged cheeks and big happy smiles that this camp with its fresh mountain air had worked wonders in only a few weeks. Without saying it, we were all grateful for having survived the rigors of Muntok.

Sister Katrinia was one of our welcomers. She called off names and assigned quarters. My family's was Huis 3, one of the brick houses on the hill. Walking up to the house, Ronald pointed out that it had no windows or doors. It looked as if the house had never been finished or was partly demolished. From the front porch, we had a clear view of the lower areas of the plantation. The interior of the house had been stripped of all its partitions. Only a few support beams held up the overall structure. The absence of bunks led us to believe we were free to claim a section on the bare floor to call our own.

Tante Suus explained that the barracks had been housing for the native workers. The brick houses, she said, had formerly been occupied by the Dutch planters. Now, one of them was our new home. But for how long?

On my tour through the house, I found a bathroom without a door. Since there was no piped water, I supposed the fixtures had never been used. Beyond the back door was a weed-covered terrace. The grounds had been shamefully neglected. The grass had grown tall, the bushes needed trimming, and shards of broken glass littered the area. It was a perfect hiding place for snakes and other crawling creatures. I visualized them lying in wait to attack anyone who dared to come close.

A two-door shed behind the house resembled an outhouse and, on close inspection, I learned that's what it was. I'd never seen one up close before, so out of curiosity I opened one of the doors. I stared in complete astonishment at the deep hole in the ground. Four sturdy beams were placed in such a way that they formed an oblong opening about three-feet square. Four poles held up the roof, a primitive deck made of layers of straw. There was no drainage as far I could tell. With the high humidity, serious sanitary problems were inevitable.

Following the troublesome discoveries about the house, I concluded that our lifestyle was not unlike that of the natives living in the *kampong*. They, too, never had the luxury of electricity or running water.

As I stood at the edge of the backyard surveying the surroundings, I heard water flowing. A small stream of crystal-clear water trickled down from the hills and rippled peacefully through the camp. I walked to the edge, stooped down, and let the cool, refreshing liquid pass through my fingers. With my eyes, I followed the water downstream as the droplets splashed over the rocky bottom. I imagined I was one of the droplets, making my way to new horizons. It was a lovely moment, and I became oblivious to anything else. A harsh call from the top of the hill startled me back to reality. "Hey, you down there!" someone shouted in Japanese.

I stood up, bowed, and, free from guilt of any wrongdoing, walked up the path to face the caller.

"What are you doing here, boy?" the guard asked sternly. "You shouldn't be here at this time of day."

I apologized in his language. The guard, surprised that I spoke Japanese, stared at me dumbfounded for a second or two. I introduced myself. Presenting myself as the interpreter confused him, so I explained that the current interpreter, Mrs. Mulder, had filled in for me. He smiled and informed me of the hours the creek would be accessible to the tenants of Huis 3.

Back at the house and uncertain about what to do next, we sat around chatting. A whistle sounded. It was loud, demanding, and incessant. We went outside and peered down the valley to see what was going on. People were waving wildly, beckoning us to come down. Sister Katrinia used a megaphone to call us down to the village square. Mother Superior was there. "I'm happy to see that you all made it here," she said. "We want to welcome you and thank God for saving you all. The sisters and I have prayed for this moment of reunion. I sincerely hope this will be our last stop because I am getting very tired of moving, aren't you?" We agreed unanimously.

A woman in the group interjected, "Wouldn't it be nice if the war ended soon?" It was wishful thinking.

Mother Superior gave us information about the camp and its rules. The mountain stream, she said, was the only water supply, and its use required special rules. The kitchen and hospital were situated downstream, and their need for water had a higher priority. A schedule of the creek's accessibility to the rest of us had been set up. Mother Superior begged us to adhere to our specific hours at the creek and to abide by the rules.

We stayed and talked to friends. Mother Superior and I reminisced a little about the tragic time in Muntok. She emphasized that we should thank God for our good fortune to have escaped hunger, death, and the many diseases. As she led us in prayer, she became overwhelmed with emotion. Two nuns gently led her away.

"She is overdue for a rest," one of the nuns murmured. "Mother is very weak and tires quickly, but her spirit is high, especially knowing that all her children are reunited again."

Before returning to Huis 3, we spoke with those who had made the journey before us. Women who had died during the voyage across the strait, they told us, were unceremoniously thrown overboard.

PART VI

MARCH 1945–SEPTEMBER 1945

Strolling along the complex and talking to various women, I discovered that most of them had always been supportive of me. I hadn't met most of them before due to my work outside the camp, but they all seemed to know me. Some expressed sympathy for my having to endure working with women older than me. Many were parents and said they couldn't imagine their children being in my position. They spoke of my courage and strength in the face of hardship and unfavorable conditions. I was both flattered and embarrassed.

Mrs. Potts, the head cook, brought me up to date about the kitchen and the camp's provisions. This camp had a greater variety of locally grown vegetables, fruits, *telor bèbèk* (duck eggs), and meats. Deer meat, horse meat, pork, and chicken had been served to the prisoners.

"With so much, maybe you need a cookbook," I joked.

She laughed. "These women have always appreciated whatever I served them. They know I don't have the luxury of spices and herbs."

With the improved provisions, a more nutritious diet was possible, but meats, according to Mrs. Potts, were problematic. Without refrigeration, spoilage was inevitable in the tropical heat and humidity. Deliveries of all meat products were rigidly inspected for that reason. She also told me that it would be impossible to preserve large quantities of fresh food of any kind, especially meat. From time to time when there was an overabundance of meat, she distributed the raw product to the women, who were all too happy to prepare some dish to their own liking.

On one occasion, the kitchen received so much fish that volunteers had to be called in to clean the load. "It was so good!" Mrs. Potts exclaimed. "I had enough fish to make a ragout and it came out tasting better than I had anticipated. It took me back to the good old days of dinners and parties. When it came time to clean up the kitchen, I was grateful to have the stream running alongside. Otherwise, it would have taken us days to get rid of the fishy smell and disinfect the place.

"After a few weeks in this camp and consuming nutritious food, a large number of women and children are well on their way to recovery. They had arrived from Muntok sick and weak. I am happy to see that they are gradually, and in some cases dramatically, improving."

Resuming my stroll, I went to the hospital ward, hoping to find my friend Tina. What I saw there was unbelievable. Patients were actually sitting up in their beds or sitting outdoors under shade trees. They chatted, laughed, and gossiped. The scene was strikingly different from the one in the previous camp. What a beautiful difference after such a period of horror. The women's return to life and happiness was amazing to witness.

Just as I was about to walk away, someone grabbed me from behind. It was Tina! We were so happy to see each other again. Over a cup of tea we talked for a while and exchanged experiences of the trip from Bangka to this place. She told me that two nuns had died during the trip and were buried at sea.

That night after supper, Tante Suus, Ronald, René, and I had our first good night's sleep since leaving the Muntok camp. We rested, warm and comfortable, on our thin mattresses. It was a night of almost-forgotten luxury. The nights of being confined on the cold, damp deck of a freighter or in a suffocating bus were behind us.

A loud knock on the wall at seven o'clock the next morning startled us. A guard reminded us it was our time to go down to the creek for a wash-up. Thirty minutes later at roll call, the Officer of the Guard informed me that Captain Hamada expected me at his office immediately. As I left, the women reminded me to ask for garden tools so they could start cleaning up the yard.

I hadn't seen Captain Hamada since we boarded the bus six days earlier. He was in better spirits than I had seen in a very long time. After we exchanged words of welcome, we sat down and reminisced about the months on Bangka. It was not a pleasant subject to discuss. We both, however, held positive feelings about the new camp. It had one particular advantage: Captain Hamada's living quarters were on the premises, making communication between the two of us a lot easier.

The first days at Belalau were peacefully pleasant. Every capable body was assigned to a work station, and the cleanup around Huis 3 was begun and completed. The rules for the use of the creek were strictly enforced. One drawback was that we had no privacy. The guards constantly stood at the highest point along the path and watched us at the creek. It was their duty. Not wanting to be at the mercy of the guards' roving eyes, the women established their own routines. Generally, the morning and afternoon hours were for washing up or doing laundry. A few preferred to take baths in the morning, but most took theirs at twilight. It was dark enough then to hamper the guards' view. Many women kept their undergarments on while they bathed. Some wrapped themselves in sarongs, as Tante Suus taught me. The most self-conscious women carried buckets of water into the outhouses to take their baths.

A week after our arrival, we discovered Ronald huddled up and shivering. Tante Suus knew it was malaria again. "He started to get this just a few weeks before we left Muntok," she told me.

Malaria, the dreaded disease of the tropics, was spread by mosquitoes, which was why we always slept under nets. "People who are undernourished," my aunt explained, "as most of us are, are more susceptible. Ronald, unfortunately, is one of them."

Ronald was in bed for three days; then a very high fever and chills set in. We piled blankets, coats, mattresses, and anything we could find on him, but he couldn't stop shaking. The fever subsided after Tante Suus made him a hot cup of tea with a squirt of lemon added to it. She insisted he drink it as hot as he could stand it to help break the fever and make him literally sweat it out. His body temperature gradually returned to normal, but it left him exhausted and he fell into a deep sleep for the rest of the day. Unfortunately, the terrible chills returned every three days or so, causing him to suffer the same symptoms over and over again.

The general health in the prison camp continued to improve. Children began to play again. Women showed renewed interest in their hobbies. Sounds of laughter rang out. In short, the prisoners were thriving, enjoying the clean mountain air and the company of good friends. It appeared, at least on the surface, that all memories of Muntok were written off as history.

Days during the wet season could be murderously hot and humid. That's how it was one particular day when I left for work. I walked out the back door of Huis 3 and a sickeningly fetid stench met me. I almost threw up. It had rained off and on for days—not hard, but steadily—soaking the soil thoroughly. A blanket of fog floated lazily in the air in no hurry to dissipate. There was not one puff of wind to blow away the obnoxious smell.

"What in heaven's name is that smell?" I asked out loud, not expecting an answer.

Mimi, one of our housemates, who was standing close by, startled me when she spoke. "It's the outhouses, those damn shit holes in there." She pointed. "And it's going to get worse. They're bound to overflow soon, if they haven't already."

I was taken aback by her anger. "Open the damn door and look in!" she continued. "Go on. You wouldn't know anything about this, of course—you have privileges we don't have." Her sarcasm was like a slap in the face.

343

Mimi was right, of course. I wasn't aware of the condition of the outhouses because I hadn't been around long enough to notice anything out of the ordinary. I rarely used the outhouse. But why pin the blame on me? Did she take pleasure in upsetting me? I couldn't understand why the unhealthy situation hadn't been reported.

Though the stench was unbearable, I held my nose and walked toward the outhouse. I wanted to obtain physical evidence to report the matter; I had to see for myself. I jerked open one of the doors. What I saw made the hair on the back of my neck stand on end. Goose bumps erupted on my skin. My wildest imagination could not have envisioned that sight. A low fog floated over and around the hole. A blanket of millions of white maggots were squirming and crawling all over each other in a vile mass. They were on the door, the walls, the beams, the floor. It was a nauseating and sickening sight. Every inch of skin on my body crawled. I gagged. I slammed the door shut and heard a group of maggots fall to the ground in a splash.

Mimi, standing in the doorway with both hands firmly planted on her hips, snarled, "Now you know what I was telling you, huh?"

I left her standing there and went in the house to see what Tante Suus knew. "Calm down, dear," she said. "What's wrong with you? I've never seen you so upset."

Explaining the circumstances, she said, "Because of the heavy rains the water level in the toilet holes rose, pushing the maggots up and allowing them to climb out. The terrible odor is caused by the high humidity, I think." Then she added, "As far as I know, the outhouses haven't been used for days. Nobody could have foreseen the problem."

The news upset Captain Hamada, and he decided to see for himself. As we got close to the outhouse, the odor overwhelmed him. He opened one of the doors and, like me, gagged at the sight. He let out several words of utter disgust in not-so-pretty Japanese!

Volunteers were needed for the cleanup, but considering the task, I knew we would run into trouble finding them. Only by offering a bonus of extra rations were we able to round up a willing group. We equipped them with protective face masks and buckets. When the trucks arrived with drums containing a deadly chemical solution for the first treatment, the volunteers filled up their buckets and emptied them out into the holes and against the walls and doors. What a nasty, filthy job for those women!

The maggots lost their grip and fell to the bottom of the pit. In no time at all, the chemicals transformed the two outhouses into a maggot graveyard. It was a stomach-turning sight.

The trucks returned the next day for a second and final treatment. Heavy equipment to empty and deepen the holes came the following day. After that process, the sheds looked like new and smelled chemically fresh.

Afterward, several volunteers of the maggot patrol were treated for intestinal disorders, but they recovered quickly without suffering lasting harm. Use of the outhouses was reduced to a minimum, and using them as bathhouses was strictly prohibited from then on.

Chapter 39

It was the end of July, 1945. Out of the blue, Captain Hamada suggested that we have a little party. Reason? Unknown.

A piano that had been stored in one of the empty brick houses was pulled out onto the front porch. One of the women was a marvelous piano player. When she started to play, the women danced around wildly. The music literally swept them off their feet and brought us all to life. Imagine! Real music! We were all in ecstasy.

My work, however, was a totally different story. Tension lingered in the air. Something was brewing, but I was unable to pinpoint it. One afternoon in early August, one of the Japanese officers came to the office intoxicated. He mumbled incoherently. I was alone in the office. He stumbled toward me, tripping over his feet. I caught him and walked him to the bunk in his room.

At first, I thought perhaps bad news from home had prompted him to drink. He kept rambling and repeating something over and over. I tried to make sense of it, but to no avail. On the way back to my office, I spotted a newspaper with the headline, "Atomic Bomb Dropped on Hiroshima." The paper was dated August 7, 1945. That's when I realized that what the drunk officer had been saying was, "It's over! It's over!"

I didn't entirely understand the headline. Did I dare pick up the newspaper and try to find out more? Was the war over? I was certain the paper held the answer, but I had to watch my step. I didn't want to arouse suspicion. Captain Hamada had given me permission to read the paper in the past, but my conscience told me it might not be wise to look more closely at this paper under the present circumstances. If someone saw me reading it without Captain Hamada's presence, they might get the wrong impression.

Time crept by that day, and my curiosity would not rest. When I couldn't stand it any longer, I grabbed the paper and began to read. The United States had dropped an atomic bomb on the city of Hiroshima, killing or injuring more than half its population.

Captain Hamada returned from his trip late that afternoon, tired and listless. Now I was convinced that the article had been responsible for the officer's drunkenness and for Captain Hamada's lingering sour mood.

That evening, while I was playing cards with Ronald and René, a call came for me to return to the office. The entire staff, including Captain Hamada, seemed to have had too much to drink. Times must indeed have taken a turn for the worse, for this behavior was out of character.

"Rick," Captain Hamada slurred, "invite a few of the women to join us, would you, please?" It was the first such request under his command. I was disappointed, but I had to do what he asked.

While I walked down into the camp, I couldn't help but think back to the parties I had attended in Djambi and expected the same misconduct here. I spoke with one of the women whom I knew to be a partygoer and asked her to pass along the invitation to anyone who might wish to come. Having no desire for further involvement, I returned to the house and continued the card game with my brothers.

I had trouble falling asleep that night. When I finally did, a suitcase dividing floor space between us and our neighbor tipped over on top of me. It woke me up. Squirming to free myself, I tried discreetly to wake up Ronald, who was asleep next to me, but nothing could stir him.

I heard a man's voice and that of our neighbor, both uttering words. Then I smelled a strong odor of liquor. I felt nothing but contempt, shame, and embarrassment. I finally pushed the suitcase back to its original position and held it there while tears rolled down my cheeks and onto my pillow. I felt so degraded and lonely that I wanted to scream. I hated both of them for involving me in their venture. When Tante Suus heard me crying, she whispered words to comfort me. She, of course, knew what had taken place.

The visitor left the house stumbling and bumping into several obstacles on his way out in the dark. It was a wonder the noise did not awaken the entire house. Or were the women just pretending to be asleep?

A few days later, there was another disturbing headline. On August 9, 1945, an atomic bomb had been dropped on a second Japanese city, Nagasaki. I was also able to decipher some bits and pieces about British command troops stationed in India being delayed in their efforts to reach prisoner-of-war camps. Reading that bit of news gave me hope. Would we be rescued soon? Could this be the end of the war?

That afternoon, Captain Hamada received visitors for several hours in his office. I did not know these people, where they came from, or why they were there. When they left, Captain Hamada called all his officers in for a briefing. The strain on their faces intensified.

Next, he asked me to call a meeting of all the prisoners. "I want every able body present," he stated. "I have a very important announcement to make."

I was terribly anxious to hear his important message. Other than the little bits of news that I had read recently, I had no information at all about what was happening and how it would affect us. The headlines that had burned a spot in my brain screamed for further elaboration, especially after the secret meetings.

The prisoners gathered in front of the office, but it was some time before Captain Hamada appeared. He looked us over somberly then blurted, "The war is over. We will all remain here until further notice." Then he left.

That was it! Short. Insensitive. We were totally stunned. Hearing the news should have caused an outburst of cheering, dancing, *hip-hip-hurrah*ing. Instead, the air was filled with a peculiar silence. It was as if we had been hit over the head and left on the spot to die. The manner in which Captain Hamada presented the astounding news was so impersonal that it did not feel at all like a liberation.

Then some women began singing the Dutch national anthem. Others cried silently, some fell to their knees to pray, and a few sobbed, calling out for their loved ones, both dead and alive. I cried and thought of my mother and wished she were here with us. I wondered where my father was and if he knew the war was over.

Naturally, I was the one my fellow prisoners hunted down for more information, but I had to tell them that I didn't know any more than they did. Many refused to believe me.

Several weeks later, when I went to work as usual, a cloud of doom hung heavily over the office. I tactfully avoided any conversation with Captain Hamada and simply tended to my duties. He watched the telephone nervously, as though compelling it to ring.

A newspaper on his desk reported that Emperor Hirohito had announced the surrender of Japan on August 14, 1945, and that, on September 2, 1945, almost three weeks after the surrender, an armistice was signed on board the battleship U.S.S. *Missouri,* anchored in Tokyo Bay.

Days passed, but still no liberators appeared to free us. We wondered who they would be and where they would come from. Patience is a virtue, the nuns reminded us, so we all waited patiently for our freedom.

One day Captain Hamada emerged from his office, wobbling. Inebriated again, he burst into tears and confessed to a plan to set fire to the camp. Whining pitifully, he admitted that he couldn't bring himself to carry it out. He couldn't do to us, he sobbed, what the war had done to Japan. I felt sorry for the man, but couldn't console him. I wasn't supposed to know all that had been going on in the world. I feigned ignorance. "I don't know what you're talking about, Hamada-san."

Eager to unburden himself, he told me the whole story. "I have received instructions to set fire to the camp and send every woman and child up in smoke." He took a deep breath. "I have been ordered to make the entire camp disappear." He again cried loudly. The sound pierced my soul, and I almost cried with him. The thought of the women and children being burned to death made me nauseous.

He rambled on, slurring every word. His distress was crushing. By refusing to execute the order, he had lost his self-respect. By disobeying, he had committed treason against his country. The only honorable act in the face of such disgrace was to commit *hara-kiri,* the Japanese suicide ritual. My heart went out to him.

"What will happen now, sir?" I asked.

He looked at me, as though to answer, but never did. He stumbled to his feet and I led him to the couch in his office, where he passed out. He was a sad sight lying there.

Chapter 40

The next day, I awoke with a profound sadness and a feeling that the day wouldn't turn out well. I should have been looking forward to better times, but knowing what I did, I could not.

Captain Hamada was seated at his desk with his arms crossed on his chest, looking at me with bloodshot eyes. His greeting was formal but humble. He was so very much unlike the Captain Hamada I had known a short time ago. *"Ohayo gozaimasu, Hamada-san. Ogenki desu ka?"* I asked, forcing myself to sound chipper.

"I've had better days, Rick, but I'm all right." He sighed. "Thank you for asking, though. I wish to apologize for my misconduct yesterday."

I mumbled something insignificant to try to put him at ease. He waved his right hand through empty space as if to tell me to excuse his mood. Silence fell.

"Did I say or do anything inappropriate yesterday?" he asked.

I hedged a bit on the answer. "No, sir, you did not. You were, as always, the perfect gentleman," I reassured him, then made an excuse to leave the room. If he didn't remember what he had disclosed to me, I wasn't going to tell him.

Still in turmoil, he came into my office a few minutes later. Knowing that he had my attention, he posed an interesting question. "If you were granted one wish, what would it be? What would you wish for?"

I searched my mind for an appropriate response, although it was rather easy to think of one. "I would wish for my family and all the others, including yours, Hamada-san, to be reunited and live in peace. War is such an ugly thing, don't you agree?"

"Naturally!" he said, pacing back and forth. A soft look came to his eyes. "I anticipated as much, and I have a plan. Now that the war is over, I am authorized to open the gates to both camps, to bring the prisoners together and reunite them. Should I do it?"

"What a silly question. To be reunited with my father after nearly three years of separation would be an indescribable joy!" I shouted and jumped up and down.

Captain Hamada enjoyed my spontaneous display. "Can we announce the news to the women, sir?" I asked, eager to run out and tell the whole world.

"Not quite yet, Rick. There's more."

"More?"

"How do you think the women would react if I allowed them to go downtown?" he asked.

My mouth fell open. I was unable to answer the question. Speechless, I stood there for a few seconds with my eyes fixed on him in disbelief. I remembered the odd feeling I'd had when I woke up that morning, but it looked as if the day was going to be a happy one after all.

"My second plan is to allow the prisoners some freedom. How does a bus trip to Lubuklinggau sound to you? To shop, or just go for a ride into town on the bus." With a boyish grin, he watched my reaction.

"Are you serious? You would allow us to leave camp and go downtown?"

"The plan, of course, must be approved by headquarters."

Could this be the first step to our freedom? What a beautiful word: F-R-E-E-D-O-M.

Captain Hamada said he would announce the plan to the women that day. Since the news was being made public in a few minutes anyway, I didn't think it would be harmful to tell Tante Suus first. I properly excused myself and ran from the office to find her. I called out her name. As soon as she came in sight I threw both my arms around her in a tight embrace.

"Are you all right?" she laughed, surprised at the sudden gesture of affection.

"I'm more than all right, Tante Suus. I'm ecstatic!" I said, and hugged her again. "You won't believe what I have to tell you." I spoke loudly and didn't care if others heard about the surprises. I couldn't help myself.

"Auntie, we'll be free soon!" I grabbed her by the shoulders and looked her straight in the eyes. "Did you hear that? Free!" I repeated, emphasizing every word. "The war is really and truly over!" I babbled on, pulling her around in circles.

"Stop for a moment, dear. I don't understand what you're talking about. We all know the war is over."

Then I told her about Captain Hamada's plan to open the gates to both camps, and about the bus trips downtown. I could barely keep from screaming at the top of my lungs.

Tante Suus stared. "Are you sure this is for real?"

"Captain Hamada is working on the details right now. To go into town on our own, without a guard. What do you think of that? And we'll be seeing Poppie soon, too!"

She was skeptical. "Those plans may not happen."

"Auntie, please be happy," I begged. "The war's over. We can go into town. You're the first to know!"

But Tante Suus wasn't the only one who knew. Several of our housemates had overheard the conversation and began asking questions, most of which I unfortunately couldn't answer. I knew no specific details.

I took my aunt by the hand and we hopped and skipped down the path into the valley to see Mother Superior. Other women and children followed. I felt like the Pied Piper carrying a bundle of good news, ready to make beautiful music.

That night in bed, although I was very happy, a sense of sadness came over me. Sadness at the thought of having to say good-bye to a group of people I'd worked with for so long, people who had come to trust me as one of them and referred to me as their "little friend."

Although the takeover by the unknown liberation forces was not yet official, we were no longer prisoners, no longer forced to bow to the Japanese military, although they were still our caretakers. Now I had nothing to hide or to fear any longer. The time had come to reveal my true identity. I wanted to tell everybody that I was Rita, not Rick. The thought of confessing to the commandant, however, was a painful matter.

Tante Suus signed up Ronald, René, and me for the bus trip into town. It was time to discard Rick's clothes and my camp persona. After more than three years, I could let my hair grow and I could again be Rita. Tucked away in our meager belongings was one of my favorite dresses. I tried it on, and it still fit although I was now fifteen and slightly taller. I decided to wear the dress to town.

When Tante Suus and my brothers saw me in the dress, I detected their uneasiness. To the four of us, this was about the return of Rita. Ronald was the first to break the solemn moment. "It was more fun to have a brother. You don't look right in a dress," he stated.

Was he expressing true disappointment at having his sister back? Or did he fear for my safety? Tante Suus said, "I'm afraid for you, dear."

"Don't be, auntie. Nobody can harm me now. The war is over. It's time to make my comeback," I said.

"Aren't you a bit overconfident?" she pressed. "How do you think Captain Hamada will react when you show up as a girl?"

Though I tried not to let on, I had doubts, too. I was as apprehensive as Tante Suus was about my being accepted as Rita by Captain Hamada and his staff, but I didn't want her and the boys to know that. By speaking comforting words to Tante Suus, I was able to cover up my nervousness.

Deep down inside there was more than just being nervous about revealing my ruse. The impish side of my personality was yearning to create mischief. Frankly, I could hardly wait to see everyone's reaction when they recognized me as the former boy interpreter. My excitement built up. Considering that the Japanese only knew me as Rick, I had to be prepared for almost anything—surprise, laughter, even rejection. Shortly I'd know how these men would react to the unveiling of a girl, a girl they had treated as one of their own gender, a girl they had even allowed into their quarters to play cards!

The day finally came. The buses arrived on schedule and parked at the front gate. Tante Suus, Ronald, René, and I walked down the steep driveway. I entered the guardhouse to sign out while they boarded the bus. One of the guards looked at me without any sign of recognition. Then he looked again. A flicker of surprise crossed his face, then perplexity. Another puzzled look followed. He squirmed in his chair.

I walked away to board the bus. The suspicious guard followed me with his eyes, and once I had disappeared into the vehicle, he turned to his coworkers and whispered. Seconds later, four pairs of eyes were staring in my direction. I was certain that as soon as they recovered from their surprise, they would tell Captain Hamada. I had waited a long time to step back into my normal life as a girl but had never expected it to be as much fun as it turned out. But the moment of reckoning—facing Captain Hamada—was yet to come. I prayed he would truly understand the reason behind my disguise.

The guards weren't the only ones surprised by Rick in a dress. Many of the women hadn't known about my secret either, but they were bold enough to ask me straight out about it now. When I told them my story, *ooh*s and *aah*s filled the air, followed by words of admiration for my having the courage to go through it all. I enjoyed the unveiling of Rita to the fullest.

When we returned from town, my first priority was to find Captain Hamada. As I entered his office, a wry grin brightened his face. He wasted no time in coming to the point.

"I have heard about your new appearance and personality. I could not believe what I was told, but seeing you in front of me now leaves me no doubt." He spoke slowly, weighing every word.

It was an awkward scene at first, but I told him the whole story and he listened quietly. I ended with an apology. "I am terribly sorry. I hope your heart is big enough to understand why I had to do it."

Then he spoke. "Now that I know you're a girl, my admiration of your accomplishments has surpassed anything else. Your courage to carry on the disguise is exceptionally unusual. It is incredible." He shook his head and mumbled, "Indeed, it is.

"You must have enjoyed playing the role of a boy," he continued. "I never suspected even once that you were not. My sincere congratulations for the flawless and exceptionally well-performed accomplishments of your mission."

His kind words were more than I had hoped for. "Hamada-san," I said, thinking this might be my last opportunity for a private conversation with him, "I don't know what will happen in the coming days, but I want to take this opportunity to thank you for a most pleasant working relationship. I appreciate the trust and confidence you invested in me. I especially thank you for your generosity in providing extra provisions for my family when we were in Muntok."

After a short silence, he said, "You have many special

qualities, Rick. You're not only a smart, hard worker; you intuitively sense what needs to be done and you get it done. Those are favorable assets, especially in one so young. Keep them and cherish them."

"Thank you, Hamada-san. Your kind words embarrass me. I hope you will forgive me for having misled you about my identity."

"I have forgiven you," he said.

We wished each other good luck. On my way out, I turned to him and said, "My name is Rita." He smiled, repeated the name, and bowed.

Epilogue

Unarmed guards escorted us on our first visit to the men's camp. Elation filled our hearts and nervous anticipation veiled our faces. The women and their children slowly filed along the winding dirt road that connected the two camps. Except for an occasional whine from a young child and the rhythmic beat of footsteps, the only sounds came from a gentle breeze stirring the tops of the rubber trees. It cast a relaxing atmosphere.

The women had made efforts to look their best for the occasion, but dressed in rags, oversize shirts, short pants, and military boots, they were still a pathetic-looking bunch. What made the difference in their appearance was that they looked happy, excited, and eager to be reunited with their loved ones.

Suddenly, someone up front pointed and shouted, "I see them! Gosh, come on, girls, I see them!" The woman almost cried saying the words. Everyone craned their necks to catch a glimpse of what was ahead. Then an invisible power pushed the line forward and the women started to run. The Japanese guards made no attempt to stop them.

At the gate of the men's camp, we were met by a group of men assigned to coordinate the reunion. They had lists of names and barracks of those who were immobile and unable to meet their families at the gate. The men awaiting our arrival were barely able to control themselves once they had found their loved ones. Couples ran into each other's arms and kissed and became oblivious to their surroundings. Some stood face-to-face, not quite knowing whether to laugh or cry, before locking themselves in loving embraces.

A very shy young man led us to the sick bay where my father was. When we reached the barrack, the young man asked us to wait. "I had better announce your presence. These guys haven't seen womenfolk for a long time. You understand." He took a few steps forward into the building and yelled, "Is everybody decent? A couple of young ladies are here to see one of you guys. We're coming in!"

It was a comical introduction, but it broke the otherwise tense atmosphere. An unfamiliar stench permeated the air. Most of the patients were covered in rags; some showed a bare chest. We passed them, walking slowly. Glimmers of excitement shone in the eyes of some. They were anticipating seeing their own family or friends.

I wondered what we would find when we reached my father. Would we recognize him before our guide pointed him out to us? Then a familiar voice called out, "Please, can't you walk a bit faster?" We recognized my father's voice. He sat like a statue in his place on the bench. He had on a smelly, threadbare, dingy undershirt. A filthy torn blanket covered his legs and wrapped around the back to hide his bottom. He had on no underwear.

My eyes filled with tears. Ronald and René ran to him and jumped on the bench, nearly knocking him over. We wrapped him in a long-awaited, loving embrace. The tears flowed freely. After our moment with him, we children stepped aside to allow Tante Suus to greet her brother-in-law.

My father was bald, and his head now seemed too small for the rest of his body. His arms and legs were grotesquely swollen, making the skin look like that of an elephant. His feet stuck out from under the blanket and his swollen toes looked like fat little sausages. His distended body was covered with scabs and scars from infected scratches caused by vermin in his clothes.

He told us all about his life in confinement and about how he had felt terribly alone in his fight for survival. Tante Suus and I both cried. By comparison, our lives had been easier because we had each other. Every time I thought I had gained control of my tears, something else he told us would make me start crying again. The last time I had cried that much was when my mother died, two years earlier.

As days passed, we visited my father often and got to know his friends and roommates. The ones who were in better shape and involved in daily activities invited us to barbecues. The gatherings were fun and helped us forget that we were still living in a prison camp.

Tante Suus shared her cooking with my father's roommates, some of whom were not lucky enough to have family visitors. She spoiled them with attention, especially with her delicious dishes, and adopted them into our family.

Meanwhile, natives hidden between trees and tree

stumps, on the lookout to barter with people traveling between camps, approached me to trade goods with them. They offered me three live chickens for my boots. I was willing to accept their offer if they would add a dozen eggs to it. They agreed and I walked away with a worthwhile purchase.

"Look what I brought you, Auntie," I said cheerfully.

"Where did you get those?" Looking me over, she noticed that I was barefoot. "Where are your boots? . . . You didn't!" she said, realizing what I had done.

"I did! I got you three chickens and a dozen eggs. How did I do, Auntie? Was it worth my boots?"

"Of course it was worth it. Your father and his friends will surely enjoy all the dishes I can make with these goodies."

With everything running smoothly in both camps, I had little work to do in the office. I visited my father and his friends often. I searched the woods for edible greens to supplement the dishes Tante Suus cooked.

One day we woke up and the Japanese soldiers were gone, as though they had vanished into thin air. Their departure took place in total secrecy in the middle of the night. I felt deprived of a proper farewell to my very special friend, Captain Hamada, the commandant of our last two camps. Most probably, I thought, he would suffer the consequences of an act of treason—not carrying out the order to burn the camp and its prisoners.

With the departure of our captors, the camp was under the supervision of four Australian paratroopers, the first allies to reach our camp. Their only job was to locate the camp and to report our condition, but to us they were our liberators.

We learned from them that the Japanese had indeed had plans to exterminate all prison camps, including ours, on or before August 31, 1945, the birthday of Queen Wilhelmina, queen of the Netherlands. But because the bombing of Hiroshima and Nagasaki expedited the end of the war, Japanese priorities shifted. They had to turn their attention to saving their own islands. The turn of events might well have been a lifesaver for us.

In a matter of days, we received airlifts of food packages organized by the Recovery of Allied Prisoners of War and Internees (RAPWI). The packages contained a variety of canned foods that we hadn't seen or tasted in years. The drops even included freshly baked bread. The food came to us straight from a military base on the Cocos Islands, a ten-hour flight away, located in the eastern Indian Ocean and belonging to Australia.

In days following, the sick ex-prisoners of both camps were transported to Lahat, a former mountain resort that had been transformed into a rehabilitation center for prisoners of war. My father was one of those patients. We said good-bye again.

The ex-prisoners who stayed behind in the camps were taken to the railway station to be transported to the city of Palembang, our final destination. Buses were waiting there to drive us to our assigned homes in the *concession,* a government-controlled area. We were taken to a house where a Japanese soldier, evidently in charge, welcomed us. He made a deep traditional bow and invited us to enter the house. He handed me a note written in English with instructions to check the contents of the house against the list on the dining table. It directed us to examine the condition of the house. Anything that was not to our satisfaction or that would require additional work was to be reported immediately.

While Tante Suus verified the inventory, I took a walk outside. We had a small grassy area for a front yard and a one-car garage at the end of a long driveway. We were in a very good neighborhood and only steps away from a large pond surrounded by beautiful homes and tall trees. A church, one house away from ours, stood at the corner of our street.

The house was neat and clean and fully furnished with beds, tables, chairs, kitchen utensils, and many other accessories. To Tante Suus's delight, there was even a sewing machine.

The Japanese soldier who dutifully followed me around behaved in a servile manner when we approached the bathroom. It was in a squalid state. Streaks of human waste covered the walls and soiled the area around the toilet. Addressing the soldier in Japanese, I scolded him for the neglect and insisted it be cleaned up. Not expecting me to know his language, he was speechless. I repeated my request as if I were Rick, conveying a command from higher up.

The little soldier recovered from his surprise and bowed several times, apologizing humbly for his poor workmanship. It took him a while to clean the bathroom.

After he was done, I signed the note and drew his attention to the blank space under *Remarks*. He knew what it meant, and seemed thankful that I had left the space blank.

Later in the afternoon a truck delivered food to us and to the other families in the neighborhood, to bridge the time until we were completely settled in. A Dutch captain and two female lieutenants in the RAPWI came to our house the next morning. The three provided us with ID cards, money, food stamps, and coupons for clothing. Even more important, they brought us news about my father. He was recovering well, they reported, and would be home as soon as he could travel.

A few weeks later an automobile stopped in front of the house. Sitting in the backseat with an air of royalty was my father. Two officers helped him out of the car and into the house. We felt blessed to have made it through three and a half difficult years. Our family was together at last, and free.

Glossary

DUTCH

concession: a government-controlled area
dame van de huishouding: housekeeper, maid
dankjewel: thank you
een, twee, drie: one, two, three
gouvernante: governess, nanny
"Het Wilhelmus": the national anthem of the Netherlands
hup: go
Indisch Meisje: someone of mixed Dutch and Indonesian heritage
kakkerlakken: cockroaches
keuken prinses: nickname for the family cook
oma: grandmother
Post Telegraaf en Telefoondienst: Dutch postal services, including telegraph and telephone
tot ziens: until we meet again
zangles: singing hour

Japanese

banzai: hoorah; long life; cheers
domo arigato gozaimasu: thank you very much
hai: yes
hara-kiri: Japanese suicide ritual involving disemboweling
hiragana: phonetic script used for writing Japanese in combination with *kanji*
kanji: Chinese characters used in Japanese writing
katakana: phonetic script used mainly for writing foreign words in Japanese
Kempetai: the Japanese military secret police
komban wa: good evening
konnichi wa: good afternoon
obi: the wide sash worn tied at the back with a kimono
ohayo gozaimasu: good morning
ogenki desu ka: how are you?
sake: Japanese alcoholic beverage made from fermented rice
sukiyaki: a Japanese skillet dish (usually involving beef)
tenko: roll call

Malay/Indonesian

anglo: small, charcoal burning stove
atap: straw roof
baboe: housekeeper, maid
balé balé: row of bamboo platforms
boekoe pienter: book of smarts; "astute book"

dogkar: Indonesian pronunciation of "dogcart," here referring to a covered, two-wheeled horse-drawn carriage

djongos: manservant

doekoe: a fruit

gajoeng: dipper

gedèk: bamboo-plaited wall

heiho(s): Indonesian guards used by Japanese

ikan asin: dried, salted fish

kampong: native village

klamboe: mosquito netting

koetoe boesoek: bedbugs

kokki: cook

Nja (short for Njonja): Ma'am

pasar: open air market

patjol: a hoe

pendopo: an open hut

Pergunungan Barisan: Barisan Mountains

ramboetan: a fruit

Saja toean, ngerti!: Yes, sir, understood!

sajoer: an Indonesian-style soup containing meat and vegetables

sampan: a light, open flat-bottomed boat of the Far East propelled by two short oars

sarong: a loose garment worn wrapped around the body

sawo: a fruit

telor bèbèk: duck eggs

tempat: place

toean: master

toko: store

Acknowledgments

I am grateful to my monthly writers' group, The Word-smiths. During the last year of finishing my book, they stood by me, guiding and encouraging each step. Their support has been invaluable in achieving my goal.

I extend special thanks to two within the group, Cindy Vlatas and Ernestine Howe. Cindy introduced me to the writers' group and later brought my story to the attention of a movie production agency. Ernestine spent many hours working with me to improve my writing overall.

Wendy Gammon and Kathleen Adams also deserve special thanks. They encouraged me to go ahead, to perse-vere, and together we worked through all the information to write my story.

Sincere thanks go to my husband, Dan, with whom I spent many evenings proofreading and data checking.